D0875621

Using Investor Relations to Maximize Equity Valuation

Founded in 1807, John Wiley & Sons is the oldest independent publishing company in the United States. With offices in North America, Europe, Australia, and Asia, Wiley is globally committed to developing and marketing print and electronic products and services for our customers' professional and personal knowledge and understanding.

The Wiley Finance series contains books written specifically for finance and investment professionals as well as sophisticated individual investors and their financial advisors. Book topics range from portfolio management to e-commerce, risk management, financial engineering, valuation, and financial instrument analysis, as well as much more.

For a list of available titles, visit our Web site at www.WileyFinance.com.

Using Investor Relations to Maximize Equity Valuation

THOMAS M. RYAN
CHAD A. JACOBS

WILEY

John Wiley & Sons, Inc.

Published by John Wiley & Sons, Inc., Hoboken, New Jersey.
Published simultaneously in Canada.

For general information on our other products and services, or technical support, please
contact our Customer Care Department within the United States at 800-762-2974, outside
the United States at 317-572-3993 or fax 317-572-4002.

Wiley also publishes its books in a variety of electronic formats. Some content that appears in
print may not be available in electronic books.

For more information about Wiley products, visit our web site at www.wiley.com.

Library of Congress Cataloging-in-Publication Data

Ryan, Thomas M., 1964–
   Using investor relations to maximize equity valuation / Thomas M. Ryan and
Chad A. Jacobs.
      p.   cm.—(Wiley finance series)
   ISBN 0-471-67852-X (cloth)
   1. Corporations—Valuation.   2. Corporations—Investor relations.   3. Investment
analysis.   I. Jacobs, Chad A., 1964–   II. Title.   III. Series.
   HG4028.V3R93   2005
   659.2'85—dc
                                                            2004020700

Printed in the United States of America.

10 9 8 7 6 5 4 3 2 1

Contents

Preface

A Brave New World
of Investor Relations

If a chief executive officer or chief financial officer wanted to hire an outside agency to help management more effectively interact with sell-side analysts, investment bankers, and portfolio managers, it would seem obvious that the best person to hire, especially if the shareholder implication of the decision were really thought through, would be someone who had senior-level, first-hand experience as a sell-side analyst, an investment banker, or portfolio manager. At least that's our view, one that seemed obvious. Yet, almost every day, corporate America's best management teams make the decision to put investor relations in the hands of professionals who don't have the appropriate background.

Choosing the wrong investor relations support can add risk to the already risky business of dealing with Wall Street. After almost a decade of seeing corporate communication blunders that lose shareholders billions of dollars in value, we became convinced of the tremendous need for a more professional, strategic, and capable approach to IR.

Along with John Flanagan, our lawyer and founding partner, we started Integrated Corporate Relations in 1998 in a small office above an antiques store in Westport, Connecticut. We'd both been senior-level equity analysts on Wall Street and covered exciting industries while enjoying the opportunity to become experts on specific companies and industry sectors. Similar to most equity research analysts during the 1990s, we worked long hours under stressful conditions to be the go-to guys who knew the companies, the management teams, and the underlying fundamentals that would presumably move our stocks.

As analysts, our job was to take information, both distributed by the company and that which we uncovered, and conduct in-depth analyses of these businesses and their earnings potential. During that process, however, we often found a costly communications disconnect that invariably penalized the companies (in terms of valuation and cost of capital) and investors (in terms of declining share price).

The culprit? The problem was nothing more than a general lack of expertise on the part of management teams with regard to dealing with The Street and managing the nuances of the stock market. All too often, there was unnecessary confusion, uncertainty, and caution, leading to an arbitrage between reality and perception.

During that process we frequently witnessed management teams struggle with interacting and communicating with The Street, and we realized that if we were privy to the details of any given situation, we could really make a difference. That's why we crossed the capital markets divide, so that we could help transform not only the perception of investor relations, but also its importance to a company's long-term success.

As former analysts, we saw the complicated relationship between corporations and the investment community and realized we were probably the best-qualified third party to give counsel on strategic IR issues. This type of advice was certainly not the job of legal counsel, who most likely never had spoken to an analyst or portfolio manager as part of his or her job. Nor was it the task of the big accounting firms that advised CFOs on other important reporting issues. Most importantly, we strongly believed that it wasn't the job of a third-party public relations firm, staffed in all likelihood with PR experts and communications majors. While these professionals may be at the top of their game in many communications-oriented situations, they simply don't have the background to advise management teams on complex capital markets–based, strategic IR issues. Nonetheless, this type of firm was dominant in the business of investor relations although there is no guarantee that the landscape will remain that way.

We came to IR because we believe that former sell-side analysts and portfolio managers have the unique experience to advise CEOs and CFOs on how to deal with the markets. As analysts, we understand how research, investment banking, and sales and trading coexist and interlock to drive profits at investment banks. Understanding this point is critical to positioning a company and advising management on how best to approach any sell-side firm. We also understand exactly what portfolio managers are looking for, and how it can change from quarter to quarter. In essence, we package the product for the sell-side and the buy-side (the buyers) because we've sat in those seats.

Currently, many CEOs and CFOs dismiss IR as too costly or unnecessary. That's a precarious stance on a communications function that, at its best, can lower a company's cost of capital and, at its worst, can destroy management's credibility, as well as hundreds of millions of dollars in shareholder value. The new world of corporate affairs must position IR at the tip of the spear, leading the communications strategy to preserve and enhance corporate value.

We created our company to improve the IR equation. In the past six years, we've gathered an exceptional team of Wall Street sell-side and buy-side professionals, including our president Don Duffy, a former portfolio manager, and James Palczynski, a former sell-side analyst. We like to think that we're redefining investor relations, and despite a mixed market over the last few years, our business has flourished. Why? We believe it's a direct result of the value proposition a group of former capital markets professionals can bring to the IR process.

We have also taken a fresh look at the practice of corporate communications in general and launched a PR group run by Mike Fox and John Flanagan. We've challenged the established practices of many of today's largest corporate communications firms that see IR on a lower rung of the corporate communications ladder. We strongly believe in shaking up that mind-set. Our view of the world is that IR strategy, focused on long term equity value, should be a force in all corporate communications decisions, providing a check and balance to PR issues that, if not handled properly, could erase market capitalization, and raise a company's cost of capital.

> "Our view of the world is that IR strategy, focused on long-term equity value, should be a force in all corporate communications decisions."

All of our senior professionals come from Wall Street. We understand the science and the art of the stock market, and we help corporate executives better direct their time and money to optimize performance, increase profitability, and spur growth. In our view, the transformation is beginning to take hold and was accelerated by the bear market in 2000, 2001, and 2002; corporate malfeasance; stepped-up government regulation; and a renewed commitment by many to fix the system.

This book is about our approach. We believe that every company executive and investor relations officer must understand certain basic communications essentials in order to facilitate efficient capital markets understanding and optimal equity valuation. IR can also play a decisive role in the competitive performance of private companies. We have helped many private companies find a voice on Wall Street without sacrificing the privileges of being private. Any private company that does not utilize IR in its strategy is missing out on an opportunity to affect its competitor's cost of capital and bolster its reputation with investment banks that could eventually take it public.

In the following pages we relay the tools we employ to help our clients maximize equity value. We call it "capital markets advisory," but in reality it's what investor relations ought to be. It starts with *definition*. In order to help a company reach its best possible level of performance, one must have a thorough understanding of what adds value to, and what detracts value from, a stock. It continues with *delivery*. Corporations must understand how sales and trading, research, and investment banking work together, and how they can take advantage of this understanding to best benefit share-holders, employees, and the company as a whole. *Dialogue* rounds out the process. This book is for the corporate executives, investor relations officers, analysts, bankers, and investors who want a better understanding of the process.

As we see it, management needs to gather advice from very experienced analysts and portfolio managers when trying to navigate the choppy waters of Wall Street. IR practices at larger agencies have become exposed for what they are: namely a commodity service frequently incapable of providing so-lutions for complex capital markets issues. We believe that we've come up with a better mousetrap for IR, and we're pleased to share our thoughts with you. We hope you enjoy the book.

Tom Ryan and Chad Jacobs

Westport, Connecticut
May 2004

Introduction
A New Approach and Why It's Important

Earnings are coming in low, the CEO's about to resign, inventory is up, and the cost of new equipment just doubled. It's a sure thing where the stock price is headed, right?

Not necessarily. When it comes to the stock market, Adam Smith's invisible hand has been known to get a gentle tug from a variety of constituencies. There's the *company* itself and the information it provides. There's the *equity research analysts* who offer their intelligence and opinions on the company and the industry. There's the *media* and the stories they present. Rounding out the mix are all of the *stakeholders*, such as employees and strategic partners, and the long arms of their actions and opinions.

All of these constituencies influence those most affected by the tug, the *investors*. From sophisticated institutions to ordinary individuals, investors depend on reasonable information upon which they can make sound decisions. The company's responsibility is to seed the substance and direct the form of this information, and IR is at the core of this responsibility.

Though the long-term value of a company's stock correlates reliably to a company's long-term financial performance, the short-term price is vital to keeping cost of capital low and maintaining a competitive advantage. We believe stock price or equity value, is the tangible consequence of an obvious, but often mismanaged, equation:

Equity value = Financial performance + How that performance is
interpreted by a variety of constituents

A company's underlying fundamentals and industry outlook are important. The company must understand its strengths and weaknesses in the context of its competitive environment to attract the investors and investment banks that present the best fit to come along for the long-term journey. How that story is told is critical. Packaging the information for each audience must be done in the same way that gifted executives package and sell their products. The bottom line is that public companies are in a sense products to Wall Street, and Wall Street is the market for public companies. Let the commerce begin.

Information alone does not determine stock price; it's also the interpretation and perception of that information. Recent stories from *The Wall Street Journal*'s What's News, Business and Finance column read something like this:

- An apparel company said its net income was overstated and that its third quarter results were lower than reported. Stock slips in a sell-off.
- A technology company's shares fell 10 percent on worries about more disclosures of accounting irregularities. Finance chief quits.
- An entertainment company's distribution deals are the subject of a grand jury probe into potential conflicts of interest. Stock price slightly up on low volume.
- An Internet company's earnings jumped 69 percent and sales surged 84 percent, beating forecasts. But its shares fell in after-hours trading on high volume.

These examples are certainly a mixed bag with some counterintuitive market reactions. The most likely reason that the entertainment company's stock didn't move on bad news is the result of a consistent and clear IR strategy and how that strategy managed expectations leading up to the event. Chances are that the entertainment company's stock was already down and that new management dealt with the problem transparently and quickly. Although there may be no catalyst for the stock (as evidenced by the low volume), the worst is likely over. The news was likely compatible with shareholder understanding of management's assumptions regarding future performance, and that's exactly the situation that company wanted to be in given the circumstances.

How about the Internet company? In all likelihood, the company had been growing quickly and ignored IR while earnings were accelerating, a common mistake. Without the proper strategy to control the sell-side, estimates and expectations increased, leaving 69 percent earnings growth as a disappointment. Too bad for the tech company's management team that was on the verge of an all-stock takeover of a rival company. Their stock just plunged, and that acquisition just became materially more expensive or out of the question altogether.

The thrust of traditional investor relations has included necessary disclosures, such as annual reports and 10-Qs, as well as communications, such as press releases and conference calls. As most IR professionals and Wall Street experts know, this approach is not enough. Companies that are increasingly aware of this fact look at IR more strategically than administratively. This strategy shift must include proactive counsel that understands the capital markets, positions the company properly, and cultivates interest and investor confidence. The goal is to heighten management credibility, generate third-party validation, and improve the company's exposure to potential investors, all to maximize equity value.

IR helps a company devise a strategy and present its story based on quantitative and qualitative attributes, competitive issues, the industry situation, and most importantly, the current valuation. In order to do this well, IR must have the capacity to act as a peer or confidant to the CEO, CFO, and the board of directors. Additionally, IR must advise on a variety of issues from union relations to project development to dividend yields to crisis management. IR must be able to solve problems and communicate issues in the context of shareholder value, and do it quickly. This is the language of the CEO, and it's the basis on which he or she is compensated and judged. And IR can't talk the CEO's language unless IR understands valuation and capital markets. Period.

Part One of this book provides a quick overview of the capital markets, the arena, its players, and how IR works with all of these areas.

Part Two covers the current environment, including what happened during the boom and bust, the rules that surfaced, and the regulatory environment.

Part Three looks at the basics of IR, including administrative and strategic tasks, internal and external communications, and the changes we see coming.

Part Four presents IR with dimension and reveals the practices that marry IR, corporate communications, corporate strategy, and ultimately equity value. In this section we answer:

*What goes on in the day of an **analyst**?*
*What are the **portfolio managers** looking for?*
*How can a company **uncover value**?*
*Why is **guidance** so important?*
*When is the best time to release **earnings announcements**?*
*Why and when should a company ever **pre-announce**?*
*How can a **teach-in** boost a company's visibility?*

*Why are Wall Street's **morning meetings** key to IR strategy?*
*What are the **landmines** that CEOs can set off with just one wrong word?*
*What is the most effective time for **insiders** to buy or sell stock?*
*How can a company best deal with **short sellers**?*
*What is **plan B** if a company can't get coverage?*
*How do mid, small, and micro-caps **stand out** in a crowded field?*
*When are **private companies** missing out if they don't have IR?*
*How can a company prevent the **whisper number**?*
*When is **bad news** better than no news?*
*Who's not being honest, and how can a CEO get **real feedback**?*

IR should be the tip of the spear of any financial communications strategy and help management define the tangible and intangibles of valuation, deliver a company story, and navigate the nuances of the capital markets dialogue to maximize equity value.

In addition, the caliber of a company's IR and the ability to untangle complex communications problems must be upgraded and handled by people with applicable experience. To us, it seems like common sense. A company that is going to hire a third party to navigate its course on Wall Street should retain someone with senior-level Wall Street experience. But then again, common sense isn't always so common.

One

Capital Markets and Their Players

A Brief Primer

This portion of the book provides a very basic overview of the capital markets: the arena, its players, and how IR works with all of these areas. The IR skills and tools necessary to manage this arena are only briefly presented here, and then discussed in-depth in Part IV.

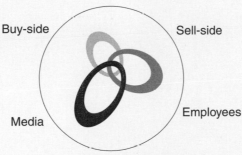

Capital Markets, Players, Stakeholders, and Influencers

CHAPTER 1

The Capital Markets and IR

No public company operates in a vacuum. In fact, many people, including regulators and competitors, generate opinions that can affect a company's position in the capital markets. Every decision a company makes, whether financial, strategic, or operational, ripples into the capital markets and affects the stock price, the competitive position, or the public's perception. Anticipating and assessing the impact of corporate actions on the capital markets, whether from an acquisition, a change in dividend policy, or a new product introduction, is the function of investor relations (IR).

The underlying premise of the capital markets is to connect those who have money with those who need money. However, this match must be made in a mutually beneficial manner. To that end, the *sell-side*, the middlemen and -women, must bring quality companies that need capital to Wall Street to sell equity or debt to the *buy-side*, managers of trillions of dollars in capital. What about companies that already have money and want to grow? They seek out the sell-side, who can help them acquire or divest of businesses or divisions. These transactions too must be beneficial to the buy-side, and to ensure that value is created, shareholders must approve these actions.

So who are the sell-side and the buy-side? The sell-side is made up of firms like Goldman Sachs, Bank of America Securities, S.G. Cowen, Wachovia, RBC Securities, Merrill Lynch, and Piper Jaffrey, to name a few. They are known as investment banks or brokerage firms, and they employ bankers, institutional salespeople, traders, and research analysts. The buy-side is composed of investors. The majority of these are institutional or professional investors, like Fidelity, T. Rowe Price, and Wellington Management, and they control huge amounts of money, usually from funds, endowments, or pensions. Simply put, they are true professionals who invest on behalf of their clients. Other investors include individuals who put their own money into the capital markets pot.

Generally speaking, companies that need money can get it in one of two ways. They can take it in exchange for a piece of the company—that is, they can sell *equity* or ownership, by giving the investor shares of stock in the company. Or they can borrow the money, and pay it back to the investor with interest, selling the investor *debt*—for example, bonds. On the other side of the equation, those who want to invest their money can do so, again generally speaking, in either *stocks* or *bonds*, and there are usually specialists in each area. (Of course, hybrid financing vehicles, like convertible bonds, are an option, but this discussion focuses just on equity and debt.)

Equity shares can be traded publicly on either the New York Stock Exchange or The American Stock Exchange, which are open auction floors, or the NASDAQ and Over-The-Counter exchanges, which are buyer-to-seller negotiated systems. Debt trades publicly on the bond or fixed income markets. A company that has equity or debt that trades publicly is subject to the rules and regulations, significantly augmented and expanded in recent years, of the Securities and Exchange Commission.

INVESTOR RELATIONS, TAKE 1

Publicly traded companies are required to provide certain information to current and potential investors. This information includes *mandated SEC disclosure documents*, such as *annual reports, 10-K filings, proxy statements, quarterly 10-Q filings*, and *8-Ks* that announce unscheduled decisions and actions. Additionally, there are the day-to-day goings-on of the company, marketing strategies, operational decisions, acquisitions, and general business fluctuations that, if deemed to be *material*, can be shared with investors.

All of these communications are supported by other vehicles such as

---

Though the SEC does not have a specific definition for material information, the term is generally interpreted to mean anything that would affect the understanding and decision making of an investor—i.e. anything that would cause a rational investor to act.

press releases, *conference calls*, and *management presentations*, whether live or Web cast.

In most cases, the packaging and distribution of this information is the responsibility of investor relations, as IR is the filter through which all financial communications come out of the company. (See Figure 1.1.)

Companies have either an IR department or an executive designated with IR responsibilities, and many companies supplement the IR function with outside IR counsel. IR counsel, either internal or external, not only administrates disclosure responsibilities but, in a perfect world, works to preserve or enhance the company's equity value. IR counsel steeped in capital markets know-how and industry-specific knowledge understands the cause and effect of stock movements and incorporates that knowledge into all strategic communications plans.

STOCK PRICES

Stock price, or equity value per share, moves up and down on company-specific financial results, macro- and micro-economic influences, and investor perception of the company. Digging deeper, however, stocks move for two main reasons: performance, both past (actual) and future (expected), and the way that performance is communicated and perceived.

A buoyant stock price is critical for any company because it can create opportunity in the form of a second currency beyond just cash to buy other companies. It can also attract the best employees and vendors and improve the morale of the entire organization. Many institutional investors only invest in stocks with large market capitalizations—that is, greater than $1 bil-

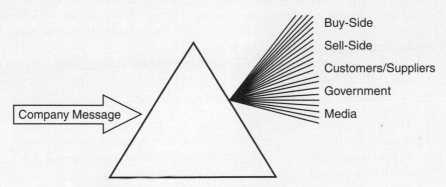

FIGURE 1.1 The Financial Communciations Filter

> "Digging deeper, however, stocks move for two main reasons: performance, both past (actual) and future (expected), and the way that performance is communicated and perceived."

lion, and sometimes $5 billion. Many investors focus only on large caps because they view them as having less risk, less volatility, and more liquidity, which allows big investors to buy and sell rapidly without moving the market. Correspondingly, companies want institutional investors to buy stocks because they usually buy large amounts, increasing liquidity and modifying volatility.

Companies with fewer shares outstanding often have to fight for exposure and awareness and work hard to support the continued buying and selling of their shares. Standing out among thousands of publicly traded companies and increase trading volume should be one of the aims of IR. Exposing the company to a wider range of shareholders can also attract the sell-side, which, from an investment banking perspective, views a high equity price as an opportunity to acquire assets for stock rather than cash or sell more equity to the public to raise cash for operations or debt reduction. All of these options or opportunities derive from a high stock price and are examples of a low-cost transactions that benefit shareholders.

COST OF CAPITAL

Though *the long-term value of a company's stock correlates 100 percent to financial performance*, a company's daily, monthly, or yearly stock price is important because it determines a company's cost of capital, and cost of capital is real money. As everyone knows, it costs money to get money— usually in the form of interest payments, or selling a piece of the pie. The cost of debt, or borrowing, is interest paid, and the lower the interest, the lower the cost of capital. The cost of equity is the price that investors are willing to pay for each share. In this case, the higher the price per share, for a constant earnings number, the lower a company's cost of capital, because the company will have to issue fewer shares to raise the same amount of money.

These relatively simple concepts can have a significant impact on the capacity of companies to generate profits and remain competitive. Keeping cost of capital low should be a major concern to CEOs and CFOs in running the business and creating shareholder wealth. It's a fiduciary obligation.

The Weighted Average Cost of Capital

$$WACC = E/V * Re + D/V * Rd * (1-Tc)$$

Re = cost of equity
Rd = cost of debt
E   = market value company's equity
D   = market value of company's debt
V   = E + D
E/V = equity percentage of capital
D/V = debt percentage of capital
Tc = the corporate tax rate

THE VIRTUOUS CYCLE OF A HIGH STOCK PRICE

If the cost of capital is determined by a company's equity value, it's pretty important to maximize that value at any given time. Beyond financial returns, it energizes employees, partners, and vendors; supports important strategic activities; influences the media; and creates a superior return on investment to that of one's competitors. This becomes a virtuous cycle. (See Figure 1.2.)

Strategic and consistent communication and outreach can have a significant and positive influence on share price, and therefore the price-to-earnings ratio or any other valuation method. This is because one multiple point on a company's market value can be worth tens, or even hundreds, of millions of dollars. For example, if a company's stock price is $60 and its earnings are $6 a share, they're trading at a P/E of 10. If they have 200 million shares outstanding, the total market capitalization is $12 billion. If the multiple goes up just one point, to 11, the stock trades at $66 a share, and the market cap is $13.2 billion, a $1.2 billion increase in value from one multiple point. Strategic positioning and outreach can accomplish that expansion.

VALUATION—THE OBVIOUS AND THE NOT-SO-OBVIOUS

There are many different types of investors with many different objectives. Some want *growth* and look for stocks with high returns and earnings momentum. Others seek *value* and purchase stocks they feel are undervalued

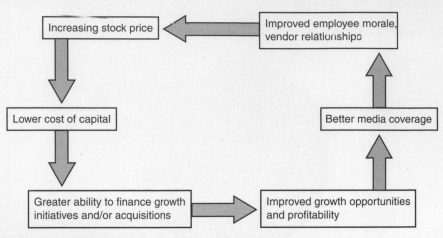

FIGURE 1.2   Maintaining a Premium Relative Multiple

and underfollowed by Wall Street. Another type of investor wants *income*, like stocks with a dividend.

Regardless of the differences, most investors take the information they are given and run it through quantitative models. Then they compare the results to other companies in the same industry and make an investment decision based on these relative quantitative indicators. This is basic information easily culled from a company's financials, which must be disclosed on its income statements, cash flow statements, and balance sheets. Anyone can get these and do their modeling.

Then there are the *intangibles*, which is where IR needs to be at the top of its game. The intangibles are the nuances of value, the managing of expectations and perception, and the ability to *define, deliver,* and create a *dialogue* about a company's financial performance and position in its industry. In fact, intangibles are an important component of maximizing value. Anywhere from *20 to 40 percent of a company's valuation is linked directly to these items*. That's a big piece of the valuation pie, and the job of IR is to help management maximize it and investors understand it. (See Figure 1.3.)

AIR TIME FOR THE PRIVATE COMPANY

Regardless of whether a company is traded publicly, or its stock is held by private investors unable to sell the shares on public exchanges, having a voice in the capital markets is important. Many private companies wait until

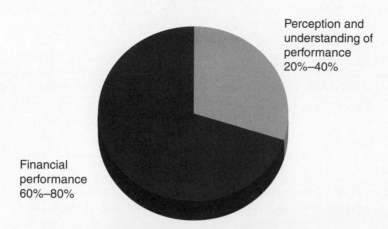

Perception and
understanding of
performance
20%–40%

Financial
performance
60%–80%

FIGURE 1.3   The Valuation Pie

they are considering going public—that is, offering their shares to the public via an initial public offering—before they incorporate IR into their strategy. This is a missed opportunity for private companies to build relationships with Wall Street and, more importantly, to create a distinct advantage and gain a competitive edge in their industries.

The opinions of capital markets professionals, particularly analysts but sometimes portfolio managers, are often quoted by the media, and the media is an integral force in shaping public perception and forming a company's reputation. Therefore, in order for private companies to have equal representation in the public eye, they have to be at least a twinkle in the eye of the capital markets. They have to get their message and mission across so that it is well-understood and incorporated into the points of view of The Street. An IR strategy is of great value to the private company in putting the message out there.

A private company has the best of both worlds. Privates can talk to the world, make predictions about themselves and the industry, and potentially affect their competition's perception and cost of capital, yet never be held to the regulatory accountability that comes with life as a public company.

INVESTOR RELATIONS, TAKE 2

Providing the necessary disclosures and information is one thing. Knowing what Wall Street expects from a company and its management team is something else entirely. The best IR professionals are inside the brains of their investors, and think like analysts and portfolio managers. By understanding valuation they can approach analysts and money managers as peers and work hard to build trust.

IR can directly improve the 20 to 40 percent of a company's valuation linked to factors outside of financial performance and bolster market capitalizations while increasing exposure and obtaining valuable third-party validation. There is a science to valuation, but there is also an art.

Two companies of similar size in a similar industry are growing earnings at 20 percent annually, yet one trades inexpensively at a 10x P/E multiple while the other garners a 20x P/E multiple. The former, in all likelihood, has credibility issues or problems understanding the investment community. The latter most likely understands the nuances of communication, how to be economic to investment banks, and how to preserve credibility in tough times. That's the art of the stock market and that's what affects equity value.

Though the uninitiated may believe that investing is a game of chance, few intelligent investors act with this understanding. Professionals on the buy-side have too much responsibility for too much money to invest aggressively with management teams that don't understand Wall Street. Investors need to believe that they will get good and relevant information clearly communicated by the company, and that the CEO and CFO understand the capital markets and how to properly circumvent issues that could be detrimental to equity value in the short and the long term.

Premium valuation results from not only strong performance, but also because of a belief in management, which reduces uncertainty. Lower risk perception means higher value, and IR can be a key factor in this equation. CEOs and CFOs should seek to establish this credibility and trust with all communicated events. It's an insurance policy on shareholders' personal wealth and management's reputation.

GLOBAL IR

Companies are expanding their communications to foreign sources of capital, and investors are culling a global range of investment opportunities. In this arena of global exchange, specific investor relations expertise distinguishes itself.

IR professionals with extensive relationships and a wide range of capital markets know-how can extend the reach to find the right investor well beyond the company's home shores.

- When is the time to think about marketing to overseas investors?
- How will you know if overseas investors will even care?
- Will the story translate?

Roam from Home

Investing can be precarious and risky from the outset. Add an ocean, a different language, a distinct currency, and cultural idiosyncrasies, and the uninitiated might consider it speculative. Generating interest from international funds that invest in U.S. equities requires knowledge of the funds' investment guidelines. Many international funds, similar to those in the United States, publish their investment outlines on their Web sites, and this information is also available from institutional investor databases, such as Thompson Financial and Big Dough.

Once a pool of potential investors is identified, IR must think through the issues that an international portfolio manager or analyst will have to address to complete adequate due diligence. Additionally, if the investment idea comes from a voice they feel they can trust—someone with whom they have a relationship or who has experience in the overseas markets—international marketing can be efficient. Companies should consider marketing with a brokerage firm that has institutional salespeople who cover that region. Thankfully, the investment bank consolidation of the 1990s created many such banks with strong overseas presence, including Credit Suisse First Boston, Deutsche Bank (formerly BT Alex. Brown), and CIBC Oppenheimer.

Experience has taught us that investment opportunities tend to travel better when a product or service of the company is already international. Companies listed on U.S. exchanges that do a substantial amount of business overseas have a much easier task translating their business, and thus their investment merits, to foreign investors.

Many large branded companies, like Starbucks and Wal-Mart, have had significant international business success and have also captured the attention of foreign investors. Some emerging companies have also done the same.

One good example is Quiksilver, the world's leading purveyor of surf and boardsport-inspired apparel and accessories. In 2003 institutional investors were reluctant to pay a higher multiple for the perceived growth of the rapidly growing global brand, so management wanted to cast a wider net. The investment merits of this smaller-capitalization growth company traveled well and attracted foreign investor interest due to their international brand-name recognition. Any portfolio manager with kids, whether living in France, Australia, or the United States, was probably buying the company's products, which made it easier to explain the investment opportunities to foreign investors.

The Tangled Web

No company operates in a vacuum. Every decision ripples through the capital markets. The sell-side, the buy-side, strategic partners, the media, regulators, and the global community are all important constituencies to be addressed by investor relations. IR with capital markets know-how is invaluable to companies addressing these constituencies and helps to maximize equity value.

CHAPTER 2

The Sell-Side Disclosed: Who They Are and What They Do

A common and pervasive misperception about the sell-side is that small- and micro-cap public and private companies need not apply. That's not entirely accurate. Though the consolidation of investment banks has created financial conglomerates oftentimes incapable of generating profits from smaller companies, we believe these "small caps" should pursue the sell-side and research coverage nonetheless. IR that fully understands the sell-side, who they are, and what they do, can help any size company, public or private, take on this challenge.

The sell-side represents an important link between investors and corporations. For those companies looking for capital, the sell-side has access to investors and the means and motivation to service them. For investors, it gives them access to investments, and even creates new products in the form of IPOs, debt issues, or secondary offerings. It also offers research, sales and trading execution, and liquidity. The sell-side's ability, through its analysts, to provide research on companies and recommend stocks underscores the analyst's importance in the capital markets. Even for the smallest publicly traded entity, a sell-side analyst can be an effective vehicle to legitimize a business and attract new investors.

That said, a company with $20 million in market capitalization will likely find it futile to pursue an analyst at one of the blue-chip Wall Street firms. Larger firms need larger fees to stay in business, and the best way to earn larger fees is to focus investment banking, research, and trading activities on larger companies; also, roughly the same amount of time and resources is needed to do the work, regardless of size. Three percent of a $20 million equity transaction is a far less attractive fee for an investment banker than 3 percent of a $200 million equity transaction. Similarly, a stock that trades 100,000 shares a day at $0.04 commission is far more attractive to trade than an illiquid small-cap company that trades 10,000 each day at best.

Each company should play in its own league and look for the best sell-side fit. Big companies should target the blue-chip investment banks, like Goldman Sachs or Morgan Stanley, whereas small companies should direct their efforts to the small, yet high-quality banks set up to service smaller public entities. Analysts and firms are available for just about any company, but what's important is finding one to support that company's goals.

THE SCOOP ON THE SELL-SIDE

The players on the sell-side are research analysts, investment bankers, traders, sales traders, and institutional salespeople or brokers. Brokers work with their clients, both institutional and retail (mom-and-pop), to assist them with, and facilitate, their investment choices. They hand-off buy and sell requests to their traders, who execute the buying and selling of stocks and bonds in the market. To help the traders manage risk—not owning or shorting too much of any given stock at any given time—sales traders are there to locate buyers when too many sell orders are flowing into the firm, or locating sellers when an overabundance of buy orders for a given issue flood the trading desk.

Following a select group of stocks with a variety of recommendations are analysts in the research department. Analysts cover or publish on a relatively small number of companies and/or industries and make stock recommendations based on extensive due diligence and analysis. These reports are used directly by the buy-side for investment guidance, although employees, customers, suppliers, and the media also look at them as key sources of intelligence.

Research can be powerful and relevant, and despite the malfeasance of the late 1990s, hundreds of extremely hard-working, intelligent, and ethical analysts work in this industry.

However, the consolidation of the investment banking landscape resulted in fewer banks and, by definition, fewer analysts. For the most part, they are being paid less, partially because of new rules that prohibit the investment banking divisions from compensating analysts. Also, analysts are under intense regulatory and legal scrutiny, both internally and externally. When many of the most experienced analysts left their practices, the assumption was made that the quality of research would deteriorate, but quality research is still very relevant and available:

- Research is still a very important source for unbiased views on any company.
- The media, trades, employees, and competitors all read it.
- Research still has an effect on visibility, liquidity, share price and valuation.
- Because of the above factors, research affects the overall cost of capital, which can fuel a company's expansion.

The sell-side also employs investment bankers. They are product creators who facilitate transactions, such as IPOs, mergers, and bond offerings that create value for companies and shareholders. In the case of an IPO, the banker essentially packages the soon-to-be public company as product and the institutional sales forces sells it to their clients, such as Fidelity. The traders then manage share inventory on the trading desk post-transaction, and the analyst publishes research on the company and assesses whether the stock is a Buy, Sell, or Hold given the circumstances.

Research and sales and trading, and the investment banking function of the business work separately, with a figurative Chinese Wall keeping information from passing between them. In concept, this agreement keeps the day-to-day capital markets function from the inside information that bankers need to do their jobs. During transactions, such as underwritings of debt or equity, the investment banks have procedures that support the intention of securities laws and keep research and banking apart. We all know now that the process broke down in the late 1990s in a rush to complete transactions and generate massive fees and salaries.

In addition to the large investment banks, there are many smaller boutiques that specialize in certain industries or investment approaches. There are also regional houses that focus on local companies and investors. Many of these offer brokerage, banking, and research services and can be great partners to smaller, fast-growing companies. Finally, there are numerous independent research firms that only publish research and have no investment banking capabilities.

IR RELATIONSHIPS WITH THE SELL-SIDE

For the IR professional, sell-side relationships are extremely important. While knowledge of how the sell-side works is a necessity, knowing how to position a company for research coverage is one of the most important fundamentals of IR. On any given day a sell-side analyst talks to dozens of portfolio managers, the press, industry professionals, and other company executives. Directing the perception of the sell-side is a highly effective means of leveraging the corporate message.

Analysts are very busy with a crowd of publicly traded companies to pick through and possibly recommend. While they want to find the best investment opportunities for their clients, they don't always have the time and resources to follow up on every interesting prospect. Given these facts, IR professionals are essentially competing for shelf space in the analyst's mind, and the best way to get on the shelf is to think as analysts do and understand how they are compensated. The IR professional typically has a small window of opportunity to deliver the company story, and that story must appeal immediately to the analyst as a stock picker. The profile of the company should also be attractive in terms of potential investment banking and trading fees, but that shouldn't be the analyst's concern given the new regulatory environment. That said, all analysts can quickly determine if a company fits the overall philosophy and focus of their sell-side employer.

THE SELL-SIDE/BUY-SIDE RELATIONSHIP

The buy-side, both institutional and retail (individual investors), execute their investments through the sell-side. They rely on the brokers and traders to execute their orders in a timely and reliable fashion, a relationship that is integral to the capital markets.

Buy-side investors also rely on the research analyst's narrow focus. While a sell-side analyst might cover 15 or 20 companies, his or her counterpart on the buy-side may own 50 or 100. Because the sell-side is insinuated into every aspect of an industry, the buy-side relies on them for market intelligence, industry information and opinions, as well as access to companies and management.

EQUITY RESEARCH

Equity research was created after the sleepy stock market days of the 1930s and 1940s, when investors were still a bit market-shy from the 1929 crash. Broker Charles E. Merrill and his firm Merrill Lynch wanted to bring the information to average American families. He thought research papers with in-depth information and recommendations on certain companies and industries would ease avenues of access to what had once been the domain of the wealthy or speculative few.

As more investors entered the market, firms continued to provide research to their sales and trading clients for a fee, but it was also a customer service offering for investors who did their business with, and provided trading commissions to, that firm. Eventually, analysts became known for their expertise and pulled investors and companies to the firm for trading and investment banking business.

Equity research provides in-depth analyses of companies, as well as overviews of the industries in which those companies compete. The analyst's objective is to do a complete analysis of a company in order to estimate its value relative to the current stock price and then make an "actionable" recommendation to investors. These recommendations are bannered at the top of all research reports and differ from firm to firm. Generally, however, there are different scales of recommendations, including Strong Buy, Hold, and Sell. In reality, there are many other ratings, including Buy, Outperform, Long-Term Buy, Moderate Buy, and Accumulate. These, unfortunately, can be the equivalent of either Hold or even Sell recommendations and are designed not to offend management teams, thereby preserving access, the lifeblood of an analyst. Without these ratings, management would certainly be bothered or angry (Sell recommendations in writing don't sit well with CEOs), and an analyst might be cut off from access and ultimately the ability to do his job. Underperform, Moderate Sell, Sell, and Strong Sell are truthful recommendations and analysts who utilize these ratings, although very rare, are real stock pickers. Table 2.1 shows the anatomy of a research report.

The IR aspiration of getting a company noticed and creating interest in the stock is best met through the analysts and their research reports, which is called coverage. Unless a company is fairly substantial, with a market cap over $100 to $200 million, getting coverage can be a battle. IR that understands how an investment bank works and can establish a relationship with an analyst is best positioned to get coverage.

The first step is to get on an analyst's radar. Analysts pride themselves on the depth and range of their industry expertise, and with shrinking staffs, many analysts don't have time to learn every fact. IR can make analysts smart by delivering timely and incrementally valuable information about the company or the industry. Even if that analyst doesn't write a research report on the company, an information-sharing relationship might result in a mention in an industry report.

In pursuit of a voice, private companies should also think about targeting the analysts. Much of the media exposure on private and public companies includes an analyst quote because analysts are seen as highly credible, third-party validators. As the analyst works to paint a comprehensive picture of the industry, the private company must convince the analyst that any portrait without them is incomplete.

TABLE 2.1 The Anatomy of A Research Report

Company Name					
(Ticker – Recent Stock Price – Exchange)					
Recommendation: Buy, Hold, or Sell					
Stock Price (most recent)	Stock Price 52-Week Range high to low	EPS Lst Yr This Yr est Next Yr est	P/E est This Yr Next Yr	Quarterly EPS This Yr v. Last	Div/Yld est This quarter
Capitalization $					

THE ANALYST'S BUSY DAY

The work begins with the daunting task of sifting through hundreds of companies to decide which ones warrant research coverage. Then the analyst visits the business; touches the product; scours the inventory; walks through the plants; meets with management; talks to its competitors, consumers, suppliers, vendors, and employees; and fundamentally becomes the expert on that company and its goings-on. Following this comprehensive due diligence, the analyst goes back to the computer and builds a financial model that estimates future performance. Then the analyst, who must be part scientist and part artist, must make an argument on the company and sector, complete with the earnings estimates, a recommendation, and a price target.

It is wrong to think that a company can't get sell-side coverage without investment banking business. Analysts want to be smart, and they ultimately keep or lose their jobs based on stock picks and the reputation they develop over time. If they initiate coverage on what they believe is a good stock pick, it means commission business for the trading desks and may mean other banking fees down the road if the sell-side firm's investment bankers meet with management and point out the firm's strengths.

That said, issuing research is a big commitment for an analyst and an investment bank. IR must do its homework and know what size companies are the best fit for sell-side firms—large caps only, small-cap stocks, or industry expertise, such as technology. Then it must package management and the company in a way that will appeal to the appropriate analyst and his or her bank.

ECONOMIC EVENTS

IR should help the analysts plant the seed for trading commissions and banking fees by creating economic events that generate these commissions and fees and create paydays for the analysts and their investment banks. There are numerous above-board ways for a company to facilitate economic events that will continually reward analysts with well-thought-out research coverage (not necessarily any particular rating), which is discussed in Chapter 24, "Meeting the Street."

THE IR IMPERATIVE

Analysts, in order to do thoughtful analysis and judge stocks fairly, need the right information, communicated clearly, from sources they trust as reliable. Analysts sometimes find people who don't really address what is needed. Some executives just don't have the time to share their story. Others don't know what analysts want or need. A few are worried about sharing information, even positive information, that might be misunderstood or misrepresented. Others have flaws in their strategy or operations and opt to keep quiet until the problems are fixed. Many companies just aren't aware of how best to describe their businesses and strategies to The Street.

A company that is going to be public might as well be the best public company it can be and do right by the shareholders. Unfortunately, in all these cases, management isn't necessarily doing what is in the best interest of its shareholders, and that's blatantly wrong.

The reason we came into IR as former analysts and buy-side professionals was to mitigate the losses incurred in translation, to help companies tell their story without being misunderstood or misrepresented, and to help analysts get the best information they could for thoughtful and fair analysis. IR's mandate is to fully understand the sell-side in the broader context of its employer, the investment bank, which is the best way to increase chances for coverage. Without this information, companies that spend lots of time and money approaching Wall Street analysts are probably wasting both.

CHAPTER 3

The Buy-Side: Institutional and Retail Investors

The nice thing about institutional and retail investors is that their objective is the same as the company's. They want the stock price to appreciate. An investor who understands the long-term investment thesis is a valuable partner because this investor takes some supply out of the supply-and-demand equation, and sets the table for a demand imbalance should the company's earnings increase.

It is not only possible, but very productive, to match specific investors with specific companies for long-term partnerships. In fact, investors who take large positions in a company's stock can have a big influence on share price. If they believe in the company and management, then they will most likely buy and hold, which can reduce volatility and keep the stock price on an even, upward keel. IR should identify, establish, and maintain strong relationships with these investors and keep track of how these investors can change with valuation changes.

THE BUZZ ON THE BUY-SIDE

The majority of the money invested in stocks comes from fund and portfolio managers overseeing formally organized pools of money. The rest comes from individual investors. For the time they hold the stock, these are the company's owners, and their perceptions and those of potential investors are what matter.

Institutional investors, led by portfolio managers, are responsible for large amounts of money that need to find a way into the market. This class of investor gets funds from foundations, endowments, pensions, estates, asset accounts for high-net-worth individuals and families, and companies with large cash balances, like commercial banks and insurance carriers. *Retail investors* have become a greater force in the market because of the advent of Internet-based trading and the expansion of retail brokerage houses. These individual investors (not to be confused with day traders, who are not true investors) can be targeted through the retail brokers and brokerage houses through which they trade.

All of these investors have different objectives. Some want security, while others take more risk for more reward. In general, investors are thrown into three categories.

Value investors look at metrics like P/E, or enterprise value to EBITDA (earnings before interest, taxes, depreciation, and amortization), and purchase stocks that have unrecognized potential and are trading at a discount to others in their industry.

Growth investors also look at P/E and EBITDA, but also look for consistent, above-average increases in market share, sales, cash flow, and retained earnings that get pumped back into operations.

Income investors are looking for current cash—that is, dividends—and all the better if the stock price appreciates and they garner a solid total return.

Some investors can't be categorized so succinctly. Factors that play into their objectives may include a focus on technology, an emphasis on environmental policies, growth at a reasonable price, or micro-market-cap investing. Aside from the aforementioned objectives that characterize investors, IR professionals should recognize the other players on Wall Street.

The first are the *short-sellers,* those who bet against a company. They sell borrowed shares and hope to buy them back at lower prices, thereby profiting.

The second are the *momentum* or *tape players* who look for quick paper gains. These players are essentially traders who buy in and out of stocks, taking advantage of short-term movements. They tend to create volatility, are not long-term-oriented, and rarely spend the time necessary to understand a company.

IR that helps management deal effectively with short-term fluctuations in the stock caused by these players is invaluable. The key is always being conservative with financial communications and focusing on long-term fundamentals, which gives those shorting the stock or trading the market less relevance.

Companies should also understand and accept that there is an army of short-term commission players on Wall Street and that management can do little to combat them. Ultimately, stock prices find the level that correlates to financial performance and perception at any given time, so management must accept that fact on a day-to-day basis and deal professionally with these groups to preserve credibility and protect value. Admittedly, that's not always easy when a big investor or board member implores the CEO to take action against a short-seller. The situation can become emotional. Having an IR effort that can identify short sellers, understand the situation, and take the emotion out of the issue is paramount.

MANAGEMENT AND THE INVESTORS

Every investor considers factors such as profitability, operating efficiencies, growth potential, competitive positioning, and management. The last is not only not least, sometimes it can be everything.

It's an old adage: people invest in people. There's a premium investors pay for Bill Gates's vision or Warren Buffett's experience. Investors like to know and trust the person managing the company and hear them elucidate their views and strategy. However, they don't want to hear them promoting themselves or the companies they run. It's a fine line, and while confidence in management leads to investor confidence, IR must help management balance this high wire.

IR RELATIONSHIPS WITH THE BUY-SIDE

IR's pursuit of the right investor benefits not only the company but the investor as well. Most portfolio managers spend most of their brain power trying to do the right thing with the millions of dollars for which they're responsible. If IR relays a company's value story in the language a portfolio manager is used to hearing, the company has a much better chance of surfacing through the hundreds of investment options piled on the fund manager's desk. Also, if the portfolio manager respects the IR representative's capability and knowledge of the capital markets, the IR team has effectively saved fifteen to thirty minutes of the CFO's or CEO's time by communicating the basics of the story. Replicated over dozens of portfolio managers, that's significant time savings that management can put into the operations of the company.

Once the portfolio manager has decided to become a long-term holder, IR that understands how to communicate with that money manager and The Street in general will position the company for sustained equity value. If the buy-side believes that management knows not only how to execute, but also how to communicate decisions so that the buy-side's investment is protected, the art and science of negotiating the market combine to maximize valuation.

That is why the buy-side, more than anyone perhaps, appreciates capital markets–based IR counsel. Strategic advisors who have sat in their seat understand investment goals and the hot-button issues that can cause short-term volatility. The IR function, without experience and information, can't possibly have this perspective.

CHAPTER 4

Employees, Suppliers, Customers

Though the buy-side and the sell-side influence stock price, both sides can agree that others in the equation are equally important to the ongoing operations and profitability of the company. These are the catalyst constituencies, the groups that in and of themselves can make or break a company.

THE STARTING TEAM

Employees are the most obvious catalyst constituency because they are a major contributor to the success of a company. In addition to developing, executing, and growing the business, they are also an active voice for the company. Aggregated, their words and deeds can carry far into the capital markets. Not only can employees have an influence on investors, in most cases they are investors.

For senior management, it's not only important to develop a long-term business plan and thesis but equally important to have employees embrace that thesis. This buy-in is essential to keeping the team on a cooperative, purposeful, and energized route to accomplishing the company's goals. Employee communications must effectively integrate with IR so that internal communications regarding business performance, outlook, competitiveness, and challenges are consistent, if tailored from investor-speak to employee-speak.

All public companies should assume that employees and team members listen to quarterly conference calls and Web casts. Employees represent the company to the outside world, in their neighborhoods and communities, as well as to important strategic partners such as vendors, suppliers, and distributors.

A telecommunications company has disclosed to investors on a conference call a cost-cutting plan without simultaneously communicating this plan to employees or preparing them for the news. Not only did the company set up the employees to hear the bad news from elsewhere, but the company disenfranchised its team members by referring to employees as "heads," stating they'd be "cutting heads" to reduce costs. Productivity and moral naturally suffered, and resume activity increased dramatically.

VERTICAL AND HORIZONTAL STAKEHOLDERS

Strategic partners in a company's supply channel are most effective if they understand the objectives and goals of the companies with which they are working. Clear and consistent communication is the key to this understanding.

The need exists to relay the company mission throughout the supply chain, from raw materials to retail. The balance of power in the supply and distribution channel varies from industry to industry and company to company. Sometimes the relationships are greatly interdependent, with all players equally reliant on the others for their very existence. Sometimes one player dominates; for example, when Wal-Mart sneezes, multiple consumer product companies catch a cold.

Management should recognize the effect that a major customer or supplier can have on the way the company is perceived, based on the company's reliance on that customer or supplier. When the lead dog is the company, IR's ability to communicate well is vital. Regardless of which organization weighs heaviest on the supply channel, every function has the direct or indirect capacity to enhance or detract from a company's value. Everyone benefits if IR is informed, understands these relationships, and works with PR or Corporate Communications to set the context for the flow of communication between the company and its strategic partners.

THE COMPETITION

Though communication to the competition is rarely direct, a company's peer group in any industry is going to see its press releases and financials, learn its strategy, and understand its business. Public company disclosure requirements necessitate that material financial information be disclosed in a timely manner, although what is and what isn't material can be a confounding process. In fact, there is no bright-line standard for materiality. The definition relies on case law. Companies want to disclose as much as, but not more than, they should, while investors and analysts increasingly demand more information. Getting this fine line right is important for all constituencies: regulators, investors, and analysts. Distributing excessive information can provide competitors with more knowledge than makes management comfortable.

THE GOVERNMENT—SEC, FASB, AND INDUSTRY REGULATORS

Created in 1934 to restore public confidence in the capital markets subsequent to the stock market crash of 1929, the Securities and Exchange Commission (SEC) was established to promote stability in the markets and protect investors. As the Commission states, "the primary mission of the U.S. Securities and Exchange Commission is to protect investors and maintain the integrity of the securities markets." In this vein, "the SEC is concerned primarily with promoting disclosure of important information, enforcing the securities laws, and protecting investors who interact with these various organizations and individuals."

The Securities and Exchange Commission is the overseer of all public disclosures. The SEC sets the template for, and provides the public with access to, these company-specific filings. The precise guidelines for SEC disclosure, as well as the rules and regulations of the Federal Accounting Standards Board (FASB), lends a uniformity to all financial statements and helps streamline and simplify the process for financial communications. Almost every business must claim regulators as an important constituency. These can be government (e.g., Food and Drug Administration [FDA], Federal Communications Commission [FCC], or Environmental Protection Agency [EPA]), labor (e.g., unions), or industry (e.g., the Direct Marketing Association). All these third parties closely examine the operations and output of a company, aiming to protect whichever aspect of the business they represent. Regulators are best served if they are being consistently heard and clearly addressed. Along with the other catalysts, IR's input into the communications with these groups can make or break valuation.

CHAPTER 5

The Media

Of all the constituencies that will ultimately pass judgment on a company, none can be more powerful or pervasive than the media. The media has the right and privilege to explore any newsworthy issue concerning public corporations and private companies and scrutinize them for the edification or pure entertainment of their audience. The media can influence investor perception, their investment choices, and stock prices. It can also affect public perception, which can then affect consumer behavior, and ultimately have an impact on a company's business. Obviously, the consequences of a company's media strategy can underscore or undermine their valuation strategy. Business and media relations efforts must follow the strategic goals of an IR program and be very aware of the company's financial performance, its investment merits, and the expectations that Wall Street places on the company.

AN INTEGRATED PLAN

The element of surprise may be an effective tactic for war and birthday parties, but it's a company's worst nightmare when the media is concerned. The most important thing a company can do when dealing with the media is to be prepared for *anything*. That means having a plan to deal with *everything*.

On the other side of the page, the media doesn't take surprises well either. A company that shares information in a timely and candid manner not only provides the media with a courtesy, but also gives the company an opportunity to create the tone and direction of the story. If that story is in line with the long-term thesis of the company, then the investor relations and communications departments arc doing their jobs properly.

When most people think of the media, they think of public relations. Public relations, communications, and media experts have the skills for selling a story. They also know best how to deal with the media, whether getting in front of a story, emphasizing key components to steer a story that's already out there, or building a platform of productive discourse in times of crisis.

These functions should work closely together to communicate with every constituency that influences the capital markets, especially the media. If IR can run its pattern toward the analysts while PR runs its pattern toward the media, the combination creates a substantial and parallel two-tiered offense that can pay off in terms of valuation, the CEO's ultimate goal.

Just as IR professionals should know how the capital markets will react to key decisions, PR professionals should anticipate the media's interpretation. This knowledge is essential, because once a story leaves the company doors, it's up to others to get it right. Because the company can no longer control how the story is told, the company should do everything in its power to make sure that those controlling the story actually understand the story.

THE AUDIENCE

Analysts are taught to dig deep to discover the company story, a quest similar to that of a reporter. Good reporters aren't trying to annoy companies; they're trying to do their jobs, which means uncovering information and the story line.

Understanding the audience is an important step in getting the media to hear and tell the story that the company wants understood. PR can help IR with its intimate knowledge of the various television, newspaper, radio, or magazine outlets and their personnel. By identifying their needs and responsibilities, and uncovering the issues of interest to them, PR and IR can position a story to stand out.

Some companies forego the conversation with the media altogether, fearful that they'll be misquoted or have statements taken out of context. But avoiding the media, or worse, promoting contention with reporters or producers, can be damaging. The media exists, and it's not going away. They will oftentimes do a story with or without management's help. The media is a necessary, and many times beneficial, conduit for communication, and companies should utilize it to their advantage. As in any industry, there are going to be mavericks out to make a name for themselves, sometimes by any means necessary. With a pulse on the media players and a proactive plan in place, IR and PR can hope to manage these individuals and keep the story on track.

POSITIONED TO BE PROACTIVE

Most companies would like the media to be all over their good news and nowhere near the bad news. Of course, it doesn't work like that. If a story is going to be told, the company wants to be first in with the information, which means a proactive approach to sharing news, good and bad.

It also means a complete approach, especially with the bad news. A company that has bad news to share should do it right away and all the way. Dribbling it out in bits and pieces can make for not only a long, drawn-out decline in stock price, but also a major credibility issue for management that can have far-reaching effects. In reality, if there is bad news, management must understand that the media and the market will become aware of it sooner rather than later anyway, so management might as well take it all in one punch and not let negative momentum build. So what would a byproduct of the slow and painful negative information dissemination be? The loss of management credibility and the decline in multiple would materially diminish the ability to sell new equity in the market. This, in turn, could weaken the company, particularly if a capital raise would have led to a merger or debt reduction.

Bad things happen to good companies all the time, and IR and PR professionals must be prepared and practiced to deal with the unimaginable. Proactive, clear, composed and candid management can take the worst of all worlds and turn the company, and the perception of its investors, toward something better.

EXPOSURE AND EQUITY

Only a fine line separates company awareness and personal exposure. An integrated approach to IR and PR can work toward making every media portrayal of the company consistent and reliable. An integrated approach should help management choose the message and the speakers that are on target for preserving or improving the company's reputation and value.

Post-Bubble Communications

*Events in the Markets and
the New World of IR*

CHAPTER 6

Greed Is Good, '90s Style

The market has seen its share of ups and downs over the decades, but the rocket ride and dramatic downslide of the late 1990s was a perpetual headline maker—another example of humankind's historical prerogative to get excited, especially as a group.

"All economic movements, by their very nature, are motivated by crowd psychology."

—Bernard M. Baruch

Manic booms shouldn't be all that surprising. There are examples throughout time, from the famed Tulip Bulb Mania in Holland in the 1630s to the soaring U.S. stock market of the 1920s. The particular spurt that took place in the United States during the last five years of the 20th century was aided by the advent of a pervasive new technology, the Internet. Regardless of years of study of tribal irrationality, however, everyone wanted in on the party, the market was going up, and there was a massive disconnect between reality and perception. The Internet became a platform of possibility for every industrious innovator on the globe. Its uses seemed infinite, and in 1995 one of the leading upshots of this bountiful playing field, Netscape, went public and doubled its value in its first day of trading.

A rash of IPOs followed, and initial public offerings briefly became an inherent right of the Internet pioneer rather than the privileged platform to capital they'd historically been. The share prices of new companies, many with no profits, and most with significant losses, soared. Traditional valuations were overlooked in favor of new-fangled metrics. Institutions, retail investors, and day traders pumped up paper values, which took on more meaning than tangible assets or real cash flow.

The market went nowhere but up, glamorizing companies with products that had hundreds of "eyeballs" but no profits, over companies with steady cash flow, solid earnings growth, and experienced management. Even value investors who relied on traditional valuation models such as price-earnings, return on invested capital, or book value had a difficult time staying on the sidelines of this gold rush. During this time, it seemed that IR took on a qualitative role, more concerned about preserving unrealistic valuations than with delivering an investment thesis based on underlying fundamentals. However, when there are no fundamentals to refer to, the qualitative road was the only one to take.

The strong economy created a perception of wealth and disposable income that steered new investors to the market. These individuals were vulnerable to the hype and weren't familiar with the cyclical nature of the stock market and its inherent risks. Nor did they seem familiar with the process of analyzing companies. Dips in the market were seen as buying opportunities rather than possible downward trends, and a heavy portion of assets were allocated to tech stocks rather than to a diversified basket of established companies.

Not only was technology the source of the excitement, but it was access to the affair. Las Vegas meets your 401(k). The Dow passed 10,000, and NASDAQ pushed through 5,000.

THE ROCKY FOUNDATION FOR ANALYSTS

The analyst's role is to evaluate companies objectively. The Chinese Wall that separates research from the investment bankers allows bankers to work with privileged, highly confidential client information, and to keep that information from leaking to research, sales, and trading. It became an odd parallel, then, when analysts started to receive compensation for sourcing investment banking transactions—in effect, breaking through the cornerstone of investment banking integrity, the Chinese Wall.

These analysts, who worked closely with many companies and had the power to make or break them with their research, started funneling those companies toward their investment bankers to raise money. That was the beginning of the gravy train, and analysts started asking more corporate finance questions than questions leading them to a better understanding of a company's underlying fundamentals. Since investment banks can receive fees between 3 percent and 7 percent of the total money raised for any given deal, it's no wonder banking became the primary focus: in most cases it's the investment bank's biggest revenue generator. A mad dash to create transactions took place.

Then a funny thing happened on the way to the investment bank. The Buy, Hold, Sell recommendation system eroded even further. Suddenly, anything other than a Buy had the potential to offend management and risk the loss of investment banking business. Strong Buy, Buy, Outperform and Accumulate were all examples of "investment banking ratings," designed to shed positive light on companies and massage the ego of many high-flying (and not particularly capital markets–savvy) CEOs whose ego might not tolerate a HOLD rating. The punchline to the joke, and the reality for almost every investment professional on Wall Street, however, was that almost any rating other than Strong Buy was considered a Sell. Though this practice is beginning to shift back again, it still holds true today in many firms.

Analysts were less to blame for these conditions than upper management at the investment banks, however. If analysts didn't play along and recommend potential or existing banking clients, they might position themselves to be fired. At the very least, analysts who didn't wave the flag ran the risk of alienation by buy-side fund managers, potentially cutting off millions in commission business for the investment bank. Finally, any rating but a Buy in all likelihood put the analyst in the penalty box with management, cutting off access and one's ability to do the job. Sure the analysts were to blame, but the entire system was broken, from the top down, not just research.

MANAGEMENT'S MUDDLE

A few corporate senior managers also ran into problems as the markets surged. Because stock options became a popular form of compensation, there was too much emphasis on short-term stock performance. Though many executives did not focus on this particular incentive, too many did. These executives who made the daily stock price a factor in their strategic business decision making, certainly made some bad ones.

Feeling the heat to meet short-term incentives, many executives set expectations high for current performance, saw their stock prices increase, and raised equity or sold personal positions. When these objectives were out of reach, a meet-the-number mentality led to unethical accounting decisions that prioritized short-term goals and the continuation of upward momentum.

In a few cases, some of which are now well-known, this short-term thinking wrought accounting frauds that ultimately cost employees and the investing public millions. The transparency and integrity of corporate governance came into question. Things had to change.

"The major damage was not done by crooks. It was done by good people , honest people , and decent people who I'd be happy to have as trustees of my will. The CEOs in America basically drifted. They drifted into situational ethics. It got out of hand."—Warren Buffett, March, 14, 2003, Forum for Corporate Conscience, referring to executive pay and corporate accounting in the late 1990s.

SNAPPING OUT OF IT

In an abrupt about-face, the market started to retreat and the boom that defined the New Economy gave way, thankfully, to the old economy where earnings and cash flow mattered. The market slid down the slippery slope of a boom unraveling. The economy slowed, discretionary income dipped, and suspicions about inflated valuations increased. Start-ups swirled toward cash-constrained positions and established companies lost their pumped-up values. Many Internet companies began to trade at a discount to the cash on their balance sheet. 9/11 devastated the economy and morale, and the economy petered into a major correction. As investors and companies adjusted to the new market, issues in accounting and disclosure dominated the headlines. The understanding that the system was broken was almost ubiquitous.

Prompted to action, the government stepped in.

CHAPTER 7

Of Rules and Regulations*

After the market crash of 1929, many regulators and investors realized that market manipulators, with their access to nonpublic information, seemed to undermine two of the key tenets of capitalism and democracy: fair play and a level playing field. In 1934, Congress created the Securities and Exchange Commission to establish and enforce rules for the financial exchanges and companies that would keep the capital markets fair and open.

For the past 70 years, the SEC has regulated the markets and monitored corporate merger, acquisition, and finance activities to protect investors. All of these activities enforce the umbrella creed that companies must disclose any material information, and this disclosure cannot, by statement or omission, be false or manipulative. Material information is generally defined to mean anything that would affect the understanding and decision making of an investor—that is, anything that would cause a rational investor to act.

The declining stock market of 2000, 2001, and 2002, and the unethical behavior of several investment banks and CEOs, brought several issues to light and drove the SEC and Congress to create regulations to promote clarity of information and equal access to that information. Regulation Full Disclosure, Reg FD, established in 2000 by the SEC, attempted to create a level playing field for all investors while the Sarbanes-Oxley Act, passed by Congress in 2002, required transparency and accountability from corporations.

MATERIAL INFORMATION

Corporations must understand and determine what information the investing public deems to be material. Obvious material information includes fi-

---

*Note: Readers seeking specifics on securities law should seek advice from securities professionals. This chapter is provided only to highlight the new rules and regulations as they pertain to strategic IR and it does not, in any way, constitute an accurate legal reference.

nancial events (such as earnings news, financial restatements), operational activities (such as acquisitions, joint ventures, research developments, new product introductions), management news (such as executive changes, insider sales), and regulatory announcements (such as new rules, approvals, and rejections). However, material information is not limited to these items, so management must be prepared, along with legal and IR, to determine materiality on an ongoing basis—in other words, which information or events must be disclosed to the investing public.

"Material information" is not defined under federal securities laws, according to the SEC. Materiality was defined in *TSC v. Northway, Inc.* In that case, the court stated, in part, that a fact is material where: "[T]here is a substantial likelihood that a reasonable shareholder would consider it important in deciding how to vote. . . . It does not require proof of a substantial likelihood that disclosure of the omitted fact would have caused the reasonable shareholder to change his/her vote. What the standard does contemplate is a showing of a substantial likelihood that, under all circumstances, the omitted fact would have assumed actual significance in the deliberations of the reasonable shareholder. Put another way, there must be substantial likelihood that the disclosure of the omitted fact would have been viewed by the reasonable investor as having significantly altered the "total mix" of information made available."

According to Section 409 of the Sarbanes-Oxley Act public companies should disclose "on a rapid and current basis, such additional information concerning material changes in the financial condition or operations of the issuer." As the SEC hones in on improving disclosure, IR must step up to guide management through the process. IR should develop a disclosure template, and when in doubt, the company should be conservative and assume almost any event is material. Along with IR, however, management must also show some degree of restraint in terms of releasing too much news to the financial wires. This can come across as promotional and adversely affect management credibility.

TO ONE AS TO THE MANY

Information is disclosed, buyers and sellers trade on this information, and the price of the stock, in theory, moves either up or down to a new value that discounts the new information. Therefore, those who have access to the information in question before others have a distinct trading advantage. To level the playing field, all participants must receive information simultaneously, which is what the SEC has attempted to enforce with Reg FD.

What the last few years brought to light was the fact that although companies may have been disseminating material information to the markets, they may have selectively disseminated that information to some and not to all. Most companies had found that the easiest way to get information out to investors was through conference calls, one-on-one conversations with fund managers, or at dinner with sell-side and buy-side analysts. This activity was standard operating procedure, and the general public was left out in the cold in the form of delayed information.

PUBLIC TALK

Discrepancies of timing and access also highlighted the confusion about inside information and insider trading. Inside information is any material information that has not been disclosed to the public. Having inside information is not illegal per se, but acting on it is. In fact, at certain times a company should not immediately disclose material information because that disclosure would compromise its competitive position and do a disservice to shareholders. However, if a company decides not to disclose certain information, then it cannot disclose it to anyone externally. Of course, if the information is related to a merger or acquisition, management will notify its investment bankers and the analyst in the sector will likely be "brought over the wall" to restrict any research activity for a set period.

REGULATION FAIR DISCLOSURE, REG FD

In October 2000, the SEC stepped in to require a timely and even approach for companies to disclose material information to each and every investor. This requirement is called Reg FD, or Regulation Fair Disclosure, and states that when a public company discloses any material nonpublic information, the company must make public disclosures of that information simultaneously and promptly. If the disclosure is selective and unintentional, then it must be made fully available quickly to correct the situation. The goal is to prevent selective disclosure and to reduce insider trading liability by preventing the misappropriation of information. Reg FD is designed to encour-

age full and fair disclosure, inside and outside the company, and to clarify
and enhance the intent of the existing laws.

Reg FD is an important improvement in the capital markets. It protects
every investor and supports executive compliance by taking any disclosure
leeway out of company hands. Reg FD allows a CEO to take charge of her
story, puts a halt to selective disclosure and pressure from Wall Street, and
gives all shareholders equal opportunity to hear the information first.

For a thorough explanation of Reg FD and Sarbanes-Oxley, helpful references include: SEC.gov, Sarbanes-Oxley.com, FASB.gov, the
Public Company Accounting Oversight Board at PCAOBUS.org, and
the American Institute of Certified Public Accountants, at AICPA.org.

This regulation has made the analyst's job tougher, however. Once in
the business of prying incremental information from management teams
over dinner or in one-on-one meetings or on conference calls, the analyst
now must work with information that is widely disclosed. The opportunities to get a proprietary scoop are more difficult than ever, which can result
in fewer "research calls" and diluted commissions. Being the "ax"—the
most influential analyst in a given stock—these days is less about a personal
relationship with the CEO and more about traditional research. Incremental information now comes from customer surveys, channel checks, and a
detailed analysis of the competitive environment. Only the best analysts can
survive in this environment, so the pendulum will ultimately swing back to
where analysts are highly respected.

THE SARBANES-OXLEY ACT

The stock market has no shallow end; everyone must do their homework
and enter at their own risk. Investors are responsible for due diligence, and
though most would like to walk through the company and kick the tires,
only a few institutional investors can. The privilege is certainly not extended
to individuals.

Financial statements and SEC disclosures are the most likely source of
reliable facts and figures. The income statement, balance sheet, and cash
flow statement are critical in this respect. Many investors have always
viewed accounting as a dispassionate science with little room for nuance,

but this is not true. When the markets were going up and executives were challenged by short-term expectations, the lines of this subjective art became too flexible. The government moved in to improve the transparency of those numbers as well as increase the accountability of the people behind them.

FASB, the Financial Accounting Standards Board, is an independent organization that governs the standards of financial accounting and reporting. FASB has established uniform guidelines for the preparation of financial reports, the standard recognized by the SEC, but in 2000 and 2001 some very serious violations of these accounting principles by several corporate executives and their auditors were discovered. These violations cost shareholders billions, and the fallout was extensive. The government decided that the corporate governance structure, the directors on the board of a company as well as its management team, needed strict and specific rules to incorporate into their accounting and reporting procedures.

In 2002 Congress passed the Sarbanes-Oxley Act. The Act created a new oversight board to which public companies and accounting firms must answer. Sarbanes-Oxley also tackles many issues of accounting, auditing, corporate reporting, financial investigations, and relationships with capital markets. In addition to many heightened demands, the law requires public companies to engage in a series of checks and balances along each stage of gathering, documenting, and certifying financial data. Each step of the process is calculated to improve internal controls, ensure the accuracy and clarity of financial reports and corporate disclosures, and encourage executives and directors to meet corporate ethical standards of accountability and integrity.

Sarbanes-Oxley, in addition, addresses the conflict of interest that results when analysts recommend stocks of companies with which their firm has investment banking business. At one time, analysts were in the habit of showing their reports to companies to check accuracy, which was not necessarily a terrible thing. Sarbanes-Oxley restricts the practice of prepublication viewing and also declares periods when analysts cannot write research on companies with which their firm is actively involved in a transaction, such as an initial public offering. The Act also requires a strengthening of the Chinese Wall.

In an attempt to become poster children of the new order, many investment banks have strict rules that prohibit analysts from even talking to their investment bankers, and if they do the conversation must be monitored. In fact, some bankers and analysts will run for cover if a person with a camera enters a room in which they both happen to be. This short-term over-compensation will most likely relax slightly in the coming years, but the impact of these new rules and the necessary rebuilding of credibility by the investment banks almost require them to run a tight ship by any historical standard.

RISING TO THE OCCASION

Both Reg FD and Sarbanes-Oxley are attempts to level the playing field for investors through equitable dissemination and transparency of information. The concepts are great, but the regulators are not perfect. The ultimate fix is good governance, solid ethics, a balanced compensation package for management, and a realization that slow and steady wins the race. This approach mitigates risk and almost ensures a premium valuation given the underlying fundamentals at any given time.

CHAPTER 8

Post-Bubble Reality

Although there were thousands of responsible CEOs and CFOs during the late 1990s, responsibility and accountability were certainly suspended for some executives during the market surge. After the pin prick, the market deflated, the government stepped in, and the communications landscape became even more complicated. Although companies, analysts, and investors agreed that practices needed to be amended, many of the new rules prompted confusion and some CEOs reacted by ceasing to interact with the market altogether. Under these circumstances, analysts struggled to unearth nuances from flat terrain, and the capital markets slipped into a rather awkward mating dance between investment banks and companies.

Most of the new rules hinged on the nuances of materiality. For example, a 245-unit restaurant chain that opened one new store did not necessarily have material information to disclose. But if this store had a prototype kitchen model that required less labor, and could dramatically improve unit economics if successful, then that could be deemed as material—particularly if a system-wide rollout was in the works that could dramatically expand margins.

Because Reg FD says that every investor has the right to know anything material at the same time and in the same way, there are a host of ways an executive can inadvertently make a mistake.

For example, on November 5, 2001, the CEO of Siebel Systems, a software systems provider, spoke about a company development at an invitation-only technology conference. Apparently, the executive thought the information was being Web cast, but it wasn't. Regardless, after the stock soared, the SEC levied a fine of $250,000.

The CFO of Raytheon was cited in February 2001 for the possibility that he released guidance to select analysts shortly after providing no guidance publicly. He resigned as a result.

Schering-Plough paid a huge fine of a $1,000,000, and the CEO paid a personal fine of $50,000, after he may have relayed negativity about estimates—not verbally, but through his body language. The SEC said he violated Reg FD "through a combination of spoken language, tone, emphasis and demeanor." Reg FD underscores the importance of a uniform approach to, and a template for, disclosure, created by IR along with management.

Similarly, with management legally accountable for every assumption, note, debit, and credit, Sarbanes-Oxley forces an eagle's eye on every corporate step and process. Given the time and effort required, senior executives often find themselves reluctant to risk divulging any information until it's been properly weighed and measured through all the checks and balances. IR should support this responsibility by ensuring and facilitating this process.

SELL-SIDE IMPLICATIONS

Post-bubble, investment banking business ground to a halt and the Chinese Wall needed to be rebuilt. The more immediate problem, however, was saving the overall business of investment banking, in the face of what seemed to be wave after wave of downsizings and consolidations. Industry layoffs were extensive, exceeding 50,000 workers. Subsequently, research budgets were slashed, research coverage decreased, and market makers—the traders on the NASDAQ who create liquidity in specific stocks by putting their own capital at risk—dropped their support of thousands of companies. Ultimately, many analysts left to work for the buy-side, investment banking, or establish their own small research boutiques.

The remaining analysts saw a new environment that included a Big Brother-esque shadow cast by New York Attorney General Elliot Spitzer, whose prosecution of Wall Street firms led to many of the aforementioned reforms. As *The New York Times* stated in an August 17, 2003, article entitled "An Analyst's Job Used to Be Fun. Not Anymore," analysts went from being the celebrities of Wall Street enjoying all the frills and perks of being lionized, to overworked "Wall Street everyman, content with a gray life of financial models and spreadsheets."

The current crop of analysts are under increased pressure to analyze companies and sell ideas to the buy-side within a rigid process that has materially reduced the means by which incremental information can be extracted. These analysts now also legally guarantee their opinion and are under intense scrutiny to pick winners and losers with equal zeal. In many cases, they've received significantly reduced pay packages for one of the toughest jobs around.

Given this new world, where the wrong email or the wrong procedure can end a career, it's important to understand what kind of companies attract sell-side analysts. They are looking, first of all, for an undervalued company that's a good stock pick. They are also looking for a company that "fits" their investment bank. For example, if the investment bank is a small regional player, they don't want their analyst to be the twenty-second name publishing a Buy rating on Disney. What possible incremental value could they uncover given the fact that Morgan Stanley, Goldman Sachs, Bear Stearns, and a parade of large firms are the first to have their Disney calls returned? Instead, the small firm typically looks for an undervalued, under-followed stock that the entire firm—including sales, trading, and investment banking—can get behind.

One of the biggest criteria, however, for any sell-side firm, either large or small, is that the analyst must believe in management and its ability to manage The Street. Analysts will only recommend companies whose executives they trust, executives with a firm strategy in place and an understanding of how The Street will react to that strategy.

BUY-SIDE

Investors are as equally reliant, and wary, of the relationships they build with the CEOs. They have millions or billions of dollars to invest, and the most recent taste in their mouth is either a CEO who fleeced the company or an analyst who brought them an IPO that imploded. More than ever, these fund managers need to know that they are dealing with credible executives who commit to communicating their results transparently, in both good and bad times. This is the first step to credibility or, perhaps, to rebuilding credibility.

MANAGEMENT MUST LEAD

The stock market is incredibly efficient at discounting news, and it's impossible to keep either good or bad news locked up for an extended period of time. If a company attempts to do so, the executive risks information leaks and the capital markets uncovering the information in advance of its proper release. This is a classic example of letting the outside world define an issue rather than the company itself defining an issue.

Therefore, in good times and bad, companies do well to communicate quickly, thereby positioning themselves to garner a higher valuation at any given time. Sitting on one's hands, locking the door, running for cover . . . these are not solid habits of an organization that wants to attract investors or build a relationship with the media or Wall Street.

Though Reg FD and Sarbanes-Oxley have made some CEOs skittish, any CEO who thinks it's better to be quiet—when bad news arises—risks losing credibility with the investment community and key stakeholders. The market has a tendency to negatively react in the short run to a company with bad news. However, the news would have come out eventually, and in reality all companies are going to have bad news. Professional investors and analysts expect it.

As difficult as it is to stand up and reveal problems and mistakes, the very process of doing so can help a company build credibility and dilute the consequence of that mistake. The Street admires the executive who stands on the frontline, addresses the issue, and gives a plan for correction. Investors, and all stakeholders, such as employees, like to hear one voice, one story, and a logical equation of truth that justifies their dollars, time, and effort.

Staying quiet on bad news and then being forced to answer yes, no, or no comment can destroy credibility and valuation, and may just land a CEO in court. For example, if the market uncovers the news, which it will, 100 savvy investors will proceed to call the CEO and CFO. When management returns those calls they'll be asked to comment on the rumor, and that's where they're stuck.

- No comment means it's probably true.
- If the CEO acknowledges the rumor as true to a specific investor, Reg FD has been violated.
- If the company denies the rumor, lying to both analysts and portfolio managers, the CEO's credibility is destroyed.

CEOs must work with IR to manage the release of company news so that the dissemination of information is always within their control. Often, if a company's business is challenging, the environment is also challenging for its peers. Getting out first with bad news can be a positive for the stock and for management's reputation. It's the difference of being proactive versus reactive, the latter of which is always more difficult.

The rules have opportunity written all over them. Executives need to share the facts, show who's in charge, and take control. Most good executives work past the tangle of traps that have insinuated themselves into the capital markets and strive for a policy of prompt, effective, and appropriate communication.

An effective IR program has to counsel that the message not only be told, but heard and interpreted in the way it was intended. This starts with an IR program that understands the rules and the environment, and how these fit into the perennial thinking and behavior of all capital markets' participants.

CHAPTER 9

Of Reason, Renewal, and Honesty

Changes in the investment community represent an opportunity to revamp practices and procedures to fuel a more efficient and fair market place. Several companies performed internal investigations and changed governance practices in advance of regulations. But for others, the ramp-up into these new ways has been slow, time-consuming, confusing, and costly. IR has the duty to work closely with the board of directors and management to clarify and accelerate the process, so that a company remains on course and the investor is the ultimate winner.

A good IR strategy works well within the law to support the objective of protecting or enhancing equity value. The complexities of disclosure rules are less important to the executive who is already communicating openly and honestly. But good communication cannot happen without understanding what these changes mean for the sell-side and buy-side. Knowing the ears upon which the information falls is key to a solid communications plan. Creating a solution that protects the company, the analyst, and the buy-side is the ultimate goal.

COMPENSATION

One area in which much of the debate has focused is compensation. A few companies, such as Boeing, Microsoft, Coca-Cola, The Washington Post, and Amazon, jumped ahead of potential legislation and immediately began expensing stock options. Pending regulations also sparked innovation around, and resurgence of, other compensation awards, such as restricted stock, performance-based options, and stock grants.

In the case of Progressive, a Mayfield Village, Ohio–based insurance company, the decision to scrap stock options in favor of restricted stock had less to do with the expensing issue than with their conclusion that options motivated some behaviors that were not in the best interest of the company.

Sealed Air of Saddle Brook, New Jersey, issued restricted stock as part of four components: cash salary, benefits, nonperformance-based restricted stock, and a management by objectives program. Restricted stock recipients paid $1 per share for the stock certificates, which vested after three years. There was no holding requirement, but management believed employees had a tendency to hold stock after the period.

Other companies that switched to restricted stock or scaled back the options program include Altria Group, Citigroup, Dell Computer, and Cendant Corp.

The most effective compensation packages tend to include a combination of incentives. Experts assert that multiple long-term goals and multiple compensation tools are the best way to ensure superior performance. IR, along with outside compensation experts and board members, should be consulted in analyzing and deciding upon the optimal compensation mix and incentive structure for any company. They should also be consulted on how that compensation mix is likely perceived by Wall Street investors.

Table 9.1 provides a summary of compensation vehicles.

IN THE BOARDROOM

Ever since Sarbanes-Oxley and Reg FD placed management and directors under the microscope, corporate governance, has been at the forefront of intense scrutiny. Independent agencies came to prominence to prescribe and oversee ways to achieve competent governance and too many companies seemed to be in constant preparation for some bad variation of standardized testing.

If a company has a credible management team and policies steeped in ethical business behavior, they'll rarely need someone else to prescribe the right methods. The company should always control its communications with regulators and the public, and this means dictating the terms of good governance for itself.

There are many issues that management needs to discuss with The Street so as not to affect current or ongoing valuation, including any and all issues among top management or directors that may be considered material information. IR needs to advise on how these issues will read on The Street. The selection of directors; the turnover of directors and management; the relations between, and the independence of, directors; and the indepen-

TABLE 9.1 Compensation Method Comparison

Nonqualified Stock Options		Restricted Stock		Performance Shares	
Grants the option to buy stock at a fixed price for a fixed exercise period		Outright grant of shares with restrictions to sale, transfer, or pledging		Shares of stock or fixed cash value at beginning of period; performance contingency	
Pros	Cons	Pros	Cons	Pros	Cons
Executive and shareholder interests aligned	May incent short-term behavior	Executive and shareholder interests aligned	Immediate dilution of EPS for total shares granted	Executive and shareholder interests aligned (if using stock)	Charge to earnings, marked to market
No charge to earnings	Dilute EPS	No executive investment required	Possible recruiting disadvantage	Performance oriented	Difficulty in setting performance targets
Company receives tax deduction	Executive investment required	No expiration to incent short-term stock price manipulation	Potential manipulation near vesting date	No executive investment required	
	Typically exercised and sold, rather than held by employees	Incites LT matriculation (forfeiture upon departurte)	Can be considered "pay for attendance" if relied upon as sole incentive	Company receives tax deduction at payout	
	Stringent vesting requirements (time-based)	If stock appreciates after grant, company tax deduction exceeds fixed charge to earnings	Fair-market value charged to earnings over restricted period		

TABLE 9.1 *(continued)*

Nonqualified Stock Options			Restricted Stock			Performance Shares		
Grants the option to buy stock at a fixed price for a fixed exercise period			Outright grant of shares with restrictions to sale, transfer, or pledging			Shares of stock or fixed cash value at beginning of period; performance contingency		
Pros		Cons		Pros	Cons		Pros	Cons
		FASB/SEC may require expensing in the near future		Equal rights with common stock (voting interest, dividend)				
				Investor perception = doing the right thing				
				Highly transparent (never underwater)				
				Predictability of final compensation levels				
				Performance-based requirements are more flexible than options (based on time)				

dence of auditors are just some of the factors that determine a weak or strong organization.

Analysts and investors look at these and many other issues to judge the accountability of the board and the accuracy of the corporation's financial statements when calculating the credibility of disclosure, the viability of policy checks and balances, and the character of the company's leadership.

Every corporate move has the potential to affect stock price. Effective IR counsel looks at all corporate decisions, interprets the signals, and gives management a balanced view of its potential influence on equity value. IR can manage the process by helping the board communicate the principles by which the company is run.

A TANGLE OF TRAPS

IR with capital markets know-how can unravel the string of complexity. In order for a company to sustain value, management's priority must remain on strategy, operations, and ultimately financial performance. Reg FD, Sarbanes-Oxley, and all the machinations of the SEC and the capital markets are best left to legal counsel and IR specialists who fully understand these arenas.

For example, disclosure of material off-balance-sheet obligations is a must, and IR officers need to work closely with the board of directors and management to advise on clarifying materiality and significance. If the timing of insiders selling shares will trigger a misread from the markets, IR should know this and suggest to management that a 10B51 selling program (featuring systematic selling over time), might be better received. If a company is making an important announcement and the stock exchange on which it trades needs to be called beforehand to halt trading, IR needs to respond appropriately. If a company has a private analyst call and a question is answered in violation of Reg FD, IR must correct the error and get an all-encompassing press release out on the business wires before the market opens the next day.

These are just a few of many basic functions IR must know as the tip of the spear in a company's financial communications strategy, not to mention understanding what the investors' concerns are from firsthand knowledge.

AND THE INVESTORS' CONCERN IS . . .

Impact. Regardless of the event, investors want to know two things: how does it boil down to earnings per share and how will the stock react? That's it. The investor doesn't necessarily care about the complexity of Sarbanes-Oxley; they care about whether the stock is a buy or a sell relative to the new event. That focus should be the goal of management: to release information within the rules in such a way that quantifies an event whenever possible.

Investors respect a management team that steps up and tells it like it is. When news is bad, investors want to know all of it, right there and then, in a quantifiable manner. Although Reg FD and Sarbanes-Oxley have increased requirements for corporations, auditors, analysts, and bankers, they serve to do much more than complicate the processes. The implementation of these regulations is an ongoing process that has blown a gust of welcome change through the capital markets.

According to a March 5, 2004, article in *The Wall Street Journal*, the change in the number of stocks followed by firms dwindled from 2000 to 2003, as follows:

Firm (global operations)	2000	2003
Merrill Lynch	3,500	2,469
Credit Suisse First Boston	3,077	2,373
Smith Barney	3,000	2,300
J.P. Morgan Chase	2,400 (FY '01)	2,260
Goldman Sachs	2,315	1,950
Morgan Stanley	2,150	1,925
Lehman Brothers	1,650	1,605

Source: WSJ Research

Budgets also generally fell, with one exception, as shown below (numbers shown are in millions of dollars).

Firm (U.S. Stock Research)	2000	2003
Merrill Lynch	$494.6	$292.4
Credit Suisse First Boston	$468.1	$284.8
Smith Barney	$478.2	$269.9
J.P. Morgan Chase	$149.2	$185.0
Goldman Sachs	$376.8	$177.7
Morgan Stanley	$386.7	$249.3
Lehman Brothers	$211.6	$160.1

Source: WSJ, Sanford C. Bernstein Calculations

POST-BOOM IR

The massive investment bank consolidation of the late 1990s created a new landscape. Where once there were dozens of players, now there are only a few. This means fewer analysts, fewer traders, fewer salespeople. It also means that smaller companies that once had to fight hard for the attention of sell-side analysts now have to fight even harder. But this also created an opportunity, because the finance professionals who left or were downsized either started their own firms or joined smaller firms. These smaller banks and the regional firms are stepping up to fill this research void, giving small and mid-cap companies another place to share their story. Understanding the shifting landscape as an opportunity, becoming the source of commission business for these smaller firms, appealing to their analysts, and gaining research coverage are essential.

Responsibility to navigate a landscape with less opportunity falls to the IR function. It must combine fundamental IR execution with capital markets advisory to help define, deliver, and create a dialogue for a company's story. If IR is doing its job, at any given time, value will be maximized, the cost of capital will be reduced, and management will better be able to focus on its business. This cycle feeds off itself, and better valuations can certainly result.

Investor Relations: The Fundamentals

Traditional IR and the Need for Change

Traditional IR: What It Is, and Why It's Not Enough

All public companies must adhere to numerous requirements in terms of communicating with investors. These include filings that the Securities and Exchange Commission requires to level the playing field for all investors. SEC filings are the raw materials of IR, and what one does with them can determine the success of financial communications.

Of course, on the one hand, a company that did nothing more than file 10-Ks and 10-Qs would be utterly uninteresting to institutions and probably never develop a strong public company multiple. On the other hand, if a company goes out of its way to explain these rather dry documents and makes the effort to target and court the right investors at the right time, the success can raise the visibility of the organization and increase the company's overall value.

Let's start at the beginning, however, and review the basics.

THE ESSENTIALS: PUBLIC FILINGS AND MEETINGS

The following list shows the absolutes that every public company must file with the Securities and Exchange Commission and the procedural notices and meetings that are a part of all public company interaction with investors. The schedules of these reports and notices are based on a fiscal, as opposed to a calendar, year.

Annual reports
Proxies
10-Ks
10-Qs

SEC Disclosures
Annual meeting

Annual report: An end-of-the-fiscal-year report to investors that includes communication from the CEO and a basic summary of business, including text on operations, tables of audited GAAP (Generally Accepted Accounting Principles) financials (income statement, cash flows, balance sheets), and the notes explaining the assumptions behind those numbers. This is an easier-to-digest, graphically designed, variation on the 10-K.

The bigger, more extensive annual reports with pages of products and strategy are becoming less relevant in today's world. They are usually the domain of larger companies that use their annual report to market their business. We tend to recommend the *10-K Wrap*, a two- or three-page fold-out that wraps around the 10-K. This approach makes sense for cost-conscious firms because the difference between a 10-K Wrap and a full-blown, designed, and distributed annual report can be tens of thousands of dollars.

Proxy: The proxy is a document that contains vital information on current company issues to be discussed at the annual meeting. These usually include elections for the board of directors, ratification of independent accountants, company plans, and shareholder proposals. Shareholders who cannot attend the open meeting cast their votes by proxy by signing and sending in the proxy's voting card. The proxy document also lists up-to-date information on beneficial and insider stock and options ownership.

10-K: An end-of-the-fiscal year report to the SEC that summarizes that year's business and financial activities, the 10-K is more extensive than the annual report.

10-Q: A summary filed with the SEC each quarter of the fiscal year, reporting the last three months and year-to-date operations.

MD&A: The Management's Discussion and Analysis is a key, required section of the 10-K and 10-Q filings.

SEC Disclosures: Required documents filed with the SEC any time a significant event has occurred. These include *8-Ks*, to report unscheduled, time-sensitive, material events, such as a merger or a change in board of directors. For private companies or spin-offs of divisions, SEC disclosures include *S-1s*, which are registration statements/filings that announce an initial public offering.

Annual meeting: The company's once-a-year meeting to which all shareholders are invited. Some companies have more than one to accommodate the geographical distribution and number of their shareholders. Management and the directors present and discuss recent issues and decisions, answer shareholders' questions, and put company plans and shareholder proposals, pre-announced by proxy, up to vote.

THE ESSENTIALS: DELIVERY VEHICLES

The absolutes are delivered, or can be made accessible, to investors in many ways, including:

The SEC
Direct mail
The media
The Internet
Conference calls

The SEC: By filing with the SEC, companies automatically make their disclosures accessible and available to the public. Created in 1984 to ease paper flow and to hurdle microfiche hassles, the government's Electronic Data Gathering Analysis and Retrieval System, EDGAR, collects, validates, and stores SEC-required public disclosures. Since 1996 all public companies have been required to file disclosures electronically, and these forms are made available to the public on the SEC Web site. Increasingly, SEC Web links are found directly on the IR portion of most company Web sites, creating even easier access to both institutional and retail investors.

Direct mail: Public companies are required to mail the annual report and proxy to all of their investors. This expense can be substantial for even the smallest of companies. More and more companies make annual reports and proxies, current and past, available on their Web sites. With the permission of their investors, many companies are transferring the delivery of disclosures and news from traditional mail to the more immediate and cost-efficient email and electronic distribution. As stated earlier, the savings can be material, anywhere from $20,000 to $50,000 for smaller companies. All that said, many companies still mail press releases and other materials to investors, a practice that is becoming less and less common.

The media: In order to stay in compliance with Reg FD, companies must share material information with all investors promptly and simultaneously. To do this, companies should issue *quarterly earnings releases* and *press releases* describing SEC disclosure highlights and other significant company events. Common sense, however, dictates that these disclosures should be disseminated to a wider audience that includes media, trade publications, buy-side organizations, and sell-side firms. IR should develop a standard press release format in combination with investor targeting mechanisms to garner optimal reach and frequency. IR should also make sure that the message and investment highlights are clear and focus on key capital markets triggers.

The Internet: Company Web sites, as well as the Web sites of agencies that provide investors with public company information, are good platforms for the communication of essential disclosures. User-friendly investor relations pages can provide current and potential investors with current and historical annual reports, proxies, press releases, 10-Ks, 10-Qs, and other SEC disclosures. Email alerts are also an efficient way to reach investors in an even and timely manner. Beefing up these capabilities not only saves money on dissemination, but it's also legally required.

Conference calls: An effective and the most common way to draw investor and analyst attention to recent company disclosures, the conference call allows capital markets players to listen to senior management summarize recent disclosures, highlights, and significant activities, as well as ask questions. We believe that a script for these calls is essential and should never be sacrificed for bullet points or off-the-cuff explanations of relevant facts. This is due to Reg FD as well as the quest to control the information that the buy- and sell-side are digesting. Because these calls are highly scrutinized, the script functions as a template for disclosure for the upcoming quarter, by providing a framework for materiality, and mitigating the possibility of an intra-quarter Reg FD slipup. For example, if management receives a call from a 10 percent investor during the quarter, they can always reference prepared remarks from the latest script, rather than inadvertently disseminate new information.

The conference call is also management's opportunity to define its company rather than wait for the analyst to do so in writing. Accordingly, the best way to create that definition is a well-thought-out script that leaves nothing to analyst interpretation. This tack gives buy-siders a welcome check and balance to sell-side research as they can go directly to the source, the transcribed conference call transcript, and get a solid understanding of management's vision. Knowing this, management should never be unprepared for this critical touch point with the institutional community.

ADDITIONAL IR TOOLS AND VEHICLES

Investors expect public companies to go beyond the SEC requirements of annual reports, 10-Ks, 10-Qs, proxies, and SEC disclosures and provide as much information as possible to fully relay the company story. Additionally, strategic partners and employees sometimes expect to receive, or have access to, a steady flow of information. Supplementary information could include the following:

Newsletters
Conferences
Road shows
One-on-Ones
Analyst days
Ads/Publicity
Web sites

Newsletters: Periodic newsletters to employees, partners, and investors are a good way to keep stakeholders informed and capture the attention of key constituencies. Interviews with executives and key management, insights into operations, announcements of product or service initiatives, technology or research advancements, consumer trends, industry updates, marketing concepts, and any other information that helps investors and strategic partners stay informed should be included.

Other forms of interim communication include *fact sheets*, sent out quarterly, that summarize the most recent company developments and financial performance. Large companies sometimes provide the sell- and buy-side with *fact books*, or supplemental disclosure forms, which literally have reams of data on the finer details of complex operations.

Although helpful to investors, these supplemental materials are most effective when disseminated consistently, no matter how the company performed. Companies that only do so when times are good and suspend information sharing when times are bad risk their reputation and company credibility, both drivers of equity valuation over time.

Conferences: Companies can sponsor, or participate in, conferences for companies and customers in their industry. It creates an opportunity for senior management to present a viewpoint through speeches, panels, or discussion groups and a platform for product sampling or exposure of services. It is best for Reg FD purposes to have such presentations Web cast to avoid unintentional selective disclosure.

Road shows: This is an effective way for management to tell its story directly to investors. Sometimes called Non-Deal Road Shows, because companies aren't raising capital at the time, these are presentations where management travels to the offices of buy-side and sometimes sell-side analysts to discuss the financial and strategic prospects for the company. The hope is to generate interest so the buy-side will buy and the sell-side will publish. These meetings also serve to establish and build personal relationships. Having the sell-side involved in coordinating these events is a good move, as it is a source of their compensation and can provide for active sales and trading support in conjunction with the meeting. The IR team should coordinate the process and potentially augment the schedule of meetings so it's done as efficiently as possible with maximum impact. However, it should be ultimately executed by the sell-side, not the investor relations agency.

One-on-Ones: Although Reg FD keeps everyone on their toes, one-on-one meetings between management and analysts or fund managers, either at conferences or on road shows, are still a productive way for investors to find the answers they need while giving management a chance to share their story directly.

Analyst days: Many companies find it helpful to bring analysts to company headquarters to hear the story, see the product, and most importantly, meet some of the other management outside of the CEO and CFO, with whom they typically interact.

Advertising and publicity: Broadcast and cable television, radio, magazines, newspapers, and trade publications are good resources for reaching a wide segment of potential investors and stakeholders. Relaying the corporate mission to a wide audience can help build awareness and name recognition that will bolster investor interest. Through publicity, companies can draw attention in media articles and news stories, and present management as interview candidates for business and news programs. In advertising, companies can showcase their corporate message, products, services, customer satisfaction, trade awards, or financial performance.

Web sites: The Internet is as pervasive as the media, but much more immediate and flexible, making a corporate and/or brand Web site an excellent way to communicate with all stakeholders. Most corporate sites have specific pages where the employees, suppliers, vendors, customers, consumers, and investors can connect and collect pertinent information. The pages for investors, a specific investor relations area, should include

Daily stock quotes
Dividend announcements
Earnings releases
Stock performance graphs
Current and historical financial performance
Company history and background

Web casts of presentations and conference calls
Archives of annual reports, SEC disclosures, and media releases
Answers to frequently asked questions
New product demos or factory tours interactive chats
Language access for global investors

Also on the investor relations pages should be information about administrative functions, such as

Stock transfer agents
Dividend reinvestment programs
Employee stock services
Shareholder stock purchase programs
Subscriber services
Company investment plans
IR contact information

The following items are optional and should be included on the investor relations pages if appropriate:

Fact sheets and books
Newsletters
Information on governance issues, such as lists of board of directors, committees, charters, policies, guidelines, by-laws, and accountability initiatives

Companies should also consider creating links to their Web site from related sites and third-party Web sites that provide data to potential investors.

OTHER BASIC IR PRACTICES

Obviously, basic IR has a lot of administrative tasks that need to be conquered, such as overseeing the preparation and distribution of disclosures and organizing conferences, presentations, and meetings. But, of course, even with these basic IR functions, simply sending out information and providing access to facts and figures does not compose a world-class IR program. Most IR professionals will tell you that that is just the beginning. In addition to the above tools and vehicles, IR professionals must engage in the following activities:

Stock Market Reconnaissance

IR's job is to keep an eye on the stock market and understand valuation. IR must follow general economic indicators, industry-specific indicators, and stock-specific issues. Stock price and stock volume, as well as specific ratios such as P/E or EV/EBITDA relative to industry competitors, help management understand market perception of the industry, the competition, and their own company's performance.

Shareholder Analysis

The makeup of institutional ownership and percentage of institutional ownership relative to the whole is an indicator of a company's image in the eyes of the capital markets. Large holdings by institutions, involvement by short-sellers, or a high degree of retail or mom-and-pop ownership indicate the kind of holders or nonholders a stock might have. Tracking investors, the amount of ownership, and movement can keep a company ahead of the market currents and help the company target the investors it wants in a cost-effective manner. Knowing who your investors are, how much money they manage, what their investment style is, and what comparable stocks they own is essential information.

Approaching Analysts

Equity research coverage is still one of the best ways to create exposure and gain credibility. Analysts are quoted by the media, referenced by investors, and queried by their own brokers and traders. The potential endorsement of coverage, and the realistic setting of earnings estimates, can lead to wider distribution of equity, greater liquidity, less volatility, and a better multiple for the stock.

Feedback

IR should constantly survey the capital markets to understand the attitudes of the sell-side and the buy-side toward the company. Not understanding perception before approaching a release or conference call is like distributing product on gut instinct. Much like a consumer products company would understand the market or customer before introducing an extension, IR should understand market issues before communicating with investors. At the end of the day, publicly traded companies are "product" to the buy- and sell-sides, and the exercise of shareholder communication should be approached as a marketing function to a degree.

RESOURCES FOR TRADITIONAL IR

Many good books on investor relations explain the requirements and resources for providing the traditional IR function to investors. These books include *Investor Relations for the Emerging Company*, by Ralph A. Rieves and John Lefebvre; *New Dimensions in Investor Relations*, by Bruce W. Marcus and Sherwood Lee Wallace; and *Best Practices in Global Investor Relations*, by Richard B. Higgins.

These texts provide clear explanations of the IR necessities. Additionally, many Web sites and associations provide IR information. Other critical resources include the National Investor Relations Institute's Web site, *NIRI.Org*, and *IR Magazine*'s *IRontheNet.Com*.

REVAMPED, RAMPED UP, AND REDEFINED

Traditional IR is not enough, however. We believe it is not only about delivering the basics, but also wrapping them in the context of valuation at any given time. For people who sit on the sell-side and buy-side, it often seems that companies don't understand what they need. Rather, companies tend to present a one-dimensional portrait.

Senior management knows the story inside and out. After all, they run the companies. However, a large number of management teams don't really know how to package their story for institutional buyers or sell-side analysts. It's unfortunate because, if a company is packaged properly, analysts just might take a chance on publishing or portfolio managers might begin to accumulate a long position. In sum, the channels and methods by which management communicates to Wall Street and Wall Street communicates to the companies should not be underestimated. Done right, the process is simply not as easy as many companies think.

Being on the inside with companies teaches that it takes more than traditional IR to build or preserve value. Though going beyond the required and voluntary disclosure of information, traditional IR can sometimes still fall short. Unless IR operates from a capital markets perspective, understanding the thoughts and processes of the sell-side and the buy-side, there will always be room for improvement.

Consider these cases in point:

Missteps in Stock Market Reconnaissance

The stock market is a funny thing, and like a pot to boil, it's best not to watch it too closely. Companies that cross the fine line between nonchalance and obsessing over short-term stock movements can make rash decisions to try and purge their short-sellers or have careless delays when dealing with sizable institutional investors. Achieving that balance takes capital markets know-how. For example, it's best for management to not talk valuation with analysts and portfolio managers. After all, they are the professionals. Rather, management should get counsel from IR that understands all of the implications and consequences of any market moves.

Missteps in Shareholder Analysis

IR that monitors share price to gauge market perception is somewhat behind the curve. Although important, stock price movement is the tail wagging the dog to a degree, and IR must know the likely impact of a company decision before the shareholders render their judgment in the form of buying or selling.

Missteps in Approaching Analysts

Having a handle on analysts' estimates and the consensus estimate helps a company stay in control of its story and engage The Street as an active, participatory voice. But analysts are not just smart, calculating evaluators, they are human beings who rely heavily on trust to devise those estimates and recommendations. Not just any approach will do. Management must control this process, as it can be a significant part of building valuation and raising capital.

The public establishment of estimates by a company to The Street, *guidance*, is perhaps one of the most essential practices of IR that this book covers. One of the biggest missteps we've seen in the relationships that companies have with the investment community is when they decide not to give guidance. This inaction stems from a management view that if they don't give guidance, they won't be measured against the numbers. The reality is that analysts must make projections with or without guidance from the companies, so companies are losing control of a number that will exist anyway. Effective IR should always counsel management to take control of that process.

Missteps in Obtaining Feedback

Though management might think they are getting clear feedback from analyst conversations, they may not recognize that the sell-side and buy-side rarely say anything to jeopardize access to management. That's because access leads to information, which is the currency of Wall Street. It enables both analysts and portfolio managers to either generate commissions, invest safely, or avoid an investment altogether. Therefore, because someone's living is at stake, Wall Street pros are wary of giving honest (negative) feedback, particularly to an emotional CEO or CFO.

This is the classic "Emperor Has No Clothes" scenario, where market feedback is filtered to the company, even though it's no-holds-barred between analysts and investors. CEOs unwilling to take constructive criticism because they think it's personal are ultimately not conducting themselves in the best interest of shareholders.

A BETTER APPROACH

IR with a capital markets background guards against many of these missteps. Companies that engage in more strategic IR know how to communicate better with the buy-side and the sell-side and materially improve chances of coverage and institutional ownership. Done right, this method and knowledge can lead to more optimal media coverage, better company morale, and many other benefits that all increase the value of the company.

CHAPTER 11

Staffing and Sourcing the New IR

In public companies, the IR function is either a department, a specified task of a professional, or a need that is fully or partially outsourced to an outside agency. Private companies looking for a voice in the capital markets might engage an investment bank or a public relations firm to raise their visibility, but usually fall short of hiring an investor relations officer (IRO).

The backgrounds of professionals performing the IR task vary: public relations, media relations, accounting, finance, and legal. One traditional route to IR has been as follows: a professional takes on the IR role, learns the company's business, devises a communications system, and then manages in-flow and out-flow from the various constituencies. Though IR was frequently viewed as an administrative function, more recently many IR professionals and senior executives have understood its strategic importance.

IR as the tip of the spear in a strategic corporate communications plan suggests that someone with capital markets experience should quarterback, or at least play a significant part in, the communications strategy. This type of ramped-up IR means staffing and sourcing the IR function with a team of people, internally or externally, who have the knowledge and skills necessary to provide the advice and execution that the competitive global markets demand.

IR professionals must be able to do the basic IR requisites:

- Oversee preparation of SEC documents
- Administer dissemination of SEC disclosures
- Develop core communications
- Create scripts and templates
- Organize conferences and events

- Manage meetings and calls
- Direct inflow and outflow of corporate information and communications
- Detect industry and competitive currents
- Track Wall Street behavior
- Discern media opportunities

To perform these essential tasks, IR professionals must be proficient in

- Accounting
- Communications
- Finance
- Investments
- Management
- Strategy
- Writing

As we've pointed out, traditional IR, born strictly out of communications, is no longer enough to ensure optimal valuation. The job requires an added skill set to really maximize the time and money spent on the function.

THE COLLABORATION

To be effective, IR needs to have an eye on the stock market, an ear on industry buzz, and a finger on the pulse of the buy-side, the sell-side, and the media. Finding this myriad of basic skills in one person, plus the scope of proficiencies and range of experiences, is no easy task. It takes a team approach.

Companies that have IR departments staffed with several professionals experienced in all of these areas have the luxury of pursuing an integrated, strategic approach to IR. But every company should at least attempt this level of professionalism. After all, valuation and management's reputation are at stake. Engaging a capable team is the first step.

An effective IR team should utilize two areas of expertise:

Capital Markets Experience—Analysts, Portfolio Managers, and Investment Bankers

The IR team should consist of professionals with senior-level capital markets experience. IR professionals who were once senior-level Wall Street analysts, portfolio managers, and/or investment bankers are probably best qualified because they understand the perceptions and behaviors of the sell-side and the buy-side; more importantly, they understand financial performance in the context of valuation. Additionally they undoubtedly have relationships with former co-workers in the markets, which is invaluable for keeping abreast of the current tides.

Public Relations Expertise—Reporters, Editors, and Broadcasters

The other vital component of the optimal IR team is public relations or corporate communications experts. Because the media is the most penetrating conduit to the general public and vital stakeholders, IR needs to work closely with PR to actively approach and address the media.

Like the capital markets experts, PR professionals know how to say what the media needs to hear, which contributes significantly to the IR strategy. In as much as IR packages a financial product for consumption on Wall Street, PR professionals create an easily digestible package for the media and other constituents.

MAXIMIZING VALUE THROUGH AN INTEGRATED APPROACH

Hiring a PR group to run the IR function can have problems at its very core. IR demands an integrated approach where IR and PR strategies are discussed and overlapped to maximize the event for all company constituents. Easier said than done, however, when budgets preclude two senior professionals from each discipline. There are alternatives, however. A solid program, particularly at a small-cap company, uses inside and outside help to achieve stated goals.

Working in-sync is the key. When hiring a traditional public relations firm to create a strategic IR plan, a company may be taking a risk. Many talented agency staffers are Wall Street outsiders looking in, and they lack the high-level experience to counsel a CEO on what the capital markets want. Another potential problem is that the functions of IR and PR can have very different goals. IR works best in a low-key, nonpromotional context delivering information systematically and conservatively wrapped in financial understanding. PR, on the other hand, can solely exist to promote and raise visibility, which can be the kiss of death on Wall Street if not handled properly.

Therefore, IR, whether internal or external, is best when fully integrated with PR. The interlocking arrangement creates the checks and balances that ensure all of the constituencies receive relevant information that manages their expectations and meets their needs.

ONE-TWO PUNCH

IR needs to quarterback the communications process to make sure that the company accurately sets financial expectations with Wall Street before the other communications plans commence. For example, if a company allows the media to run with a story before The Street is formally apprised of its financial consequences, analysts might quantify the story and translate it into earnings per share guidance, without management's blessing. For example, the newspaper might read: "Profits to Soar Next Year." Wall Street pros don't really know what that means. Their job is to quantify language like that. We see "Profits Soar" as a PR win, yet an IR loss.

To that end, dealing with The Street is more clear-cut than dealing with the media, because the analysts don't need the dramatic angle or story the media must have. The Street provides an unfiltered, straightforward, credible, third-party platform from which the media can build its story. The fact that reporters often get their quotes and sources off of analyst research creates an opportunity for the company to reach the media through Wall Street. Having the company story out on research and in the minds of analysts establishes the company's thesis and maximizes any PR effort.

Company strategy usually pans out over long periods, often three to five years at a time. IR must patiently build and execute its plan dovetailed with corporate communications each step of the way. But at other times, the whole strategy and its execution can be formulated and communicated in a few minutes, such as in the case of a merger or a takeover bid. Although either timeframe calls for a plan, quick-fire reactions to situations can define a company. And that's when, and why, IR and PR should have a structure within which they can work together.

HIRING IR

As stated, an IR department that is fully staffed with capital markets and PR experts is best, but this is usually a luxury of only the biggest public companies. What about the micro, small, and mid-caps?

Each company should field the best team possible. One way to bring these people on board is for a company to go directly to the capital markets and the media and hire these professionals. Even after paying the inevitably high price to obtain these experts, the new hires still have to do a lot of catch-up on the company, its operations, its metrics, its industry, the competition, and the marketplace. One solution is to transfer a current employee, who knows the operations, into the IR space to work with these experts. This strategy is not bad, nor is it the holy grail.

INTERNAL VS. EXTERNAL IR

In order to cost-efficiently obtain an effective, experienced, and integrated IR/PR team, every company, whether it has an internal investor relations officer or not, should consider hiring outside IR counsel with capital markets experience and the ability to work with corporate communications. An internal IR point person, whether it's the CFO or a designated IRO, can help steer these efforts and ultimately be responsible to Wall Street.

The advantages of integrating internal and external IR are many:

- Specific, productive expertise of a team
- A deep bench of capital markets and public relations experience
- Advisors on the front lines, aware of current capital markets and media tides
- Viewpoints beyond an internal, company perspective
- Go-betweens who garner honest feedback from capital markets and media
- Specific industry knowledge
- Multiple databases that would be cost-prohibitive for one company to purchase
- Checks and balances to ensure communications are specific to each constituency

The integrated approach takes ample risk out of the communications equation and frees up management to focus on operations. External IR can see what the company, steeped in its own story, doesn't have time to see and be a nay-sayer in a sea of yes men. External IR can also support the IRO or CFO by doing reconnaissance, tracking shareholder shifts, and executing the necessary strategy relative to valuation.

What all this leads to is that IR is about intelligence. The IR staff, whether internal or external, needs sources and resources. The best sources are the market professionals, the players on the sell-side and the buy-side.

Another is the industry, specifically strategic partners in the arena who might have insights into competitors and consumers. Awareness of industry goings-on is invaluable.

In addition to relationships, there are other valuable forms of intelligence, such as shareholder databases. Some of the good ones include Big Dough, Thomson Financial's First Call, Reuters, Bloomberg, IBES, the trades, and news services. You cannot do the job, let alone do it well, without this information, and those who are at the top of their game know how to interpret the data.

ONWARD AND UPWARD

Ultimately, the goal of IR, which is fully aligned with the CEO's, is to maximize equity value. Professionals who understand how to do this are the professionals an IR department needs, regardless of company's size.

Too much is at stake to not take this course—a company's next equity raise, employee motivation through option value, or preventing a hostile take-over, to give a few examples. By maximizing stock price the company is in a better position for all of these scenarios.

The basics of disclosure, event, and presentation administration need to be supplemented with strategic IR that ingrains itself into every aspect of corporate decision making. Once the basics are understood and the team is in place, it's onward and upward to a new approach to IR. That is, IR at the tip of the spear in terms of maximizing corporate communications and, ultimately, equity value.

CHAPTER 12

Grasping the IR Evolution

The difference between traditional IR and this book's view of IR is the difference between hope and control. Both approaches incorporate basic IR functions, but traditional IR more than the present approach hangs its hat on chance. In other words, the approach advocated here gives the dice to the high rollers and bets with the house. Part IV shares several specific strategies that IR should employ to mitigate risk and position the company to maximize valuation.

Any company that does not approach the IR function as critical and strategic is not acting in the best interest of its shareholders. Now, of course, some smaller companies are so focused on their bottom lines that they refuse to believe they can afford a sophisticated IR effort. Yet these same companies have armies of lawyers, consultants, and accountants. IR is right up there with those professional service providers and equally, if not more, important as it relates to valuation issues.

Accordingly, the cost of any IR effort, no matter how sophisticated, is nominal relative to the prospect of damaging the company's valuation by even one multiple point—a penalty that would, for example, translate to $50 million of value for a company with 50 million shares outstanding.

OUT WITH THE OLD

The stakes are extremely high in corporate America today, and the payoff can be equally great. That's why every company, big and small, public and private, needs to infuse a more sophisticated approach to their IR programs. The new IR is a voice to and from the stock market, interpreting the signposts, negotiating the hazards, and picking the best routes (see Table 12.1).

TABLE 12.1 The New IR

	Traditional IR	New Approach
Strategy	Supports strategy and makes sure it's communicated to the key players.	Helps create strategy, with the benefit of understanding its impact on the markets.
Story	Crafts and communicates an investment thesis based in operations and marketing strategies. Built from the executives' perspectives, sales-oriented.	Crafts, communicates and helps create a complete investment thesis that hinges on valuation. Shuns promotion. (See box on Dress Best Shops.)
Stock market reconnaissance	Maintains a dutiful eye on the stock market.	Understands valuation and daily market volatility. Can discern if fluctuations are due to buy-sell imbalances, or correlated to the underlying fundamentals of a logical peer group.
Shareholder analysis	Tracks stock ownership, names, and amounts, through any number of available databases and resources.	Tracks investors. Also creates investors by looking at multiple comp groups based on size, business model characteristics, balance-sheet strength and valuation.
Approaching analysts	Knows the value of analysts, but often approaches them qualitatively.	Makes sure that guidance is set conservatively and the story is "packaged" properly before approaching anyone. Mitigates risk.

TABLE 12.1 *(continued)*

	Traditional IR	New Approach
Feedback	Considers feedback an important part of the job. Success is based on peer relationships in the capital markets which may or may not exist.	Has peer reltaionships with bankers, analysts, and portfolio managers. Those relationships are driven off the ability to talk valuation.
The CEO	Supports the CEO, helps senior management sell the company strategy, and provides information from The Street and the market as they know it.	Provides senior, strategic, peer counsel to the CEO. Both cheerleader and devil's advocate. Coaches the ego out of management. Comes in at strategy creation to advise on best possible choice for shareholders, and helps the board quantify decisions and educate The Street.
Managing the event	Reactive, at least from an analyst's perspective. Lacks experience or information to be proactive.	Creates the company story and defines it with analysts before anyone has a chance to write it. Specific, conservative guidance to control, in as much as possible, the variables. Sophisticated targeting to attract new buy-side and sell-side blood.

TABLE 12.1 *(continued)*

	Traditional IR	New Approach
Smaller caps	N/A Some micro caps, small caps, and mid-caps conduct IR as an afterthought. When regulations were more lax, did little more than bare necessities, such as SEC disclosures and annual meetings.	Knows no public company can ignore IR. Uses conference calls and other cost-effective strategies to enhance a company's multiple, which can mean millions of dollars for company value as well as other benefits that far outweigh the cost.
Private companies	N/A Most private companies do not have formal IR programs because they don't publicly trade equity or debt and don't have to report to anyone outside of the company.	Knows that a voice in the industry is invaluable and that analysts are still the best road to validation and awareness. Helps define and distinguish offering to advance agendas, such as distribution, promotion, or financing, to gain competitive edge.

Finding the Company Story

Dress Best Shops is a retailer that experienced four quarters of terrible same store sales results. The stock had gone from $20 a share to $13 and was on course to earn $1 per share in 2004. Management pulled inward, refusing to talk to The Street, because it felt that it had no story to tell. Over time the company had done well, but at this point, they were opening stores at a slower pace and they weren't quite sure why their sales were poor.

It just so happens that the stock was trading at 13x the $1 earnings estimate for 2004. This was in-line with other retailers, but they had $11 per share in cash on their balance sheet. Wall Street was thus valuing the operating company at $2 per share or 2x forward earnings, literally a risk-free situation on par with a Treasury Bond. Plus, the company had a great dividend and the opportunity existed for significant equity appreciation over the next two to three years.

Contrary to management's belief, Dress Best Shops was a very exciting investment opportunity. The lack of risk made it a perfect situation to get analyst coverage, as well as buy-side interest. And that's exactly what happened, in that order, because good IR is always economic to the sell-side first. After they publish, and get the credit, the buy-side gets involved.

TRANSFORMING IR

IR cannot be only an administrative function. It needs to work strategically, report directly to the CEO and CFO, and insiuate itself into the practices and strategies of the company. IR in many cases should be equally, if not more, savvy with regard to the capital markets than the CEO or CFO, and should constantly be on the lookout for anything that could damage or enhance valuation. IR worries about the stock; the CEO should worry about the business.

IR offers more than a plan, comments, or insights, it offers a tactical description of how to get things done, how to achieve the desired result. IR works through each quarter to support the decisions of senior management and to qualitatively and quantitatively convey the story of these decisions to all stakeholders.

IR should be management's confidant, value detective, ear to the street, bridge to the industry, strategic advisor, and insurance policy, much like outsourced legal and accounting. Capital markets and public relations professionals with experience on the other side of the table are a good start to executing the new IR.

To paraphrase a line from Sean Connery's character in the movie *The Untouchables*, implementing and executing a strategic IR strategy without a capital markets background is like "bringing a knife to a gunfight." In order to maximize equity value, companies must have intelligence and understanding of the market, transparency, a comprehensive long-term plan, and the management credibility and financial performance to bring in results.

Strategic IR is a critical cog in this process and if done correctly can add another trusted and valuable management leg to the stool. The management team and the public company are the product, and IR packages that product for Wall Street consumption.

Investor Relations

Maximizing Equity Value

Positioning IR to Succeed

The often costly disconnect of information, from company to analyst, and the gap between true value and the investors' perceived value, can bring people into the investor relations field. Those people should not only have communications skills but also have the ability to understand the capital markets and value companies as an investor would. Capital markets professionals seem to have the best background for the job in that they have a unique understanding of Wall Street and specifically how investment banks operate. It's tough to obtain that skill set in any other way.

STRATEGIC IR

An improved investor relations program, grounded in capital markets experience, can help a company achieve a higher level of strategic communications, which consequently should position a company for maximum equity value at any given time. This expansion of multiple lowers a company's cost of capital, positions it for more favorable financing terms, broadens its potential shareholder base, increases chances for analyst coverage, and increases the wealth of all stakeholders, including employees.

In addition, everyone benefits when the IR function is approached with firsthand capital markets knowledge. Analysts feel comfortable knowing that all possible events, good or bad, will be communicated properly with the right messages. Portfolio managers feel the same way because their investment is presumably protected from a communications misstep. Finally, management wins because they build credibility with the markets, a major factor in determining multiple and valuation.

IR RESPONSIBILITIES AND OBJECTIVES

The type of IR described in this book requires that the team know how to anticipate Wall Street needs and stock movements, be able to read financials, model quantitative factors, appraise qualitative elements, garner sector and industry intelligence, develop investment highlights, nurture capital markets relationships, harness honest feedback, think analytically, and communicate clearly and credibly, both verbally and in writing. It's quite a basket of responsibilities, requiring a professional who has strong buy-side and sell-side know-how, the conviction and knowledge to convince a CEO or CFO of the proper course of action, and the ability to act as a peer and confidant on high-level business decisions.

Strategies to maximize equity value are specific to each company. Even so, the process should be systematic and thorough. This section of the book, Part IV, which gives an overview of this new way of practicing IR, is broken down into three sections (see Table 13.1): *Definition* (chapters 14 and 15), *Delivery* (chapters 16–20), and *Dialogue* (chapters 21–25).

All three aspects of IR, Definition, Delivery, and Dialogue, overlap, intersect and constantly change because stock prices and valuation are always changing. IR's function is to integrate these three tasks into a cohesive, comprehensive strategic discourse with the capital markets, one that supports the mission of the company and prompts Wall Street to keep its vision on the long-term goals and operating performance of the company.

DEFINITION

Every company needs to communicate who they are to the capital markets, the media, employees, vendors, and so on. In order to do this, IR must undergo a process similar to that performed by analysts and portfolio managers: an IR audit. An IR audit deconstructs the current company view and rebuilds it from the bottom up to create a story that serves as the company's face to Wall Street given the current valuation.

Defining a stock to Wall Street is actually not so different from marketing a product to a consumer; much of the success lies in packaging. Packaging the product takes some skill, starting with learning about the product's strengths and weaknesses and defining its value relative to its peers.

For example, a company that chooses to develop a sports drink and places it on the shelf next to Gatorade does so if it believes that the sports drink will appeal to consumers and deliver value. To that end, sports drink

TABLE 13.1 Description of the Three Ds

Definition	Delivery	Dialogue
The IR Audit	Preparation	Maintaining and building
Review disclosures	Guidance	relationships
Interview management	Targeting the audience	
Identify comps	Integrating with PR	Meeting The Street
Determine relative value	Infrastructure/Disclosure	
Get capital markets		Event management
feedback	Action	
Gather industry	Earnings announcements	Banker mentality
intelligence	Conference calls	
Excavating value	Pre-announcements	

XYZ may have 20 ounces versus Gatorade's 16 ounces yet cost half the price. If the drink does the job for athletes just like Gatorade, XYZ is probably a bargain and consumers will be very interested. A stock is no different. A company that knows its peers and understands its value relative to those peers can do a better job of communicating its value story. Defining the company through an IR audit is the key to this process, and it sets the foundation for communicating to the outside world.

DELIVERY

Targeted communication involves several levels and vehicles. The company should be committed to actively presenting itself to the appropriate audience with a commitment to conservative guidance, transparency, and consistency, in both good times and bad.

An integral part of this step is finding the professionals in the investment community who might be interested in the company. Once a company recognizes, based on valuation and growth prospects, if it's a growth or value vehicle and to what degree, it can discover its audience of potential sell-side analysts and buy-side funds. When this segment is identified, IR can approach them.

Reaching out to the target market includes a commitment to basic correspondence that includes earnings announcements (and pre-announcements when appropriate), conference calls, non-deal road shows, or material press releases. These points of the delivery stage are the make-or-break fulcrum upon which the company's investment thesis relies.

DIALOGUE

Packaging the product, targeting the audience and telling the story are all a good start, but the ongoing dialogue with investors and analysts is critical in supporting the approach. Dialogue includes nurturing relationships with capital markets:

- Collecting not just feedback, but constructive, strong, honest criticism
- Staying on top of Wall Street's ever-changing industry perceptions and hot buttons
- Balancing management's efforts for awareness vs. promotion
- Recognizing communication that distracts from the message

This dialogue requires the IR professional to break down the buffer around the CEO and become a confidant to both senior management and their Street counterparts, stripping away any illusions that company executives may have about their standing on Wall Street. Access to management is essential, and very few portfolio managers or analysts are going to jeopardize that access by criticizing the CEO or CFO when they deserve it.

This speaks to the classic "Emperor Has No Clothes" tale. CEOs and CFOs need to know what the crowd is saying, and IR should be the conduit. Additionally, IR is responsible for helping senior executives deliver bad news, keeping short-term disappointments or mistakes and their ramifications in perspective, and focusing on long-term goals. Investor relations cannot be the domain of a reactive administrator or a comfort zone for yes men or women.

Pre-Definition Decisions

CEOs and CFOs need to take IR and corporate communication very seriously. Approached strategically and with a capital markets perspective, IR staffed with the right professionals will position any company to preserve valuation, enhance shareholder wealth, build a company's reputation, and prolong and/or enhance a CEO's or CFO's career.

However, before a structured IR program can begin, every company should address its infrastructure needs, which almost always depend on the size of the entity. An effective IR/PR program can be done internally, externally, or through a hybrid approach that marries the best of internal expertise with an outside agency. Regardless of which avenue management takes, however, every public company, and many private ones, should plan a Wall Street–savvy strategic program to communicate to all stakeholders.

MEGA CAPS

Most stocks with market values in the tens of billions bring the IR/PR function internal and staff it, on the IR side with CFO-caliber people, and on the PR side with experienced corporate communications executives. They can afford to subscribe to all the information services, and run a very tight, self-sufficient program. A company of this size should never fully outsource the capability, nor would they.

However, every public company experiences the "Emperor Has No Clothes" syndrome where buy-side and sell-side analysts avoid honest, unfiltered feedback in an effort to preserve access. And on the corporate communications side, even the biggest of firms need to audit their practices and see if the media and other stakeholders perceive the company on par with the internal group. For that reason, mega-cap companies should consider complementary, cost-effective outside help that can deliver the current Street perception and help craft a response plan to all constituents.

LARGE CAPS

Stocks with a value between $2 and $10 billion are middle ground in our view. They could outsource the IR/PR function, but they are so widely held with so many moving parts to the business that they will invariably benefit from having one or two full-time, internal people on the job. The internal staff in this case is most likely senior enough so that any outside agency must also be staffed with experienced senior-level counsel, or it will be cost prohibitive (that is, not worth the incremental expense).

As a rule of thumb, the smaller the company, the more help it should seek from the outside. Not only is the independent feedback and outside perspective critical, but all the information services, which can run into the hundreds of thousands of dollars, can be accessed at a lower price. For even a large-cap company, there is no reason to buy these services internally. A good bet under this scenario is to hire a qualified third party to deliver and interpret the information and create a plan to act accordingly.

SMALL CAPS

Companies whose valuations are below $2 billion typically do not have an internal investor relations group and may have a sparse corporate communications group that's tucked into marketing. In IR's case, the CEO and

CFO split the duties, and it's usually done with the help of internal administrative support.

In our view, this situation almost always calls for an expert third party. An outside agency can deliver on all the administrative aspects of the company's IR/PR strategy, provide all the financial information service needed, and most importantly give the kind of advice that will protect management from making a mistake when communicating its story to the capital markets, the media, or any other stakeholder.

When the CEO or CFO takes on these corporate communications duties, they almost always move down the priority list. The primary job of a CEO or CFO is to run the company and deliver the expected financial performance. When they also have to manage the IR function that simply introduces risk into the equation, and Wall Street doesn't like risk.

IPOS

Initial public offerings are a whirlwind for a small company. Creating the S-1 document—the SEC document that describes the business and its historic financial results —is an absolutely hectic time. Moreover, there are endless meetings with bankers, lawyers, and accountants preparing management for its two-week road show that actually sells the shares to the buy-side and raises the needed funds.

With all this distraction, management must not forget the corporate communications function. Upon pricing, management will find itself in a strange new world with buy-side and sell-side analysts calling for appointments and information, and reporters clamoring for the next story. In addition, the CEO may catch employees watching the daily stock price, becoming more obsessed with the market's fractional movements than with their jobs.

This scenario is trouble waiting to happen as management, with no communications plan whatsoever, finds itself spending 20 to 25 percent of its time reacting to events as a public company, rather than decreasing that percentage by being proactive. To make it more difficult, this situation usually comes at a time when management has tremendous pressure to deliver stellar financial performance.

We believe companies that find themselves on the road to an IPO should get an IR/PR team involved two to three months before the start of the road show. IR can create the company's infrastructure to be public, create a 12-month plan, and implement a system that actually allows management to run the company without significant interruption—including dealing with shareholders and analysts, the media, and employees, as well as developing a crisis plan so management looks calm and polished no matter what the circumstances.

This type of proactive communications planning is how companies garner a premium valuation: the goal of the CEO and the goal of all shareholders. The most cost-effective way to do this for a small-cap IPO is usually a very qualified third party. It's at least half the cost of bringing the function internal in most cases.

HIGH YIELD

As we mentioned, private companies with public debt must adhere to all SEC regulations, including Reg FD, yet many of these CEOs tend not to take corporate communications as seriously because they are not overly concerned with the investment community's perception of their debt. After all, equity value equates to personal wealth and bonds normally do not.

That said, if the company intends to issue public equity in the future, its credibility with bondholders and other stakeholders will make a difference in its potential equity valuation. Also, even if the plan is to stay private, bonds influence cost of capital, and to ignore the role of communications is to ignore the maximizing of shareholder value, even if they are private investors.

PRIVATE

We believe that all companies should take IR/PR seriously. Every company needs a solid PR group to highlight the products and the brand and drive market share and profitability. However, private companies also have an opportunity to get their point of view across with Wall Street by developing a limited, but smart, IR outreach program.

The pursuit of one of the best forms of third-party validation, the sell-side analysts, will pay off for these companies. Analysts are always looking for new companies and a new understanding of the industry, and often they are happy to publish a company's point of view in their research, regardless if they agree with it.

INTERNATIONAL

International companies have a big opportunity to raise their exposure in the United States. However, the United States has new disclosure and reporting rules and the game isn't necessarily the same as overseas. European or Asian management teams must have the right information and the proper plan to guide their IR process in the United States, including targeting and meeting with the right institutions.

Proactive communications in the United States by international companies is welcomed by domestic institutions and the U.S. media. If successful, it also gets the international company's growth strategy factored into its multiple, and most likely into the multiple of its U.S. competitor. This, by definition, affects the competition's cost of capital. For example, after meeting with an international company that has a convincing growth strategy, maybe the U.S. portfolio manager will only be willing to pay a discounted multiple for the U.S. competitor that's currently trading at a premium. That's well worth the effort. As with all companies, the international company's story must be properly packaged and told in the correct manner to the right audience, or the communication strategy is defeated before it begins.

THE APPROACH TO STRATEGIC IR

The gist of strategic IR, for every company, any size, public or private, is smart and timely communication to the right audience. This communication, based on an understanding of the valuation process and the intricacies of capital markets, helps companies maximize equity value. For that reason IR can be more art than science, and an explanation of this approach, from IR audit to a long-term cycle of discourse between the company and its constituencies, can help companies garner the best value at any given time.

It starts by answering the question: how are companies valued?

UNDERSTANDING THE ART AND SCIENCE OF VALUATION

Investor relations officers must have a solid understanding of valuation before the definition process can begin. However, that does not mean just the mathematics of P/E or EV/EBITDA; it means a comprehensive understanding of the two slices of the valuation pie that are constantly in motion.

While financial performance is the primary determinant of value, a certain component of valuation deals in intangibles. This part of valuation has to do with perception, either good, bad or indifferent.

In our view:

Equity Value = Financial Performance + How That
Performance Is Interpreted By a Variety of Constituencies

"Earnings, and expectations about them, have become the major driver of stock prices."

—Barron's, March 22, 2004

How do we know that perception plays a part in valuation? Well, a fairly standard method of valuing companies is assigning a P/E ratio based on future earnings estimates. If fundamentals were the sole focus of investors, P/E would probably mirror the EPS growth rate. Yet often, one can see two 20 percent "earnings growers" in the same industry, with one company trading at a 10 P/E and the other at a 20 P/E. This disparity, in many cases, is the result of perception.

Valuation is both science and art. The science factor is financial performance and the standard valuation measures that are assigned to all companies. The art element is how that financial performance is communicated (how, when, what, to whom, and by whom) relative to expectations.

We strongly believe that the art portion of valuation can make up anywhere from 20 to 40 percent of the total valuation at any given time. This is a huge piece of a company's market cap, worth tens of millions of dollars in shareholder wealth. Managing the art portion of the equation is ultimately IR's responsibility; that person, either internal or external, needs to know what they're doing (see Figure 13.1).

All things being equal, Wall Street would assign a multiple to earnings or cash flow based solely on the company's financial outlook and there would be no need for IR or corporate communications. But this isn't the real world, and IR should help the company control the variance.

Management, along with IR, should be wary of several traps when managing the art side of the art/science equation:

■ A company that identifies the wrong comp group—or worse, fails to identify any comp group at all—allows The Street to define its relative

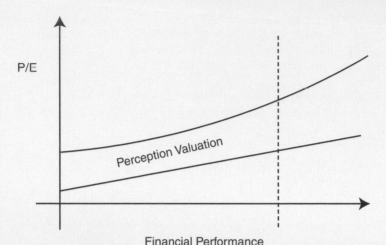

FIGURE 13.1 The Art and Science of Valuation

positioning. This stock's price will often trade at a discount if it's valued in the context of a group-multiple that's too low for the company's shifting business model, market potential, and/or prospects.

■ A company that doesn't specifically target the appropriate investors. By not finding investors who buy similar stocks and have objectives that are in line with those of the company, management might be missing the opportunity to corral dozens of large, long-term buyers. They are also wasting time and money in the process.

■ IR that allows management to establish optimistic guidance or no guidance at all. Either of these scenarios increases the risk that management will regularly miss estimates over time, the ultimate bogeys by which every company is judged. For example, in the "too optimistic" category, a 20 percent earnings grower that guides investors to expect 25 percent growth will rarely get the same multiple that a 20 percent grower will get if it prompts investors to expect 15 percent.

IR's job is to balance the fine line between optimism and realism because when that line blurs, valuation suffers. To that point, aggressive guidance that normally leads to a higher short-term stock price can be very counterproductive. It often forces an analyst to downgrade the rating, attracts short sellers, and increases the risk of volatility, all of which can be distracting and a massive time drain to management.

THE MANAGEMENT PIECE OF VALUATION

A substantial part of the 20 to 40 percent that is attributed to perception relies on management, pure and simple. Considerations include:

Can I trust management?
Do they return calls in a timely manner?
Are they forthcoming with information?
Do they appear to answer questions openly and honestly?
Have they executed against what they have communicated to their financial markets?
Do they seem promotional?

If management has developed credible relationships with The Street, then investors and analysts are much more willing to listen to a company and maintain support should a marginal event transpire. The Street needs to believe that management is consistently accessible, honest, and straightforward, no matter what the circumstances.

For example, if a company misses earnings by a penny or two, some analysts would downgrade the stock. However, those that know management and have built a relationship over time may give management the benefit of the doubt and maintain their rating (especially if the company is in the practice of pre-announcing anticipated misses, as we discuss in chapter 20). This benefit of the doubt can take years to accumulate—and can be erased in one day with one poorly handled communications incident—and IR needs to continually regulate the way the management team conveys confidence and capacity.

Management must meet the credibility checklist:

Accountability: Shuttling blame usually has the opposite effect. Devise a plan to turn weakness into opportunity, and communicate the issue with The Street.

Transparency: Be simple and clear. Concisely present financial statements that focus on the health of the business, add incremental information that highlights the major driver of earnings, and relay specific explanations of objectives and strategies.

Anticipation: Be proactive. Catch-up and spin are exhausting and ineffective. Stay in front of salient news and employ a policy of proactive communication, such as the earnings pre-announcements. A proactive plan saves time and money.

Visibility: Slick management teams who come across as promoting their stock present a risk. Promotion does not generate sustainable value. While CEOs must be dynamic enough to generate interest, their job is not to talk about valuation and promote the stock. The CEO's job is to deliver earnings and to articulate results and future strategy transparently and in a timely fashion, good or bad.

Ego: Management should check egos at the door and be open to suggestions from IR and The Street. Ultimately, an unhealthy ego and a know-it-all attitude are judged as major flaws by professional investors and analysts.

The capital markets are an arena of conviction. Management actions, or sometimes their very presence, can materially move a stock. For example, a new management team with a reputation for success comes to a company, and up goes the stock. A turnaround specialist takes over the reigns of a broken-down company and stabilizes the business, and institutional demand increases. A CEO is distracted by another venture, and owners get skittish. A CFO gets defensive or emotional on a conference call, and Wall Street backs away.

If management runs the company and, along with IR, properly packages and articulates the financials and the qualitative story to The Street, they will slowly and steadily build credibility and value. IR must control deviations in perception and maximize opportunities to garner a premium multiple.

Establishing the valuation begins with the IR audit.

Definition

CHAPTER 14

The IR Audit

The Street is looking for an investment opportunity, and the group that positions and communicates that opportunity is investor relations. Before any interaction between The Street and the company can occur, though, a company must define its current position and future plans. This is the definition stage of IR and it starts with the IR audit.

The IR audit is the first step in self-realization for companies and the first step in honing their peer group. The audit stems from the valuation methodology Wall Street professionals use, and the goal is to undertake the same exercise as the folks who will be buying or publishing on the company's stock.

In the audit, IR should

- Review disclosures and analyze financials
- Interview senior management
- Identify comparables
- Determine relative valuation
- Get capital markets feedback
- Gather industry intelligence

To best position any company in the context of other companies around them, IR must understand all it can about the company and its philosophy, determine relative value, and collect salient information and outside perspectives. Then, once the company has drawn up as much knowledge and intelligence as it can, IR takes the final step of the definition stage and excavates, crafts, and positions the value story.

The following are steps for the IR audit, regardless of the size of the company and regardless of whether IR is handled internally, externally, or a combination thereof.

STEP ONE: REVIEW DISCLOSURES, ANALYZE FINANCIALS

Definition begins with superior knowledge of the company. Even the most entrenched IRO should begin by reviewing all company disclosures and releases, including historical filings, company reports, and news coverage, as well as past and current financials. Among these resources are:

The last 10-K: This gives the best and most detailed view of the business. IR should look for competitive advantages, barriers to entry, consistency of performance, the business model, historic margins, historic sales, and EPS performance. Additionally, by surveying recent transactions, mergers or acquisitions, and debt repayment or share repurchases, IR can see if management has historically created value in the base business.

The last two 10-Qs: This gives significant quarterly information since the 10-K filing. The 10-Q is not as thorough as the 10-K but gives a great update on the business, particularly in the MD&A (management discussion and analysis) section. Also, the income statement, the balance sheet, and the cash flow statement are all on display in the 10-Q, and all the year-over-year comparisons are laid out for the investing public. IR should review the Qs for all of the above items to gauge sequential and year-over-year performance.

The last two earnings releases: IR is looking for content and style here. Specifically, is it formatted correctly (not too long or too short, not full of unnecessary quotes) and written properly (simple yet informative, not looking as if a legal team wrote it or an accountant wrote it)? Are the appropriate metrics highlighted in a way that is easy for Wall Street to digest? Additionally, IR should check what time of day it was released. Companies should schedule both the release and the conference call after market hours. As we discuss in the Delivery section, timing of the release and conference call is critical to minimizing risk.

Stock chart: The historical stock performance should be studied for an idea of how the price has reacted to earnings over time. It should also be studied for an idea of where the stock is during the definition stage. Is the stock at a 52-week high or low? Somewhere in the middle? The recent price and current valuation play a large part in determining the strategy when it comes to the delivery stage.

The board of directors: IR should also know who's who and look for any recognizable names. A high-profile former CEO or someone known on Wall Street for previous successes is a great point to highlight to the world.

Following the review comes the interview.

STEP TWO: INTERVIEW SENIOR MANAGEMENT

IR can only go so far on SEC disclosures and press releases. Management has to fill in the blanks and talk about strategy. The IRO and/or outside IR counsel should sit down with management and learn the executives' philosophy on business and the current and future plans for the company.

In addition to gaining valuable information, these interviews help IR gauge the executive's capacity for dealing with analysts and portfolio managers and can play into the decision about who will talk to The Street and when. The content of the interview should be as follows:

- Ask both the easy and tough questions. The latter is important to understand how the CEO reacts under pressure. Also, the CEO would rather field a tough question from a team member rather than from a portfolio manager when he's unprepared.
- Methodically go through the top line and the drivers of the business. If the company has several business units, IR needs to go through the top line of each.
- Discern management's thoughts on its competitive advantages and barriers to entry—first-mover advantage, patents, experience, and relationships of the sales force.
- Discuss marketing, market share, and advertising. Do those expenditures translate to the bottom line? Does the business respond to promotions? How has the company taken market share from competitors and under what circumstances?
- Ask about culture and the principles management attempts to instill in the company and the employees.
- Talk through the expense side of the income statement with both the CEO and the CFO together. Go through every line and talk about how these line items, such as Selling, General, & Administrative (SG&A) expenses, marketing, will increase relative to sales. Try and get at the operating leverage of the company. If sales go up $5 and the expenses only go up $1, that's leverage and a great selling point to Wall Street.
- Interview the CEO and CFO about the balance sheet. How much cash is on hand? How much net cash does the company generate every quarter, and what does management plan on doing with it? What's the historic return on equity? Does it sit in the bank and earn 1 percent, or is it reinvested in the business? Is it used to buy a business or repay debt or repurchase shares? These critical questions will definitely be asked by the sell- and buy-sides.

The interview process should make the SEC disclosures come to life and give IR a better idea of the overall company and the competitive landscape. The interview also allows IR to gauge how solid management will be when presenting. Can they answer the tough questions? Does the CFO have the numbers at her fingertips? Is the CEO straightforward or evasive? After the interview stage, IR might decide that if the CEO hits the road, his lack of immediacy with the numbers would require that the CFO go along for every meeting.

THE STAKEHOLDERS

From an overall communications perspective, the opinions of all stakeholders in the supply chain, including vendors, customers, employees and consumers, can have a profound effect on the value and morale of the company.

IR must keep tabs on the pulse of these stakeholders, yet gathering this information is no easy feat. The responsibility of all good corporate communications leaders is to establish simple, two-way avenues of communications.

For stakeholders such as vendors and customers, IR should work with the appropriate internal manager to comb through internal or external communications to obtain their opinions as well as initiate relationships with specific point people willing to extend honest feedback. Employees can be reached through newsletters, presentations, and other internal communications, but employees must also be encouraged and motivated to upstream opinions to management, rather than leak them to the public. Frequent management employee question-and-answer sessions can be arranged and monitored by IR in the same way that IR executes these presentations for investors.

Information from key stakeholders is invaluable. Management should incorporate the factors that support their position, or, if it does not like what it hears, adjust the reality to improve the perception of those in the know.

Hard-core finance or stock junkies who might think this approach is a little "touchy-feely" should think again. The culture that Sam Walton nurtured at Wal-Mart made the company a world superpower capable of generating over $1 billion in revenue per day. The same goes for Bill Gates, who challenges the best and brightest to maintain a culture that innovates faster and better than the competition. A solid, open culture enhances value and creates a long-term, vibrant company. One of the major problems of the 1990s' stock market bubble was overreaching management teams and their financial backers being more concerned with building and selling companies rather than building a long-term, sustainable business and culture.

STEP THREE: IDENTIFY COMPARABLES

After reviewing corporate disclosures and interviewing management to add depth to the picture, IR can move to the next step in definition: determining the comparable group. To do this, IR should create a spreadsheet with a dozen or more companies, in the same industry or with the same business model, and with a similar market cap. These companies are commonly referred to as *comps*.

Every sector trades within a given multiple range, usually related to business model characteristics and outlook for profit growth. Traditionally slower-growth industries, such as consumer staples or industrial manufacturing, tend to trade at lower multiples than the historically faster-growth industries, such as technology and health care.

A company identified with the wrong peer group may be trading at a multiple that actually discounts their true value. This problem is especially pressing if the company has been locked into the multiple of a slow-growth industry when the company is actually thriving. This situation happens for one of two reasons. Either the company has been positioned incorrectly, or the company is relatively unique and the peer group needs to be established.

Identity

Companies that are covered by several analysts should look at each analyst's coverage universe. If one analyst covers a group of stocks that is much different from another, then that's an indication that the story might need refinement.

Companies should make sure they are reaching the appropriate audience, which means studying comparables that are more in line with their business and looking closely at operations, sales and service structure, intellectual protection, size, and so on. The conclusion may initiate a change in the tag line and an overhaul of communications.

A Horse of a Different Color

Though some companies have clear business propositions and fall neatly into peer groups on Wall Street, many do not.

For example, a national landscaping company may be the only one of its kind that's publicly traded. There aren't ten publicly traded landscaping companies that IR can analyze to determine relative valuation. Creativity or outside help from Wall Street is needed here. In this example, IR might realize that the landscaping company has a national infrastructure that services individual homes, which is similar to that of Rollins, Inc., the parent company of Orkin Pest Control, and also similar to The Brinks Company's division for household alarms, Brinks Home Security. These companies, presumably of the same size (give or take $100 million in value), are very much alike and have the same capital needs and similar margins—they are good comparables. Wall Street tends to give these businesses similar multiples.

In other situations, two peer groups are needed. If a company fits well with one group because of its industry, but also another because of its business model, IR can consider offering both groups up for comparison. Shuffle Master Gaming is a company that designs and distributes products to the casino industry, so their initial comp group is made up of casino equipment manufacturers. However, their focus on patented technological solutions and their recurring revenue business model make the company appealing to buyers of technology stocks, so a second technology comp group might emerge.

It's simply an exercise in valuing a company two ways with the hope that there might be inefficiency in the marketplace relative to one of those comp groups, leading to a buying opportunity.

Companies with multiple divisions or brands, or ones that both manufacture and sell items through retail, do not fit so neatly into any box and may be muddled in the mix of a peer group that represents only part of the company's business. In this instance, IR may want to establish a new peer group altogether, perhaps even defining a whole new industry, and look for companies with similar makeups for comparison. Even more radical, IR may want to suggest a new valuation methodology.

Imagine a company called Spare Change, which had a unique business proposition that was not well defined by The Street. Spare Change provided financial transaction processing services primarily in supermarkets, although The Street didn't really compare them to similar companies. In fact, the analysts who covered Spare Change (see Table 14.1) were an eclectic group and lumped the company into categories that included retailers and general consumer products companies.

These three analysts all spent their time following different companies. The research universes suggested that Spare Change would be better positioned with a more appropriate analyst base.

At that point, the IR Audit took hold of the company's definition, narrowed it down to electronic transaction processing, and suggested not only a clarification of the company itself, but also the industry in which it competes. This instigated a reconsideration of Spare Change's peer group and

TABLE 14.1　Analysts and Companies

Analyst 1	Analyst 2	Analyst 3
Spare Change	Spare Change	Spare Change
Ediets	RMH Teleservices	Checkfree Corp
Imax	Valuevision	GTECH Holdings eFunds
PF Changs	Scientific Games	Global Payments
Nautilus	Danka Business Solutions	
New Frontier Media		

positioned the company for an upward adjustment of its multiple. The new valuation goal was more in line with financial services comparables rather than consumer products like tissue or toothpaste.

A company moves closer to optimal value when it is trading at the multiple that correctly corresponds to its business characteristics. Additionally, a new definition may open the company up to other coverage universes, creating a reason for more analysts to consider it.

Just a few years ago, one of the largest leisure craft retailers was perceived more like a manufacturer and consequently received the lower manufacturer's multiple instead of a higher retailer multiple. Investors saw risk in high-ticket items, but management had done an amazing job of generating consistent financial results over time, suggesting that the retail multiple was appropriate. Once discovering The Street's perception of its business, IR repeatedly communicated the correct retail positioning to investors, backed up by numbers: store-level return on investment and same store sales. Fortunately, the company is now measured against other hard goods retailers, but it didn't happen overnight.

Another client, a small sports equipment manufacturer, had always been viewed by The Street as competing in a tough industry with low multiples, about an 8 P/E on forward-year earnings. After looking more closely at the business model, IR recognized that this company was not much like the other players in the field, many of which were waning under the weight of their outmoded product offerings or high infrastructure costs. This company had, in fact, evolved beyond its peers and was more of a lifestyle company with a brand name that could easily be leveraged across a host of other products.

Other companies compared better to this firm, and so IR repositioned it into a new group and changed all financial communications accordingly. This sector traded at triple the multiple of the company's original sector and positioned the company as relatively undervalued as management built the business.

Creating this new comp group was a great new start, and a fresh perspective for the analysts and their sales forces. If that repositioning exercise had not been undertaken, The Street would have likely continued to define the company in a low-multiple industry. Taking control and redefining its own comp group repositioned the company to significantly increase shareholder value.

Redefining and repositioning both in terms of qualitative presentation and quantitative metrics can add value. Once the appropriate group is established, all communications of the company must relate to the new comparables.

STEP FOUR: DETERMINE RELATIVE VALUE

Once the comparables are chosen, IR must use valuation skills to determine the company's relative valuation. Is it overvalued, fairly valued, or undervalued relative to its peer group? The story that's ultimately crafted depends on that answer.

The *valuation comparison* is a comparison of financials across the company's comp group. IROs should construct a spreadsheet of all comps and their market cap, stock price, last year's earnings, next year's earnings estimates (the analyst consensus), long-term debt, last year's EBITDA (the con-

> Recently, many gaming companies adapted a valuation argument created by Daniel Davila, an analyst at Sterne, Agee, & Leach. Mr. Davila made a credible argument that the best gaming companies should be compared not only to each other, but also to other entertainment-related companies like hotels and entertainment conglomerates, both of which, historically, have traded a premium valuations to the gaming sector.

sensus), and next year's EBITDA. IR should double-check all of the P/E and EV/EBITDA formulas, and those two columns yield relative valuation. This comparison chart gives a snapshot of relative value and helps a company see where—high, low, or in the middle—it trades.

STEP FIVE: GET CAPITAL MARKETS FEEDBACK

After having read up on the history of the company, held interviews with management, and run a comp analysis that helped to determine the relative valuation, IR should figure out the reason for the valuation. The first source is The Street.

If the company is undervalued, is it because they are terrible communicators or is it a negative view of management? Is there a perceived competitive threat?

Wall Street professionals have seen companies come and go. They've witnessed the cycles as those companies either emerge or sputter, grow or struggle, and are familiar with both success and failure. While most would argue that no one can ever know a company as well as its management team, smart CEOs should realize that an outsider's perspective is sometimes needed to help the insider see most clearly.

IR should first find out who on the buy-side owns the stock and which analysts cover it. Then give them a call and start asking questions. Some portfolio managers and analysts will have time to talk. Perhaps they feel that management's compensation is too weighted toward options, the company's business is threatened by a new competitor, or the CEO isn't credible, and they wouldn't buy the stock on that basis. Perhaps they ultimately think that the company is inconsistent with no credibility, routinely overpromising and underdelivering.

The Analysts

Analysts are the go-to folks for anyone who wants to gather industry and company-specific knowledge. Although they may not cover every stock in a given sector, they do know about most of the companies and have a good idea about their value.

Therefore, a quick phone call or a conversation with the analyst at an industry conference can help the company's IR professional form an idea of how the company's story is perceived relative to its peers. If an IR professional has some helpful and specific industry knowledge that he or she can provide to the analyst, this helps the analyst learn something too. Perhaps seek out this IR professional and his or her company as a go-to incremental knowledge or channel check. Over time, this relationship can certainly lead to better feedback.

STEP SIX: GATHER INDUSTRY INTELLIGENCE

Finally, IR needs to know what the investor community expects from a sector and the companies in that sector. No matter the valuation method, all companies are judged relative to other companies. There's simply no better way to determine how much to pay for a stock. And rarely are two industries alike. Each has its own competitive issues and dynamics.

The final step in the IR audit, before developing the company story, is industry intelligence.

History

Any executive, analyst, or investor can attest to the fact that the history of each industry surfaces incessantly. The stories of who came first, who came before, what's been done, and who did it texture the dynamics within the sectors and are often cited as precedents for evaluation of current actions. If anyone else, another company or an analyst perhaps, knows these precedents, the company is best served to have someone inside its walls who knows these things too.

Current Conditions

In order to gather information on the industry in which the company competes, IR should collect information from a variety of sources. These include SEC filings; analyst research reports; conference call transcripts; the industry trade papers; company communications, such as employee newsletters and conference and convention minutes; and conversations with consumers, customers, and vendors.

During this review, understand what the disclosures say about the other businesses. IR may have discovered, during the review and interview steps of the IR audit, that her company had rock-solid growth of 20 percent per year and the same projected going forward. Yet this growth doesn't seem as impressive if, after reviewing the filings of the peer group, other companies are growing at 30 percent, have better balance sheets, and have invested in new technologies.

In addition to the disclosures of public competitors, IR should investigate all stakeholders in the industry, including suppliers, vendors, financiers, and so on. Trends are always emerging. Consumer behavior patterns, supply channel efficiencies, government regulations, financing issues, and other topics that affect every player come up in a sector. IR must have an ear on the latest and greatest because it helps in defining the company to Wall Street. Moreover, it can be assumed that the buy- and the sell-sides are also abreast of these items.

Street Perceptions

Within the sell-side and the buy-side are pods of industry specialists and personalities who differ as much as the industries themselves. In addition, the expectations, the salient issues, and the valuation techniques vary from one industry to another.

Especially in the definition stage, IR must help management understand how The Street is looking not only at the company, but at the sector. An objective for restaurants is not an expectation in consumer products; a hot issue in footwear may not even spark a twinkle of recognition in aerospace and defense; a metric in retail is going to differ from any measure that's central to the technology sector.

IR should know how The Street is measuring the industry so that the relevant topics within the company can be uncovered and highlighted. This information is unearthed by reviewing the conference call scripts of industry players and reviewing questions that analysts and portfolio managers ask. It's also done by reviewing research reports and monitoring First Call estimates for an upward or downward bias.

THE RESULT OF THE IR AUDIT

After uncovering all the information it can, determining relative value, and collecting perspectives, IR should be able to identify if (and why) the stock is undervalued, overvalued, or fairly valued relative to its peers. For the purposes of discussion, assume that a company is growing profits at 20 percent but its stock is near a 52-week low and its multiple is 10x on a P/E basis. The next step in the definition stage is discovering how to shrink the valuation gap between the multiple and the company's growth rate, which just so happens to be the average multiple of the company's peer group.

For example, let's say that from all the information collected, the IR audit has determined that XYZ Corp. is a terrible communicator. The CEO doesn't know when to stop selling, which plays poorly on Wall Street. In addition to poor communication skills, the buy-side perceives, falsely by the way, a threat from a new competitor, and finally the company has $40 million in cash and hasn't declared a use for it in over two years.

The next step would be to rebuild the story. IR should

- Uncover positive value
- Counteract any concerns
- Correct any misconceptions
- Package the company into a carefully crafted message

In the XYZ Corp. example, rebuilding the story would include establishing conservative guidance that helps management build credibility by achieving self-set earnings estimates over time, developing a presentation that highlights diversification in the business and shows that the competitive threat really is insignificant, and encouraging management and the board to announce a share repurchase authorization to put the balance sheet cash to work in an accretive manner. These steps, initiated by management and the IRO, should pay dividends in terms of closing the aforementioned valuation gap. In all likelihood, Company XYZ's multiple will expand and close in on the 20x range, adding tens of millions of value to shareholder wealth.

Another example of an audit to success story is Cinderella Story & Sons, a fairly new company to the public markets. They had a product that had penetrated a variety of channels and surfaced into consumer awareness. They had a good business proposition and a unique operating model, but The Street was not viewing it enthusiastically. The stock price was down, and Cinderella didn't know why.

An IR team conducted an audit that included a review of the disclosures, interviews with management, identifying the comparables, determining relative value, getting capital markets feedback, and garnering industry intelligence.

Once the problems were found, IR addressed them one by one and decided that Cinderella Story & Sons needed just a few adjustments. The company reevaluated its profile and changed its tag line to fit into a peer group that was more in line with the products they offered. This group also traded at a higher multiple, which the company justified by showing similar growth drivers that matched the comparables in that group.

IR also recommended that management renew its focus on free cash flow generation capabilities, their balance sheet, and their investment in long-term growth initiatives. This repositioned the company as a great value stock—that is, not growing necessarily, but generating free cash flow, paying down debt, and carrying a much more attractive risk/reward profile than a company with a growth multiple.

By conducting an IR audit, companies can set themselves up to rebuild their story. With a focus on company knowledge, industry intelligence, and relative valuation, IROs will find that when they are fully informed, they have the right tools to advise a busy CEO, and the confidence to talk to even the most sophisticated analyst.

CHAPTER 15

Excavating Value Post-Audit

The IR audit almost always leads to a more refined definition and, more often than not, positions a company to maximize the equity valuation at any given time. From this reality, IR should always dig deeper and use its capital markets expertise to excavate, craft, and position the new story.

EXCAVATING THE STORY: EXAMPLES

The following is the story of a real company (with a fictional name) that realized the importance of excavating the story.

Uncovering the Pearls

Nightingale Inc., a health care company, had a common story. The management team was running the company with a well-developed long-term strategy, but they didn't know how to connect with Wall Street. For eight quarters in a row, their stock had gone down right after their conference call.

IR became involved to help them hone in on their story and deliver it in a professional manner to the right constituents on The Street. The IR audit revealed that Nightingale had a big short position, and the short sellers were there for good reason. The negatives were apparent right away, already factored into the low stock price.

First, the company was using its cash to finance its customers, a move Wall Street never likes because it is a perceived high risk distraction from the core business. Management announced that they were dismantling this financing arm of the business.

Second, the company had a customer that was responsible for a majority of its sales, but this customer was a division of a much bigger pharmaceutical company, which was spinning it off to shareholders. The Street had predicted this to be a negative, but management knew that it would now be a larger part of this smaller company, strengthening Nightingale's powerbase in the relationship.

Third, The Street had always viewed one of the company's product lines as too specialized with no growth opportunities. Though the market was highly fragmented, Nightingale was the biggest manufacturer of this product and demand was growing annually, representing one-fifth of the company's total revenue. IR recommended adding this narrative to its story, explaining that Nightingale was the industry leader in a growing market.

Fourth, Nightingale had acquired a business with a good product and a bad management team. Short sellers specifically thought it was a terrible business headed right down the drain. During the IR audit, management was asked why they bought the business. The CEO said it was a good product, just badly managed. The company had decided not to talk about this new division on its conference calls because though they were working to stabilize the business, it wasn't meeting its numbers. In the meantime, when Nightingale marketed the product to some of its customers, they discovered it was desired by some of the biggest players in the industry.

The IR audit uncovered a whole new story for Nightingale. By redefining the company, management took control of its destiny, improved its credibility with The Street, increased its stock price and valuation, and erased the time drain, anxiety, and pressure of handling things poorly.

The moral of the story: a company can never assume that Wall Street fully understands its business. In order to uncover potential value, IR professionals must conduct the audit and look for the gems that analysts and buy-siders are looking for.

The next story shows a sample of valuation factors that may provide IR with an opportunity to uncover real value to increase perceived value and the stock price.

Define the Business: A Diversification Case Study

Picture a company that thought it had its definition right, but The Street really didn't understand the business. Zippa! is a popular apparel brand that started with a trendy, seasonal product and was identified by analysts as a company that generally sold its wares through one retailer. However, Zippa! had spent several years diversifying into other products, other brand names, and other distributors. Yet, when the retailer with which they'd initially been identified began to perform poorly, so did Zippa!'s stock price, even though, by that time, the retailer represented only 10 percent of sales. What the market somehow missed was the increasing diversity in all aspects of Zippa!'s business.

An absolute must in buying and owning stocks for the long run is to balance one's portfolio with a diverse basket of assets. Portfolio managers do this every day to generate consistent returns and balance risk. The first step with Zippa! was an IR audit that focused on the numbers, as they never lie. The business actually was very well diversified, which minimized risk in four different areas of the company.

Brands: Zippa! had over a dozen brands, yet only two were well-known and highlighted by the company. Putting numbers behind these brands, IR noted that seven years ago, the two popular brands made up 95 percent of sales, as compared to the current contribution of 65 percent.

Product categories: Zippa! came on the scene selling a certain kind of apparel that was very popular for teenagers and, at that time, made up 100 percent of its business. This clothing had experienced a decline in appeal, and The Street was generally a seller of any and all companies associated with this product. But the fact was that as the company matured, this product represented only 5 percent of revenues, which made the company much less vulnerable to the decline in the product's popularity. Not only that, but Zippa! makes hundreds of products, all of which contributed significantly to the revenue stream.

Distribution channel: Zippa!'s product flowed evenly between specialty retailers, independent retailers, and department stores. It was not, contrary to Street opinion, dependent on specialty retail and one particular chain. Putting numbers to these channels showed that there were enough pieces to the pie and that a decline in any one was not enough to materially hurt the business.

Geography: The marketplace with which Zippa! had insinuated itself was more expansive than The Street was aware. Since its genesis the business had expanded globally, and half of its revenues came from outside the United States. In other words, the domestic problems in the industry were affecting other companies much more than they were affecting Zippa!.

Therefore, out of the audit process came the fact that Zippa deserved to be in a bigger-cap, global comp group. What also came out was that the valuation gap between Zippa! and these new peers was the result of a lack of Wall Street understanding with regard to the company's diversification.

Stay On Core

Another IR audit focused on a client that was operating more like a REIT (real estate investment trust) than a retailer because they owned much of the real estate under their stores. The feedback from Wall Street said that this took focus off their retail business because of the heavy debt load and because many of their competitors had recently gone bankrupt. A capital markets perspective told the IR professionals to suggest a series of sale/leaseback transactions: sell the stores and lease them back, and use the cash from the transactions to decrease debt, which would shift investor perception. In other words, the transactions would change their positioning from a real estate player to a retailer, positioning the company for a better valuation and a lower cost of capital.

Change the Multiple

IR audits can yield a new way to value a company. To that point, under certain circumstances IR may want to present the company in a different light. If it has traditionally been valued by the price-to-earnings method, yet it's a capital-intensive business, then earnings may not be the right financial measure. Rather, cash flow or EBITDA should be used because of interest and non-cash depreciation expenses.

Companies in capital-intensive businesses, such as the leisure sector, transportation, and media, incur high levels of depreciation (a noncash expense) because they own lots of assets. They borrow on bank lines and may have higher interest expense at any given time relative to their peers. Because these below-the-operating-line variables can make a P/E comparison less meaningful, these companies must highlight their cash flow and describe their results in terms of EBITDA (earnings before interest taxes depreciation and amortization), deemphasizing earnings to a degree. This encourages analysts to value the company the following way:

Market Cap plus Long Term Debt Net of Cash divided by EBITDA

This approach better represents the performance that any company can wring out of its capital structure and doesn't penalize them for borrowing, buying, and growing.

In every industry, and sometimes from business to business, the definition of cash flow can vary. When talking company numbers, management always needs to walk through the components of an equation and reconcile those numbers to generally accepted accounting principles.

Separate and Consolidate

The IR audit can also flush out partial ownership in other companies, encouraging a *sum of the parts valuation*, which can often result in a valuation that is higher than the current stock price.

One situation where this may benefit the company is when the business has some divisions that are more capital intensive than others. In these cases, the sell- and buy-sides may not look at earnings per share because they are not an accurate reflection of the true health of the business. Depreciation and amortization, taxes and interest costs, need to be added back to net income to more accurately reflect the company's performance, so analysts and investors like to look at cash flow or EBITDA.

When some divisions or businesses are capital intensive and others are not, the IR audit must detail separately the highlights of each divisions. This may prompt The Street to attach a multiple of EBITDA to the capital-intensive divisions and a P/E on the rest. Subtracting the debt and dividing by fully diluted shares outstanding often results in a valuation that is not only higher, but more realistic than the current stock price.

Another situation where breaking out operations is helpful is when the company has ownership in a completely different business, the profitability of which may not be readily apparent on the income statement. Because every industry is valued differently, some companies may find that the earnings or cash flow from some of their subsidiaries may be valued at a higher multiple than the industry in which they primarily compete. Highlighting and properly valuing this portion of the earnings can add value to the stock price.

Blue Chips, a client in the leisure sector, owned 40 percent of a company in the gaming sector, which trades at a higher multiple than the broader leisure sector. Management was not highlighting this portion of their financial results because they did not know to look at, and communicate the value of, this sector differently from their own.

One of the first and very interesting things anyone would notice when looking at Blue Chips' financials would be that its earnings were disproportionately higher than its revenues. The earnings from this minority ownership was on Blue Chips' income statement as equity income, under the equity method of accounting, and it flowed right down to their operating line.

What investors did not notice, but what IR promoted, was that Blue Chips' passive investment was in a sector that investors value very highly. An IR audit did a valuation of the subsidiary, applied the sector's average comparable multiple, and gave a dollar amount to the 40 percent Blue Chips owned.

In other words, IR broke out this portion of the earnings that the minority ownership represented, recalculated it as an EBITDA number, and suggested a more relevant, higher multiple. By reevaluating just this fraction of Blue Chips' overall earnings IR showed investors that the stock price was trading at a discount to its fair value and suggested a new way to look at the company—another successful repositioning that was due in large part to IR's audit process.

Heal Broken Margins

Some companies have persistent margin problems with performance ratios that are lower than their peers'. This problem cannot be dismissed in a company's communications, or the company will in all likelihood trade at a perpetual discount. Once acknowledged, the company needs to figure out a way to fix the margin problem and then announce this specific fix to The Street.

A company can have the shiniest new brand on the block, but when it comes down to it, profitability is what The Street cares about. Therefore, if a company has lower margins than its competitors, its stock price will probably suffer. A clothing manufacturer, Vested & Co., had the lowest operating margins in its industry by at least 500 basis points. The company was focused on growth, doing great at building its brand and increasing market share, but The Street was not glossing over the margin problem. Because profitability was not great, Vested & Co. was undervalued.

Valuation is a demanding taskmaster, and it serves the company to fully explain key areas, particularly if there is any doubt. Vested & Co. was putting together a plan to increase its operating margin and bring it to parity with the rest of its peer group. IR audited the plan and helped management quantify it. The company could shed its "value" status and transition to growth, and thus the shareholder base would likely turn over. Further, because the stock was trading at a deep discount to its peers, even if the margins didn't improve, the stock had probably bottomed out and there was very low risk for buyers.

That's strategic IR.

Pending Profits

An IR audit for Vision View Inc., a company in the entertainment industry, zeroed in on a particular accounting nuance that exposed otherwise subtle value.

The company installed large systems on-site for its customers so that Vision View's product could be distributed to consumers. In this case, a great deal of debt was built up as Vision View paid for these installations.

The IR audit charted the backlog, revenue, earnings, and debt for Vision View going back five years. Initially, the company lost money, but as the installations increased, and particularly when they crossed a certain unit level, earnings went up and debt went down. The construction of these installations almost ensured the promise of future revenue for the business, and the IR audit uncovered the fact that earnings were less important than backlog.

This historical tracking, a precedent of revenue recognition, made the company's product cycles more understandable, took some perceived risk out of this stock, and increased the value, thereby lowering the cost of capital.

FROM DEFINITION TO DELIVERY

Once a company has gleaned definition from the IR audit and rediscovered the value or growth story it can package to The Street, the company is ready to deliver that story. In preparing for delivery, management must start with establishing earnings guidance, the driving force of successful investor relations.

Delivery

CHAPTER 16

To Guide or Not to Guide: That Is the Question

Information has been collected, relative value has been determined, and IR has helped the company define its investment story. The next step is communicating that story. Delivery is the act of reaching out to Wall Street. This stage of IR ideally puts the company in a position to increase visibility and create value.

The *first part of the delivery stage* is making sure that all the pieces of the package are in place. *Preparation for delivery* involves

- Establishing company-backed earnings estimates through *guidance* and managing expectations, through investor relations and corporate communications, to that guidance.
- *Targeting the audience* of analysts and portfolio managers.
- Setting up a communications process that *integrates PR and IR*, in which the two functions coordinate as a united front and develop the appropriate messages. This should lower the communication risk for the entire organization.
- Evaluating *infrastructure* needs to do the best job possible at the lowest cost, and double-checking with legal counsel that all *disclosure* policies are in place.

The *second part of the delivery stage* is reaching out, which includes providing the investment community with information and access to management through *earnings announcements, conference calls*, and, when appropriate, *pre-announcements*.

IR should be spearheading each step of the delivery process. Although some management teams choose not be overly interactive with the world, the fact of the matter is that all CEOs and CFOs are highly judged on (1) all communications that derive from headquarters and (2) whether or not they communicate to Wall Street's standards.

The delivery stage of IR is really the tool for value creation. Delivery fits in organically with all of the steps of IR and is anchored around the schedules, disclosures, and engagements that a company has with the capital markets. The objective is to do it better and more effectively than the thousands of other companies trying to surface through all the white noise of publicly traded companies.

GUIDANCE

Guidance straddles definition and delivery. In the definition stage, while developing the investment message, management and IR must also review internal budgets and determine the impact that future plans will have on the bottom line. This should be mixed with a qualitative communications strategy that together with a conservative quantitative outlook allows portfolio managers and analysts to make investment decisions. Developing this part of the message, the financial guidance, is the bridge between definition and delivery and sets the tone for all communications to follow.

Guidance is certainly a controversial topic, and even some of the most respected investors in the country have advised against it. Yet, guidance is a critical part of the pact between a public company and its investors, and an issue that management teams should take very seriously.

THE LINCHPIN OF EFFECTIVE IR

Before going into further specifics of delivery, it's a worthwhile exercise to dig deeper into guidance, because it's one of two or three issues that IR and management must agree on before actually delivering its message to The Street.

Guidance is ultimately about managing expectations and positioning a company conservatively in the capital markets. It also is a value-creation tool used to build credibility over time. What comes with building credibility over time? In most cases, a higher multiple, a better valuation, and increased wealth for management and shareholders.

For various reasons, however, the positive impact of guidance is lost on many management teams, so they have chosen not to issue estimates. Unfortunately, this leaves analysts on their own to build models and make assumptions. That fact increases risk for the buy-side in that analysts are publishing estimates that may be too high for the company to achieve.

IR professionals who are former analysts know how confusing this can be. A lack of guidance can leave the sell-side in a sea of potential misinterpretation, forcing them to establish their own parameters, and often causing doubt about management's forecasting capabilities.

In other words, analysts don't like the absence of guidance, and here's why. They are asking the buy-side to put investor money to work based on their recommendations. Analysts are also asking their institutional sales forces to trust them with their ideas, and call institutions to generate Buy and Sell orders. If management is too promotional with guidance or doesn't give any at all, it puts the analysts' credibility in jeopardy, and these are the people the company needs most over the long run. Particularly in the case of no guidance, where management refuses to quantify the future, the analysts end up completely blind in developing forecasts.

Management input has always been an important part of the process. The analyst is someone the company wants to protect whenever possible, and protection in this case means conservative guidance based on conservative and transparent assumptions. In the case of aggressive guidance, where there is no guarantee that estimates will be achieved, management may ultimately burn the analyst by materially missing numbers and in turn torpedo the trust between analyst and sales force and analyst and portfolio manager.

A good relationship with the sell-side can help a company and protect shareholder value over the long run. That's why Investor Relations must bring a capital markets perspective to the argument and make sure that the CEO and CFO are fully informed on the debate.

GIVING GUIDANCE

Guidance establishes parameters for investors and analysts rather than allowing those investors and analysts to establish parameters themselves. These forecasts, which might be for the upcoming quarter and/or the upcoming year, are usually set and refined during earnings announcements or in any given quarter when management is tracking materially away from the consensus view.

The not-so-subtle point of guidance therefore, is to make sure that management is the only party that sets the bar by which the company is measured. Because analysts will publish estimates regardless, management should seize the opportunity and take control of an earnings number that will exist anyway. Allowing the analyst community to set that bar in a vacuum is just too risky. Now more than ever, with many inexperienced analysts at the helm, management should always define itself or the company risks being in position to miss estimates and jeopardize its equity value and cost of capital.

SHORT-TERM GUIDANCE VS. SHORTSIGHTED GUIDANCE

In our experience, the companies that do not practice guidance tend to do so under one of two misconceptions. The first false belief is that guidance forces management to run its business based on short-term earnings expectations. They think that the obsession with short-term results is Wall Street's fault, and companies don't want to play that game. In reality, there's no game to be played; many executives simply don't understand the nuances of the stock market. The second hurdle to guidance is that management thinks it's impossible to forecast that far in advance.

Wall Street's game-playing—the focus on short-term earnings during the boom days of the market—wasn't Wall Street's fault at all. It was primarily the fault of management teams, who in most cases had compensation incentives tied to short-term stock performance. People do exactly what they are paid to do, and if a CEO has a truckload of three-year options, he or she will probably do whatever it takes to deliver a high stock price in three years.

Compensation issues aside, however, management teams have always been fully empowered to adopt and implement strategies that put long-term shareholder returns ahead of short-term results. Yet, just because these decisions may produce weaker near-term earnings and a temporarily lower stock price, it doesn't mean that management should either worry unnecessarily about the short-term drop, particularly if the drop was caused by investment in the future, or stop guiding The Street. Their new guidance can simply be more conservative based on higher spending for important future initiatives.

The second reason that some management teams opt out of guidance is because they aren't confident in their forecasting abilities. Fair enough. However, Wall Street understands that no company can predict with certainty what it will earn to the penny this year or next. But what companies should do is make assumptions on the variables that they can control, estimate what they can't control, and put forth an estimate, or better yet, a broad estimate range. The SEC's Safe Harbor provisions and other legal disclaimers protect that estimate and range, and as the quarters go by, management should commit to systematically refining it further, either up or down, to reflect current business. It's transparent and informative, and Wall Street often rewards that behavior with a premium multiple.

Lack of guidance, in our opinion, can be a sign that management either

---

Setting the Range

Some executives, when giving guidance, will choose a range straddling their internally budgeted earnings per share number. That is, if they think they'll generate $0.13 per share for a quarter, they'll choose to communicate a range of $0.12 to $0.14 believing analysts will pick the middle of the range. In actuality, companies should understand that there are many factors that they do not control, and given the fact that no one knows the future, they should be more conservative. For example, if management believes they'll earn $0.13, the communicated range should be at most $0.11 to $0.13 per share. This positions the company to release earnings at the high end of the range if in fact they earn $0.13 as expected. However, if something happens out of management's control that adversely affects earnings and causes the company to generate $0.12 per share, at least analysts will acknowledge that management hit the middle of the range and view it as a successful quarter. Under the original $0.12 to $0.14 range, management's results would be at the low end of the range and would most certainly be viewed as a negative. The key takeaway here is that management controlled the process in either case and was fully empowered to position itself for success.

---

can't forecast its business or for legal reasons isn't willing to talk about the future. In the latter case, if the lawyers simply dominate the debate and make the decision, management should be extremely careful about intraquarter conversations with analysts and portfolio managers regarding the business. Without formally disseminated guidance, these conversations set the stage for a Reg FD violation that can cost from several hundred thousands of dollars into the millions. Even that cost is not reflective of the damage to reputation that would come with a slip-up of this nature.

THE NUANCES OF GIVING GUIDANCE

The following story about Big Muscles, a company in the fitness sector, illustrates how a management team came to realize the importance of giving realistic, conservative guidance:

Going Down to Go Up

In November 2002, Big Muscles was trading at $14 per share and management was telling The Street that its earnings for the following year would be $2.60 per share. For anyone who's ever worked on Wall Street, those numbers just don't add up.

To that point, IR told the CEO that if Wall Street believed the $2.60 estimate, the stock would be at least $20 per share. The CEO said that he was sure they'd deliver on that guidance, even though the CFO had doubts. Without access to the numbers at that time, a reasonable guess was that the company would earn $1.00 or so for 2003, not the $2.60 per share that management backed. Why? Because the market has a funny way of knowing the truth and a business like this was probably worth between 10x and 20x earnings, or $10-$15 per share, right where the stock currently was trading. The market had already figured it out and management was about to find out the hard way, but unfortunately IR can't always convince a CEO on a mission.

As suspected, at the end of the first quarter of 2003, Big Muscles realized they'd need to adjust guidance to $1.50–$1.60. IR strongly suggested they go even lower, because analysts and investors were still wary of the numbers. The stock was trading at $11 per share at this point. Based on experience and the stock price, IR suggested guidance of $1.00, which is what the market was intimating they would earn anyway. Despite the material revision, the stock likely wouldn't go much lower, and some investors and analysts might even start to believe again. Management disagreed with this advice and went out with their guidance of $1.50 to $1.60 per share.

At the end of the second quarter, Big Muscles missed estimates again. IR attempted the same conversation, but added that Street intelligence was saying that both the sell- and buy-side thought the company was out of control, they had zero trust in management, and thought they were "completely unrealistic."

The CEO ultimately lost his job. The new CEO asked the CFO to review forecasts and lay out a conservative estimate, a number he could give with 95 percent confidence. The stock would not go down, IR presumed; rather it would stay at $11 or actually go up as the short sellers covered. The CFO's number was $1.00–$1.10.

The Street was still expecting the earnings number for the year to be $1.50, but during this call, management came out, took the heat, and announced that it missed the second quarter, and new estimates would be $1.00–$1.10.

The Street reacted noisily and investors called management to vent. Analysts issued negative reports.

Following the call, IR gathered intelligence that Wall Street, despite the frustration, felt that this was guidance management could deliver on. Some actually implied that they might get positive on the stock again. The next day, after the conference call, the stock went up 10 percent.

Three months later, on October 28, 2003, management held a conference call to announce the third-quarter numbers. The new CEO delivered the good news that the company had beaten the quarterly estimate by a penny. But he also detailed ongoing challenges, talked about the turnaround, gaining control, and stabilizing growth. He clarified that this would take 9 to 12 months and that there would be no growth until 4Q of 2004. That is, he gave conservative, realistic guidance.

The next day, the stock traded 2 million shares versus its usual average of 200,000 and it shot up to $16 per share. The analyst headlines read: "Fog Is Clearing, Raising Rating to Market Perform," "Signs of Life in 3Q, Worst May Be Behind," and "Turning Around?"

One analyst wrote: "Yesterday, October 28, after the close, Big Muscles released its 3Q earnings of $0.20, which was in line with company guidance and ahead of the consensus of $0.19, we were on the low end of the street at $0.17. We raised our rating on Big Muscles as management seems to have stabilized business, with hopes of a return to growth in coming years."

And though most of the sell- and the buy-side felt the company still had problems, and maybe kept their neutral ratings, they now believed the management team finally had a plan to turn it around, and they applauded it in print. One who'd said he'd despised the company for an entire year and once called the executives "a band of fools who couldn't shoot straight" said he was going to raise his rating from market underperform to market perform.

This was a clear case of a CEO who felt aggressive guidance was somehow going to fight off short sellers and keep the stock price at propped-up levels. In reality, this CEO was not open to IR advice and didn't really understand the nuances of the stock market. By refusing to adopt a conservative guidance philosophy, he increased the overall risk to shareholders and, as many have said, lost his job in the process.

Figure 16.1 shows an example of how a company can release guidance to the sell-side, buy-side, and media as part of an earnings release.

THE CONSENSUS NUMBER

Analysts assess guidance and factor management's input into their own analysis when modeling earnings estimates. More often than not, they take management's lead and use the company's assumptions and oftentimes the actual earnings estimates for their own predictions. Right there, the power of guidance is revealed.

These numbers get played twice, however: once in each analyst's research report and then again as part of the consensus estimate, which is an average calculated from all analysts' forecasts. The overwhelming majority of investors and the financial media judge a company and management based on the average number, also known as the First Call consensus estimate. In as much as a company can control it, they should attempt to give specific guidance to analysts, with the end goal of influencing the First Call estimate. Again, why should anyone other than the CEO or CFO set the performance bar?

That's not to say that analyst estimates can't be higher or lower than management intended. Analysts are free to publish what they want. However, if the consensus estimate is too high, either management did not adequately communicate why the estimate should have been lower or one or more of the company's analysts are being aggressive for other reasons. Because they are commission players, some analysts attempt to stand out from the crowd by posting a higher estimate than that which has been blessed by management, which leads the buy-side to wonder if this analyst knows something that the other analysts don't and may lead to a phone call or a new relationship. This is great for the analyst and can mean greater compensation levels. But these heroics can skew the consensus estimate upward, causing the company to miss earnings even though management was conservative with its EPS forecast.

That's why an argument of the underlying assumptions is so critical. The company gets on record with its own assumptions, and should a miss occur because of the analyst, management is largely forgiven.

THE CONSENSUS WITHOUT GUIDANCE

Wall Street's job is to boil everything management says down to an earnings per share estimate and place a valuation on those earnings. Therefore, when

Octagon Inc. Reports Third Quarter Financial Results
Raises Guidance for Fiscal 2003; Introduces Guidance for 2004
A Sample Section of a Release Updating Guidance

Octagon Inc. updated its guidance for the fourth quarter ending December 31, 2003. The Company currently expects fourth quarter sales to range between $28 million and $30 million and diluted earnings per share to range from $0.06 to $0.08, inclusive of the estimated $0.04 per share negative impact of the preferred stock repurchase and subordinated debt pre-payment. In comparison, during the fourth quarter of 2002 the Company reported sales of $25.8 million and earnings per share of $0.13. It is important to note that last year's fourth quarter results included a one-time after tax gain of $168,000, or $0.02 per diluted share, related to the final settlement of the Hexagon litigation. In addition, due to the timing of the Circle Square acquisition, which closed on October 20, 2002, the Company paid slightly more than one month of interest on the borrowings associated with the purchase. In the fourth quarter of fiscal 2003 the Company expects to pay three full months of interest on the aforementioned borrowing, aggregating approximately an additional $650,000, or $0.03 per diluted share. Also, given the timing of the Circle Square acquisition, there are no substantial incremental royalty savings between the fourth quarters of 2003 and 2002 as the vast majority of fourth quarter royalty savings were already realized last year. Accounting for these various items, the fourth quarter 2002 diluted earnings per share excluding the $0.02 gain on litigation settlement and including an additional two months of interest of $0.03 would have yielded a pro forma diluted earnings per share of $0.08; whereas, the expected fourth quarter 2003 diluted earnings per share excluding the $0.04 for debt repayment and preferred stock repurchase would yield a pro forma estimate of approximately $0.10 to $0.12, a 25% to 50% improvement compared to the $0.08 pro forma 2002 amount. See the accompanying table entitled "Pro Forma Diluted Earnings Per Share Comparison" for a presentation of the reconciliation in tabular format.

The Company also raised its guidance for the fiscal year ending December 31, 2003. The Company now expects 2003 sales to range between $113 million and $115 million and diluted earnings per share to range from $0.62 to $0.64. The Company expects its Circle Square sales to be $74 million to $75 million, Simple to be approximately $8 million and Triangle to be $31 million to $32 million.

A Sample Section of a Release Providing New Guidance

The Company is introducing guidance for fiscal 2004. Octagon Inc. currently anticipates its fiscal 2004 sales to be in the range of $126 million to $132 million, including $82 to $84 million for Circle Square, $9 to $11 million for Rectangle and $35 to $37 million for Triangle. Octagon Inc. currently expects its diluted earnings per share for fiscal 2004 to range from $0.92 to $0.96.

FIGURE 16.1 Guidance Examples

a company announces a strategic initiative without quantifying that initiative, it may be interpreted to mean $0.03 per share to one analyst, $0.05 per share to another analyst, and $0.15 per share to another. These numbers, in all their disparity, are figured into the consensus number and posted on First Call. These First Call quarterly earnings targets are generated constantly, whether or not a company has issued guidance.

A company that announces a material event without quantifying the event for Wall Street loses control of the estimates and increases the risk that the bar will be set where it can't be achieved.

NOT TO MENTION REG FD

Formal guidance on conference calls and in press releases is also for Reg FD purposes in that it acts as a company's template for disclosure.

During the spring of 2003, a technology manufacturer made a public announcement about a particular initiative, and used the qualitative term "significant" to describe its impact on the company's future performance. This claim was not backed up with quantitative guidance and it led to confusion among the analysts, who then called the company to follow up on the quantitative translation of "significant." The company defined the word, but only to the analysts who asked, to mean a rate of change of 25 percent or more. According to the SEC, the company "violated fair disclosure rules by communicating material non-public information in a manner inconsistent with Regulation FD." Had the company just quantified that statement in a public forum, they never would have been in a position to violate Reg FD.

More generally speaking, any company that practices no guidance, technically, would not be able to take private calls from analysts who, as part of their jobs, must constantly refine their future numbers. It makes management look evasive, it's a legal risk, and in our opinion decreases the odds that new analysts will publish and makes the institutional buyers of stocks uneasy. Therefore, a pretty good argument can be made that not giving guidance penalizes a company's valuation and carries with it about just as much risk as giving guidance, which confounds most corporate legal teams.

FIGHTING OPTIMISM

Anyone who plays golf knows that, in a money match, a 15 handicap who claims to be a 20 will win before the match begins. Some players do the exact opposite and brag about their game, stating that they are a 17 handicap when they are a 20. Of course, this golfer has lost before the match begins.

Guidance can be the same way. Before the year begins, every company has the opportunity to influence the First Call consensus through a conservative, self-set bogey. This allows management to establish an estimate that is achievable.

Management may not want to give certain guidance, however, because they believe the number is too conservative and the stock price will suffer in the short run. In fact, many CEOs are just too optimistic or promotional as part of their job. So when IR suggests leading with 15 percent growth when the CEO believes growth is 25 percent, they bristle.

The reality is that if the CEO started with lower guidance and raised it throughout the year as business tracks to internal budget, the price and valuation would most likely be stronger. The other benefit to starting conservative is the fact that throughout the year, conditions out of the company's control invariably happen to negatively affect earnings. It's a nice feeling for management to be able to keep guidance intact while others are guiding downward.

Aggressive guidance can also be bad for the business, not just Wall Street. For example, if a company refused to guide to an IR-recommended 15 percent earnings growth and wanted to issue 25 percent because it felt the odds of achieving that number were 50/50 and only "a couple of things would have to go right to make the number," that would be too much risk. Initially, that level of guidance would, in all likelihood, propel the stock upward. However, Wall Street, as it always does, would come to discover the risk. That vulnerability would potentially attract short-sellers, discourage sell-side analysts from publishing (why write research for a hold rating that won't generate commissions?), and cause the buy-side to stay on the sidelines. That's too much at risk for a 50/50 chance.

THE CONSERVATIVE TIGHTROPE

Companies need to communicate in a way such that their assumptions and estimates are interpreted as they are intended. In order for the value story to be heard as truth, and for management's credibility to be enduring, management has to walk a fine line. That's a line between being conservative enough to keep expectations from getting out of hand and being too conservative and giving The Street a reason to question management candor. Sandbagging is unacceptable, but it's far different from being conservative.

During the late 1990s, many companies tried to sandbag estimates so they could easily beat them and make everyone happy, every quarter. Unbeknownst to management, that behavior becomes expected, for example, if management usually beats the estimate by 10 percent, a 9 percent overage is a disappointment. When that happens, simply meeting guidance is considered negative, and a company can expect its stock to go down. It's a terrible cycle of pleasing The Street. Management should perform, guide, and deliver in a conservative, not grossly underestimated, fashion.

Guidance is a subjective and highly strategic pursuit, but the results are tangible in the following ways:

- In general, conservative guidance positions any company for a Buy rating from the sell-side. Also, it rarely lets the stock price spike, a source of volatility. A slow and steady appreciation in share price is always preferred.
- Conservative guidance allows the sell-side to feel confident and publish on a company's stock. The analyst will look his/her sales force in the eyes and tell them that management is great at dealing with The Street, they are conservative, and business is good. They'll do the same with the buy-side.
- The credibility management builds by meeting the bar they've set for themselves goes right to valuation, right to employee morale, right to vendors, and right to the media, which will tend to write more positively than negatively over time.

A great example was a recent Deutsche Bank research report on GTECH Holdings, the on-line lottery operator in Rhode Island. The headline of the report read: "GTECH Reports Solid 4Q, but Management Remains Firm on Conservative Guidance." In addition, the third bullet in the first page reads, "Citing the integration of four acquisitions this year, management has set the bar low. After having beaten FY04's initial guidance by 14%-18% by year end, we think management is maintaining its pattern of underperforming and over-delivering."

Finally, "All in, while we would have liked guidance to have been higher we believe estimates will likely increase over the remainder of the year, consistent with the last two years of earnings trends. In addition, we believe management has historically been conservative." The leisure analyst rated the stock a Buy and in the report looked for 25 percent appreciation.

This type of conservative guidance attracted the sell-side, investors became involved and management looked great, building credibility over a long period of time. So who engineered this strategy? Well, GTECH has a great management team and IR function, but it doesn't hurt that the chairman was formerly a very well-respected sell-side analyst.

In our opinion, conservative guidance can fuel a powerful cycle, where equity value is maximized, Wall Street benefits, and the entire organization becomes stronger. It works in many ways, such as:

- Management establishes conservative guidance, which lowers the risk profile of the stock.
- The sell-side analysts see an undervalued story and begin to publish.
- The buy-side analysts get involved, also looking for companies positioned to succeed.
- Management then meets or exceeds First Call consensus, which they had a major hand in influencing. At the same time they make another argument why estimates should remain low for the upcoming quarter and year. Again, they are positioning themselves to succeed.
- Employees see the results and are invigorated, and vendors want to be a part of success.
- The media latches on and writes favorably, which fuels productivity, pride, and an organization with momentum.

And that leads to better earnings.

This pattern of building credibility with conservative guidance ultimately can position the company for a better valuation than its peers and a lower cost of capital.

CHAPTER 17

Targeting the Audience

With the company's message defined and the complicated issues surrounding guidance decided upon, its time to target analysts and investors.

UNDERSTANDING THE STREET

When IR targets the buy-side and the sell-side, it should zero-in on the analysts who cover the company's industry or peers, and the portfolio managers that buy similar stocks. The initial investigation should start wide, then narrow in on a specific group.

In the spirit of casting the widest initial net, IR should pull together the names of all sell- and buy-side analysts in the comp group/sector and compile them into an email distribution list. Though the list will change from quarter to quarter, it's a good basis for ongoing communications. Even if the company has a small market cap and three of the analysts in the sector only follow mega-cap stocks, the mega-analysts should be put on the list. They won't cover the company or survive the next round of targeting, but IR wants those analysts to be aware of the company. It may lead to a dialog someday, as the company grows. IR should put anyone who's relevant on that distribution list because the incremental cost in time and money is virtually zero.

TARGETING THE BUY-SIDE

To discover its own shareholders, IR can comb through any number of databases and create an *Institutional Holders Report*, which essentially measures the buy-side and shows the value and percentage change in stock *held by the*

largest institutional investors. A large chunk of smaller-cap stocks are usually held by just a few dozen institutional investors, and their stakes, as a
number of shares and as a percentage of the company's total outstanding
shares, are publicly available.

After discovering the company's top shareholders, IR should run a peer
analysis and identify the top shareholders of its comp base. This cross-reference of ownership puts the pieces of the puzzle into perspective. If an institution does not own the company's stock, but is buying many other companies in the sector, there is an opportunity to target this institution as a
potential buyer.

In addition to just knowing whether or not the buy-side institution owns
the company's stock, IR must determine the following about the institution:

■ Amount of capital being managed
■ Investment style, for example, growth or value investor
■ Portfolio activity, specifically as it relates to the company's industry (are
   they buyers or sellers during any given quarter?)

With that information in hand, IR can zero in on the right buy-side institutions and connect management with the right PMs. Without that information, IR is guessing, the entire effort is compromised, and the time and
money spent visiting the wrong institutions can be a complete waste.

As a basic example, let's take a restaurant chain we'll call The Bubble
Factory. Table 17.1 lists the large institutional investors and their ownership
in The Bubble Factory and the Bubble Factory's Peer Group: California
Pizza Kitchen Inc. (CPKI), Red Robin Gourmet Burger (RRGB), and PF
Chang's China Bistro, Inc. (PFCB).

It's obvious because of the representative ownership in the other companies in this peer group that a few large institutions could own more of The
Bubble Factory.

When it comes to approaching the specific funds, IR should deliver, in
advance, a one-page profile of the institution which is available from certain
databases. As an example, if The Bubble Factory were to meet with Baron
Asset Management, they should know some basic information, as shown in
Figure 17.1.

TARGETING THE ANALYSTS

In terms of measuring the sell-side, the IR team can tabulate trading volume
in the stock by investment bank to see which firms are trading the most

TABLE 17.1 Institutional Ownership in Peer Group

Institution Name	Equity Assets	CPKI	RRGB	Bubble	PFCB	Total
Fidelity Management & Research Co.	552.41	$22,770,800	$27,596,712	$5,009,611	$181,624,203	$237,001,326
Capital Guardian Trust Co.	139	$54,913,000			$33,138,822	$ 88,051,822
American Century Investments	67.132				$86,503,199	$86,503,199
Forstmann-Leff Associates	2.955		$47,725,681		$27,313,477	$75,039,158
Westfield Capital Management	3.5721				$74,101,940	$74,101,940
T. Rowe Price Associates, Inc.	135.5		$11,942,304		$58,938,072	$70,880,376
Barclays Global Investors, N.A.	760	$9,576,320	$8,132,147		$45,156,289	$62,864,756
AIM Management Group, Inc.	60.365				$60,075,756	$60,075,756
Strong Capital Management, Inc.	20.54	$22,435,640	$9,724,265	$51,498	$20,982,971	$53,194,374

Source: Bigdough.com

BARON CAPITAL GROUP INC.

Reported Equity Assets (U.S. $B):	6.951
Inst. Qtr. Commissions:	$2,511,706 @ 0.05/Share
Reported Commissions:	$9,608,000
Institution Type:	Investment Advisor
Market Cap:	Small-Cap, Mid-Cap
Styles:	Value and Theme
Average P/E:	Low
Average Yield:	Low
Portfolio Turnover:	Very Low
Asset Allocation:	100% Stocks

Overview

Baron Capital manages the Baron family of mutual funds, as well as separate equity portfolios. The firm is primarily a small/mid-cap theme-oriented investor that looks for stocks with growth characteristics with a value orientation. Baron defines small-cap as those with market caps between $100 million and $1.5 billion and mid-cap stocks as those with market caps between $1.5 billion and $5 billion.

Strategy

The firm begins its investment approach with a top-down screen to identify what it calls "sunrise" industry sectors which are sectors expected to benefit from social trends and demographic changes. Baron then follows this with bottom-up research seeking U.S. stocks with: (a) high incremental returns on investment; (b) undervalued or unrecognized assets with appreciation potential of 50% or greater in the next two or three years; and (c) significant positive cash flows. The firm prefers meeting with management prior to stock purchase and often maintains that relationship after the purchase is completed. Baron Capital conducts all research in-house. The asset allocation for the firm is 100% equity.

Supplemental Information

Baron Capital Group, Inc. is the holding company for BAMCO, Incorporated and Baron Capital Management, Incorporated. BAMCO is the investment advisor to the Baron Funds. Baron Capital manages portfolios for individuals and institutions. The firm's 13F which is filed under the name BAMCO, Incorporated reflects equity holdings for the mutual funds.

FIGURE 17.1   Baron's Profile

FIGURE 17.1 *(continued)*

Security Name	Industry Name	Value	Shares	% Held	% Port	Qtr End
CAKE Cheesecake Factory Inc Com	Restaurants	$159.3M	3,456,700	6.6742%	2.292%	12/31/03
KKD Krispy Kreme Doughnuts Inc COM	Restaurants	$120.1M	3,497,800	5.7328%	1.728%	12/31/03
PNRA Panera Bread Co Cl A	Restaurants	$42.1M	1,083,550	3.8137%	0.606%	12/31/03
PFCB PF Changs China Bistro Inc Com	Restaurants	$20.2M	401,000	1.2335%	0.290%	12/31/03
CKR Cke Restaurants Inc Com	Restaurants	$17.3M	1,750,000	3.0375%	0.249%	12/31/03
CPKI California Pizza Kitchen Inc Com	Restaurants	$13.0M	650,000	3.4074%	0.187%	12/31/03

Source: Used with permission from Bigdough.com

stock of the company. A measure of each analyst's knowledge is often the ability to sell an idea to the buy-side, and the firm's willingness to back that investment idea with capital on the trading desk.

IR should know the following about an analyst:

Coverage universe
All ratings within that universe
History of recommendations
Average market cap the analyst covers
Preferences

In this selection process, the most important thing for IR to know is who matches up best with whom. Analyst support is not necessarily a numbers game. It is a strategic effort that segments and filters until a narrow group of high-impact prospects emerges. IR should assemble all analysts who cover the sector, evaluate their coverage universes, and make a decision who to target.

No other medium penetrates the buy-side and the media with as much credibility and substance as the sell-side's equity analyst. Despite all the negative publicity, institutional investors read a substantial amount of sell-side research. They may not always value the exact investment rating, but they do pay attention to financial modeling and content.

The result of coverage is awareness, access, and credibility—all of which generates interest that, one hopes, creates demand for the stock. And the research report can go beyond the buy-side and the media.

Other sell-side firms often read other firm's research, which sometimes can lead them to call the company and possibly initiate research of their own. The industry, including competitors, suppliers, vendors, and customers, may also read this research, and it gives the company tremendous third-party validation and endorsement. Finally, research reaches employees and validates their mission which helps the overall company—more so when it's positive, but a negative research report can also be a huge motivator. We've seen negative reports circulated to employees and tacked up on their walls as a reminder to work even harder. In either case, research coverage can lead to a very prosperous cycle (see Figure 17.2):

This cycle interrelates with guidance and can break down if guidance is ignored. If guidance exists, however, and it's conservative, the company is positioned to perform up to expectations or to outperform those expectations. Guidance also attracts the sell-side and increases the odds of positive research reports as earnings targets are met. Therefore, both guidance and targeting work together in this stage of pre-delivery to increase the odds that

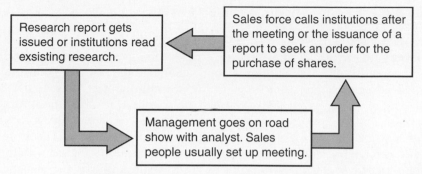

FIGURE 17.2   The Virtuous Cycle of Research

everyone involved in the process, from management to the analyst, is positioned for success.

THE RESEARCH HURDLE

Even before the consolidation of the investment banks, getting coverage was never easy. While there are hundreds of analysts, there are thousands of publicly traded companies. Additionally, most institutional investors will only invest in companies with large market capitalizations, that is, valuations that are over $1 billion. Thus, if the larger sell-side firms want to generate trading commissions, then their research should probably cover the companies with large market capitalizations. That approach potentially leaves thousands of publicly traded companies with no coverage.

That explains why many smaller companies don't pursue analysts at larger investment banks. However, many investors buy stock in companies with market capitalizations under $1 billion. In fact, these investors specifically seek out the mid-, small-, and micro-cap companies. As a result, many sell-side firms work with these investors and these companies, and there are research analysts who provide coverage. Finding these analysts is important to a good IR effort because the benefits are too worthwhile to ignore.

Some IR professionals do not have a full appreciation for how tough an analyst's job is. IR often lacks a first-hand understanding of what analysts do on a daily basis, how they are paid, and what they are looking for from IR and from management. In preparing for delivery, IR needs to understand these factors, because they can make the act of approaching the analyst simpler and more effective.

THE ANALYST'S MOTIVATION AND INCENTIVE

An analyst gets paid to make good stock picks and to generate trading commissions for the firm. There are several reasons that portfolio managers run their commissions through certain banks, including the analyst and institutional salesperson's relationship with the portfolio manager; the analyst's knowledge on any given stock; and, certainly, good trade execution. Analysts must also create access to management teams, providing the buy-side with an opportunity to "hear the story from the horse's mouth." Therefore, good research based on a superior industry understanding coupled with the ability to deliver management teams to the buy-side is key. IR and management must understand this when they target and approach any analyst.

THE MIND, AND DAY, OF AN ANALYST

Sell-side analysts overwhelmingly are absorbed in one industry or sector. They know the industry's history, the current situation, the dynamics and the players, and they know it all in-depth because they live and breathe their coverage universe every hour of every day. To be the expert, and more importantly, to get paid, analysts not only must know their sectors well, they also have to know them better than anyone else.

A day in the life of the analyst is spent delving into the intricacies of a company and an industry, which means due diligence, analysis and spreadsheets, conferences, traveling, talking to CEOs, touring factories and kicking the tires, listening to employees talk about the latest innovations or development, dialing for discourse with investors, reading the trades, observing the consumer marketplace, spotting trends, fielding calls from institutional salespeople and traders, inputting numbers into valuation models, deciding on buy, hold, or sell recommendations, and writing them into a readable, compelling report that says something useful and incremental. Pressure and stress are just a few of the occupational hazards, because millions of dollars are on the line with every stock pick. Therefore, if an analyst seems impatient or abrupt, it's par for the course.

The relationship in a sell-side firm between the analyst and the institutional sales force is tenuous because the salesperson's reputation and ultimate success depends on the information he or she receives from the analyst. This situation creates a climate with the potential for the analyst to be hero one day and a dog the next. A bad pick can alienate the analyst internally (not to mention externally with the buy-side), dramatically affect his or her compensation, and possibly jeopardize his or her career. That said, the analyst needs to be right and is counting on management and investor relations to be straight-forward and consistent.

Therefore, a thorough understanding of the analyst's day-to-day duties is needed after targeting, but before the approach. Management must understand the leap of faith an analyst is taking when picking up a stock and how anything but honest communication can destroy the fragile process. The same goes for the buy-side. IR and management may only have one chance to attract the attention of a portfolio manager, and when they do, they better act as they understand that person's job and understand what he or she has to deliver to shareholders. That increases the odds of ownership, positions the company to diversify its analyst base, and makes the most of IR expenditures.

CHAPTER 18

Integrating with PR

After making the decision on guidance, gathering the target list of analysts and portfolio managers, and understanding how best to approach them given the understanding of their mindset, IR should coordinate the attack with PR to ensure that the communications function is uniform. Doing so can help companies avoid costly mistakes in its communications efforts.

In many cases traditional IR lacks the capital markets expertise to be effective. An integrated IR and PR effort maximizes the time and money spent on corporate communications, and generally speaking, lessens the risk profile of the company. Both must work under the same story boards, lockstep in strategy, and deliver the same message to all constituencies.

The PR component of corporate communications must touch many constituencies, the media, employees, and the trade, in a parallel process with IR where both help and neither hinders the other. Unless the PR professionals understand the overall objectives of a CEO and board, which is to increase long-term shareholder value, they can certainly inject risk into the equation.

Accurate and favorable coverage in the media helps both public and private companies validate their investment thesis, build their brand, attract and retain talented employees, and build reputation capital with other key stakeholders, including customers and communities. PR can also boost the equity value of the company if it contributes to the perceived value of the equation. Because it can be so important, then, PR and IR efforts must work in a seamless fashion to ensure consistent delivery of key messages, which requires fully refining the story, preparing executives to carry that message to the media, and a proactive outreach program to generate interest in the form of media exposure and press placements.

Media and The Street can feed off each other in a very effective one-two punch. If a company has done its work with Wall Street and then wants to go out to the public with information, through the media, they have the analyst's favorable research (as long as guidance was conservative) on which to build. In fact, research reports and analyst recommendations are reliable third-party sources for reporters. Therefore, if done properly, the media can be an effective source for the capital markets, generating broader awareness and attracting potential investors and new analysts. PR and IR as an integrated communications approach offers checks and balances to make sure that each is helping the other to put the message forward as effectively as possible.

MEDIA MACHINATIONS

Media exposure can be a blessing or a curse. When delivering the message that underscores the company story, exposure is a boon and a powerful conduit to exposure and awareness. When delivering a message that undermines the company story, the media can become the bane of the company's existence.

Media channels—television, radio, magazines, Web sites, and newspapers—are the most effective avenue to the general public. The media's reach and frequency capabilities, combined with access to the largest number of people over the widest range of demographics, makes it the incomparable, unparalleled, and possibly unsurpassable channel of communication throughout the world. The media is so powerful that, many times, a company's success or failure can be in its hands. But the media can be friend, foe, fair, unfair, or just plain fickle. It's not a universe that any company, public or private, can leave to chance.

BASIC PR

Basic PR includes a *press kit* with a company backgrounder, executive bios, fact sheets with the company history and a summary of major milestones, and a guided discussion of key messages, including the basic corporate messages and the specific issues of the moment. The job of basic PR is to gain attention for the company through placement or profiles in the media, calculating which media vehicles are best and aggressively pursuing these relationships.

Knowing the various *outlets* and targeting each one is another basic. National television networks, radio shows, regional and local television and radio stations, newspapers and magazines, and trade magazines and newspapers can number in the thousands. These outlets get many of their stories directly from PR professionals, but also from press releases, earnings announcements, conference calls, and industry investment conferences. A company's PR effort must pick and target the outlets that matter most.

PR and IR should be present during the executives' *media training*. Presentation skills—specifically, good rhetoric and persuasion—are not to be taken for granted. Interviews can be distracting, and preparation is critical to ensure that executives answer questions with authority and integrity, while relaying a compelling value proposition, anchored around talking points. PR and IR experts who know how to prepare and deliver the message to these outlets should prepare executives for this task. One without the other would do a sub-par job in all likelihood.

Media training sessions involve executives in front of a camera so they can see what they actually look like in an interview. Executives invariably find this extremely helpful. Likewise, PR professionals should interview executives for a print story and then write the story they would have written as reporters. This exercise shows them how that interview would have come off in the press. When some executives say things that result in a negative statement, they often think they have been misquoted. This mock print story shows them when they weren't and emphasizes the importance of specific, rehearsed talking points. PR professionals can also prepare executives by finding out the background, style, and story objective of the reporter and then conducting a full prep session with sample questions that reflect this approach. Call it media reconnaissance and media boot camp.

PR AND IR

As much as PR tries to understand and meet the needs of the media, the objectives of the company are the priority. If a public relations effort will derail an investor relations effort, or vice versa, then that effort is certainly hurtful to the company. Therefore, an integrated PR/IR plan, with routine communication between the groups, is absolutely key to the successful overall communications strategy of the company. Without the integrated approach, there's simply too much reputation risk in the equation.

For example, a PR professional might time a news release to meet a reporter's deadline. However, this may not work best for IR, which would rather delay the same announcement until the market is closed. The integrated effort, one in which the two functions work hand-in-hand, makes both efforts more effective, maximizing time and money for senior management.

UNDERSTANDING THE AUDIENCE

The PR portion of any communications effort should ideally include professionals who came from the media so that they understand the responsibilities and objectives of the reporters, their editors, or the producers. This same philosophy is recommended for IR, that is, having the IR professional come from a capital markets background.

Reporters are responsible for finding good ideas that interest their readers or viewers. In selling a story to the media, the company needs to consider the demographic of the reporter's audience; the personality of the newspaper, magazine, or television program; and the style of the particular writer or reporter. With that legwork done, the company should then position the story so it makes sense to the reporter, with an angle that is valuable.

Ideally, a company should get to know the reporter's history and reference an article or story that the reporter previously covered. The company can then speak specifically to how the story or angle would be of interest. Reporters are swamped with hundreds of story pitches a day, so a company that has a grip on the reporter's mindset is of great value. A company that gets it right the first time can build a strong relationship.

Knowing the reporters is a never-ending process. Unlike analysts who work in one sector for most of their careers, reporters constantly switch beats, jump across departments, or move to new outlets. The company's PR effort must be vigilant in its efforts to stay up-to-date on the huge pool of who's who and who's where.

IR and PR should also initiate media opportunities, frequently scanning newswires and PR Web sites that list the stories, angles, and sources for which reporters are looking. By providing useful and interesting news, not to mention some industry education, the company can establish itself for a reporter as a reliable resource going forward.

Once a company's IR and PR efforts have proven themselves with the media by delivering good, quality information, that relationship can work the other way too. Producers and editors need stories and often call companies to provide that story, quote, or fact. When the audience is calling the subject, the PR team has done a good job of establishing itself with the media.

PERSONALIZING THE PITCH

Companies pitch the media on many different levels, from hard news such as a financial release of earnings to soft news features such as an executive profile. The key is to make the news, whatever type it is, actually newsworthy. Most of the time, the media is looking for something novel, distinct, creative, and exciting. If it's financial earnings, then the company should emphasize the most distinct and interesting aspect of the story, such as increasing same store sales ten quarters in a row or something that dramatically makes the company distinct from its peers.

Every story plays differently to each type of media outlet as well as the specific segment or section that will carry it. Moreover, a pitch for a news article is going to be far different than a pitch for a feature. A story that works well for finance plays differently for general business. Corporate or executive profiles may work in one arena, a division or product profile in another. The various platforms provide an opportunity for the company to pick certain parts of the business or various executives to highlight, which means there's fertile ground all over any given company for finding a story. Therefore, the company that wants media attention should harvest the people and activities in the company that might be news and literally create the story. A pending patent, a project development, or an innovative executive are all prospects.

State Government Utility Organization (SGUO) had just concluded a survey that led to a new public program. *State Capitol Press*, the local newspaper, had a reporter who was an expert on the issue and he wanted an exclusive. This was an important newspaper for this client, but it didn't represent the kind of media outlet that would give legs to the story. SGUO needed a broader scope and a solution that would be respectful to the State Capitol Press, yet still keep the story fresh so that the organization could reach out to the wider media.

None of the ideas on how to give everyone what they wanted made everyone happy. Then IR and PR zeroed in on the specific needs of the reporter who wanted the exclusive, and considered the angles that would appeal to general media.

The solution? Cut the news up.

The story became the two halves: survey results, and the program that would stem from that research. The *State Capitol Press* reporter received the exclusive to the survey results, which satisfied him and also gave the Utility Organization good publicity in its hometown. Then, a few days later, we unveiled the program initiative at a press conference. The local reporter had his breaking news, and the story found a greater audience.

Timeliness and exclusivity are requirements that PR should always consider. For some stories, on some days, some of the media want exclusives or they won't take it. Other times, everyone takes the same story the day it breaks. When PR has to make the choice of one outlet over another, they must weigh the importance of each channel over the long run.

Window Shops, a small, publicly traded clothing retailer, was pursuing a geographic expansion strategy through an acquisition of a privately owned regional chain. Window Shops' stores, which were located in small towns and rural areas, provided top global brands at a discount. Because Window Shops was small and relatively unknown, the media was, most likely, not going to pick the story up on their own.

The company needed an angle.

Given the current climate, the industry, the economy, and general trends, IR decided that media outlets might like something very Americana that spoke to quality and value. The tag line: "Where Main Street Meets Fifth Avenue" was developed. It was pithy, yet loaded, clearly identifying the stores as quaint, but sophisticated. A place that provided the everyman (and everywoman) with access to glamour. The American dream in a nutshell.

Several national media outlets called for the story.

Then came the appeal to the business media. Window Shops had recently emerged from bankruptcy, and the acquisition was a calculated, yet courageous, move. The business media might find this strategy, especially during a difficult economy, inspiring and interesting; the angle, "Big Bold Move for Small Town Retailer," grabbed the attention of the targeted media outlets.

Simultaneously, IR translated the story for Wall Street, focusing on diversification of earnings, accretion, and conservative expectations. Ultimately, the analyst's enthusiasm for the acquisition gave the media the third-party quotes needed to validate the story.

Many times, repurposing a story with a different angle isn't enough. But given a little flexibility and creativity, PR can get both birds in the bush.

UNCOVERING THE ANGLE

During the IR audit, the PR function should conduct a PR audit to uncover the media value proposition, which means finding the story and what makes it interesting and entertaining—in other words, hunting down the angle. Similar to the way IR hones in on the specific needs of investors, PR should tailor the story to meet the demands of each outlet. Timing and content are planned out, and a coordinated execution strategy should ensue.

STAYING AHEAD OF THE STORY

The best PR stays ahead of the media.

Novel Novelties, a toy and hobby manufacturer, was changing its selling season from four times a year to three. This move made sense for them strategically, as it would create operating efficiencies and eventually increase their margins. In the meantime, though, it increased their inventory levels and decreased inventory turns in comparison to the previous year.

Anyone reading the company's numbers would see increases and decreases in all the wrong place. The potential headline, "Inventories Sky Rocket at Novel Novelties," needed to be quelled.

After the market closed, IR distributed a release announcing the change in Novel Novelties' selling season with an explanation of the skewed comparison. It included a presentation of how well other companies, who'd done the same thing, had fared. A release to the general media stated a similar positioning, and the analysts were now on board to back it up with quotes. The IR and PR preparation stemmed the potential headline.

Another example is Green Slipper, an apparel company that planned to enter the entertainment industry even though its competitor, Red Shoe, had failed in that arena. IR knew that the strategy would work for Green Slipper, but that the company needed better positioning than its competitor had.

Following an overblown launch orchestrated by a stand-alone PR agency Green Slipper's stock dipped. The company's instinct was to continue onward, but downplay the move—in effect underpromising with the hope of overdelivering. The important point was for Green Slipper's stakeholders, specifically employees, to explain, differentiate, and support the move.

The PR effort provided an angle to the media: Green Slipper's new strategy would promote the brand as more of a lifestyle than a product. The IR effort took a similar story to The Street. As a result, the stock rose, rather than sank, like their competitor's had.

The joint efforts of PR and IR made the difference.

The following story illustrates the preventive measures of a combined IR and PR effort to stave off a potential flood of bad press for Orange Foods, a restaurant company.

The Looming Threat of Bad Press

Orange Foods had a potentially negative media story nipping at its door. The founders of Orange Foods had recently bought it back from the corporation to which they sold it and brought in a new CEO.

The company was doing well, but the CEO set aggressive targets with Wall Street and was overpromising future success on a somewhat loose foundation. The CEO was soon chasing his own tail, making short-term moves to deliver on his promises and, in the meantime, damaging the financial performance of Orange Foods because necessary spending had been curtailed. The founders and the CEO parted ways, and the founders took over the reigns. They set to work immediately to fix the problems and were successful.

During the transition, though, Orange Foods had a potentially damaging story on its hands. Orange was a very visible company, and investors seemed keenly aware of the instability at the corporate level. Our IR and PR teams worked together to reduce the risk to the company's equity value.

The problem was twofold, the potential flood of bad press and the angle the media would take. Every reporter was knocking on the door for the story and aggressively pursuing management for quotes. The last thing anyone wanted was to subject management to such an onslaught, or risk a maverick expose.

The solution was to go to one specific reporter who IR knew well and give her everything, the entire story, as an exclusive. The angle pitched was heavily focused on the return of the founders and their desire to come back and reinforce their original vision. We knew this reporter would blow out the story, creating big news for her newspaper, but the story was now about a company promising quality and the executive instability was overshadowed.

Her paper printed the story, the information was out, and now it was old news. No one else wanted to write the same story after the fact. The other reporters went away.

CLOSING THE LOOP

PR must engage in market intelligence similar to IR. By collecting the media coverage and creating an overview and strategy for the company, executives can see how they are viewed by the outside world and how well they are getting their story across to the media. PR should also collect this image and perspective data from other constituencies, such as vendors, customers, and consumers. Sometimes, in addition to educating the company, feedback can also create a story opportunity.

For a company that provided business software, IR gathered feedback, both criticism and testimonials, from its strategic partners. One of the company's customers shared an interesting story about how the firm's software solutions attacked some problems it had and added value to that customer's bottom line. After placing this story on the software company's Web site and in media marketing materials, several reporters picked up on the angle of the difference one company can make, and the software provider received some positive press. This common PR method should be utilized whenever possible.

PR AND GUIDANCE

IR and PR are mirror images of each other in that they both position a story, and they both reach out to constituents that are powerful and very busy. IR and PR are not jobs for the inexperienced. Companies spend lots of time, effort, and money on the process. Management wants to maximize this spending, and the best way to do so is through conservative guidance to Wall Street.

Conservative guidance has the power to take risk out of a stock. It also has the power to bring conviction out of the analysts as they write flattering reports about the company and argue that it's undervalued. Therefore, when the media is doing a story on the company and looks to the research reports, third-party validation is there in a very positive way.

Another reason conservative guidance can help the communication effort is that managing expectations conservatively will likely position the company to match or exceed estimates for several quarters in a row. If a reporter then shows up to do a negative story on the company or management, there's no way he/she can avoid the fact that management has matched Wall Street estimates for four quarters straight and delivered for shareholders. Similarly, if the reporter were to do a positive story, that string of successes puts an exclamation point on the article.

Without guidance or with aggressive guidance, it's totally a different ballgame. A reporter can make a negative article very negative by highlighting quarterly misses or an inconsistent earnings pattern. Also, positive stories can be tempered by management's lack of financial performance. Therefore, without conservative guidance, the entire media strategy is at risk, potentially wasting time and money as reporters focus more on management inconsistency than the intended purpose of the article, the company's positive outlook.

That goes for employees and vendors too. Obviously, employees develop pride and satisfaction from the solid financial performance of the company. Conservative guidance increases the chances that internal PR will relay positive quarterly results, rather than inconsistent results. The latter can be very frustrating to employees, affecting performance, morale, and possibly turnover. Vendors want to be a part of the success as well, and stringing together several positive quarters relative to guidance may keep those vendors loyal. Subtle communication via PR to all vendors may result in increased loyalty and, in all likelihood, better negotiating leverage for management.

Providing conservative financial guidance sets the table for an integrated PR effort that successfully can feed the media, employees, and vendors, thereby elevating the performance of the entire organization. It's a key factor in the delivery stage of communications.

CHAPTER 19

Infrastructure/ Disclosure Check

The last bit of preparation before the delivery stage is quickly reviewing infrastructure needs and disclosure. With an eye on cost efficiency, IR must have the right people and the right tools at its disposal to do the job. IR is also responsible for double-checking all disclosure policies and working with internal counsel to find the most prudent and commonsense approach.

SUPPORTING IR

First and foremost, IR must have suitable *personnel*. Staffing the IR function properly is paramount to its success, and, as we mentioned previously, each company, depending on its size and characteristics, has different requirements for the job. We can't emphasize enough our belief that a person with senior-level Wall Street experience is most qualified to sit in the IR seat. These professionals have the understanding it takes to maximize value, which is, after all, the objective. Therefore, in a very large company, there may be a team leader, reporting to the CFO, and several professionals underneath, most likely with finance experience. In smaller companies, the team may just be the CFO, an administrative person, and an outside agency.

Second is the need to secure relationships with the most proficient and capable *vendors*. At the heart of successful IR is information. Doing the job without it is almost impossible. Therefore, secure the best and most cost-effective information services around. Bloomberg terminals offer more financial information than an IRO would ever need in all likelihood. They offer stock price, historical charts, analyst coverage and ratings, earnings releases and other announcements, board of director lists, and lists of comparables. Their functionality also allows the user to create comp lists in Excel and run relative valuation exercises, a big part of the definition section.

First Call is the second essential service. Although it offers some of the same information as Bloomberg, First Call posts the analyst estimates that are widely regarded as the benchmark. First Call is also the source for analyst research, and access to that research allows IR to scan Wall Street opinions on every company in the industry, which can be especially valuable around conference calls to gather intelligence about Wall Street's perception in any given quarter. It can also be valuable as an information source for industry events. For example, First Call may be the fastest source for learning that a competitor has just launched a new initiative. For a CEO or CFO, the speed of information is critical, and executives always look good to Wall Street if they have already heard the information and have a calculated response.

Big Dough.com is the final essential service, at least on the IR side. It offers descriptions of the buy-side, identifies portfolio managers and analysts, and details how much money they manage or what stocks they cover. Finally, Big Dough.com allows a shareholder comp run that shows the IRO's company juxtaposed with five or six other similar companies. The exercise shows institutional accounts that don't, but should, own the IRO's stock.

Other information services that are helpful include Web sites where one can view all upcoming financial conferences and request transcripts from recent quarterly conference calls. On the PR side of the house, numerous databases track reporters, find obscure articles, and target stories.

The cost for all these different services, as well as a full-time, internal IR staff, can be quite high. For larger companies, this is certainly not a problem, but for companies with market capitalizations under $1 billion, outsourcing might be the best way to go. This assumes the agency has these information services and has a point person who understands Wall Street enough to interpret the data and plot a cost-efficient and targeted strategy for management.

Third, IR must also review *disclosure policies*, which may require sign-off by legal counsel and buy-in from senior management.

The company must decide issues such as who is authorized to talk to The Street and when. IR should work with senior management to set up internal policies regarding interacting with The Street and the media. An important policy is that only one or two executives should ever represent the company in public, and all other employees on their first day of work should sign a document that they won't interact if approached. If the company always has a systematic way of talking to The Street and a template or system for discourse, then the company knows and controls everything in the public domain. This mitigates the instance of leaks to Wall Street or the media and should make it abundantly clear that talking to analysts could be the equivalent of trafficking in inside information. This framework for dealing with the outside world must be in place for every interested party.

READY TO GO

With the support services in place and disclosure reviewed, IR is ready for Delivery.

CHAPTER 20

Delivering the Goods

Once IR and management have determined conservative earnings guidance, a target audience, a uniform approach with PR, and all the necessary infrastructure and disclosure needs, the stage is set for delivery. The basics of delivery are earnings announcements, conference calls, and pre-announcements.

Long-term investors manage their risk by assessing management performance as frequently as possible. They like to know what they can expect and when they can expect it. Moreover, if things are going to materially change from what's expected, these money managers want to know as soon as possible. Predictability is good, surprise is bad, and when it comes to performance, the pattern of delivery can sometimes be as important as the actual results.

To that end, earnings announcements should never be a big surprise, especially if the company has established guidance and committed to refining that guidance throughout the year.

But even with the most conservative guidance, some factors are still out of management's control, such as the weather or the economy. Even under negative circumstances there are always ways to make bad events not so bad. The ways and means of disclosure can have a profound effect on valuation over time.

EARNINGS ANNOUNCEMENTS

IR must make its company's story stand out above the thousands of publicly traded companies that interact with Wall Street everyday. To do this, to make an initial contact interesting, IR must reach out and grab the audience.

The most basic piece of the delivery stage is the *earnings release*, the vehicle through which quarterly earnings results are expressed and distributed to investors. Because the majority of public companies are on a calendar year, the announcements are usually clustered around the same four periods each year (late April/early May, late July/early August, late October/early November, and February/March), with the sell- and buy-sides geared up to handle the high volumes of information in these short windows. Because the volumes of reporting companies are so large, analysts look to quickly review the press release, take from it the key points, and move on to the next reporting company. The release must be concise, contain only the most important information, and supply a dose of context with a brief management comment. It must also include financial tables—outlining results and any other information that management believes will help shareholders better analyze the company.

Content

The earnings release is widely distributed to the buy-side, the sell-side, and the financial media. (Appendix A offers two examples of earnings releases.)

As with any press release, the headline describes the purpose of the release and should act as a hook to draw investors' and analysts' attention ("Octagon Inc. Reports Third-Quarter Financial Results"). The subheads should highlight the quarterly performance and/or the most material content in the release: "Exceeds First Call Earnings Per Share by 23% / Management Raises Guidance for Fiscal 2004." These subheads are important because the news wires tend to pick them up and highlight them. In the above example, everyone is aware that Octagon beat its earnings estimate significantly and that the full-year expectations are being increased. If the increased guidance portion of the release had not been packaged as a subhead, however, odds are high that the media outlets might have ignored this very material piece of information.

The second part of the release should include bulleted highlights from the quarter, such as revenue growth over the prior period, EBITDA if appropriate, Free Cash Flow, new customers acquired during the quarter, and anything else management believes is a critical driver of the business. However, the limit is about five items, so IROs should prioritize and settle on metrics that the analyst and portfolio manager would want, not necessarily items of which management is most proud. The key here is to deliver the right message in a succinct fashion.

After the highlights, a quick paragraph can appear describing the results for the quarter as they relate to revenues, net income, and diluted earnings per share, and the year-over-year comparisons. That section should be followed by a quote from the CEO that talks about the quarter.

Next, a paragraph can outline other drivers for the period, such as new customer counts, average weekly sales, and strategy points. Still later might be a paragraph discussing the balance sheet—cash balance, long-term debt, and shareholder's equity. The final quote should be from the CEO and is most effective when talking about strategy and his or her overall vision for the company and shareholders. Finally, before the financial tables, a guidance section should appear that addresses the upcoming quarter and the full year. There should also be a full description of the business in safe-harbor language that protects forward-looking statements.

Remember that this is only an outline. The final product must be a combination of IR, management, and legal counsel. However, be succinct and avoid endless paragraphs of information or language that doesn't immediately imbed itself with investors. While too many quotes can also be a distraction, in the past, they were less important because analysts and investors could cull the specific information from releases or just call management to gain additional insight. But subsequent to Reg FD, management must be more careful about the added color they give in private calls. For that reason, the release and the quotes are both templates for disclosure, so any direct word from the company must be deliberate and thought out.

THE CONFERENCE CALL

Conference calls are one of the most common and expected vehicles for communicating quarterly financial performance. Before Reg FD, an overwhelming majority of larger companies conducted them, but not every small-cap company followed suit. These days, nearly every company conducts them, and all companies Web cast them.

The simultaneous Web cast allows everyone to be on the call, from big institutional investors to individuals who own 100 shares. It's an opportunity to listen to management explain quarterly results and convey their vision of the future. More importantly, because it reaches the masses, the conference call and Web cast function as the company's disclosure template until the next quarterly call. In other words, if it's discussed on the conference call, on record, the CEO, CFO, or IRO can talk about it on private phone calls, at exclusive Wall Street conferences, or in one-on-one meetings. The conference call is the ultimate safety net for Reg FD.

In terms of structure and content for the call, the first section should be an introduction from the IRO or legal counsel that includes who will be on the call, what topics will be covered, and a reading of the Safe Harbor language that protects the company should actual performance not match forecasts. This section should be followed by the CEO, who discusses the quarter in general, and addresses mostly qualitative initiatives that went on during the three month period. Next up is the CFO who discusses in great detail the top-line and its drivers, a line-by-line examination of expenses (not only as a percentage of sales but versus the prior-year period), a balance sheet review, and guidance. Finally, the CEO wraps up the call, but before Q&A, he or she should comment on strategies and plans for the upcoming quarter and year and leave the audience with three or four points why the company is interesting at this particular point in time.

Analysts and portfolio managers know that the conference call is the most efficient and effective way for management to communicate with The Street, and because of this importance, the calls must always be scripted, with topics and speakers specified and limited.

Scripting the Call

Part of the analyst's job is to distill the company's message into a persuasive and credible opinion and share that view with clients in the investment community. Therefore, IR should draft the conference call script with this perspective in mind.

The IR professional should ask, *If I could write the analyst report after the call, how would it look?*

This approach underscores the necessity for making key points and highlighting the positives of the business in a way that the analyst and portfolio manager are used to seeing. To that point, the script must be realistic and credible, but take license to discuss strategic or operational initiatives with enthusiasm. The hope is that these highlights make their way to analysts in the next morning's First Call notes in the same manner that they were presented. In fact, that's the entire goal of the call: getting management's exact point of view in the analysts' research coverage, and having them understand and buy into the strategy, all while keeping their First Call estimates within management's range.

As stated, the number-one rule for conference calls is that every word must be scripted. In fact, management should begin preparing the script, with IR, about three weeks in advance so that the CEO and CFO are fully prepared. Why script every word? Because the call should last only 20 to 30 minutes, and without the script CEOs can frequently get off message and speak in tangents about issues that may not be relevant to the call. In that case, management has just wasted one of its four annual earnings calls by rambling and looking unprepared. Our hunch is that analysts and portfolio managers will pick up on that fact and think twice about getting involved.

Staying on script is also essential because today's conference calls are transcribed, widely distributed, and scrutinized. Oftentimes, portfolio managers want to read the conference call transcript, hear about progress from management directly, and check that view with the sell-side. That's why scripting each word, rather than working off bullet points or ad-libbing, is necessary. Transcripts are a new form of research report complete with estimates from management, and it's a huge advantage if IR views it as such. (Appendix B offers an example of a conference call script.)

Writing the script is a process that includes the following steps:

Management discussions: Executives are constantly crunched for time, and SEC requirements don't help that process at quarter's end. IR's lead on preparing for the conference call helps management begin the process and avoid mistakes that can accompany a last-minute rush.

Therefore, three or four weeks before the call, IR should talk to the CEO and CFO, review the performance for the quarter, and determine what topics will be most relevant for the call. These would include strategic issues, financial performance, and a recap of material announcements during the period. Once discussed and approved, IR then has an idea of what management believes is important or material to communicate.

Also, although other departments within the company should not speak on the actual call, they should be represented. For example, if an important marketing initiative is launching in the second half of the year, it should be discussed and scripted into the appropriate section. Or if the controller has a better interpretation of why an important expense line-item didn't meet expectations, it can be discussed with IR and incorporated. When senior management can speak in detail to these issues, analysts are impressed and left with the perception that management is very much in-tune with the business and running a tight ship. The comfort level that affords investors is so highly coveted by sell- and buy-side analysts that a premium multiple is often paid for stocks where management is communicating at such proficient levels.

During the internal due diligence, IR has to set the tone of the call and judge everything relative to valuation. Much information will be contributed from the definition stage, but it's always worth a quick revisit as definition can change frequently, in tandem with stock movements. For example, if things are going poorly for a company and the stock is already down, the strategy for the conference call is very different than if the news is bad and the stock is at a 52-week high. Capital markets experience and expertise can tell management in what context to deliver the news.

Street recon: IR that is tapped into Wall Street perceptions already knows the overarching messages that should be stressed or defended in any given quarter and will incorporate it with the messages that come from the original meeting with management.

IR should query as to the specific concerns that analysts and investors have regarding the company—for example, recent expense escalations, off-balance-sheet debt, or the effectiveness of a certain marketing campaign. Also, IR that has the connections to seek out and understand the "bear story" on a company is invaluable and allows management to address specific negatives on each call.

The process of collecting information from analysts or portfolio managers can be very difficult, however, in that Wall Street professionals have little time to share their perceptions, particularly around earnings season. Accordingly, IR must build long-standing relationships, and capital markets knowledge increases the odds that those relationships will develop. Talking the language of the portfolio manager or analyst is the best way to start an intelligent dialogue, garner real feedback, and pass it on unfiltered to management.

Writing the drafts: Once IR has spoken to management and the outside world, it should take the lead in writing the conference call script, adhere to an agreed-upon format, and deliver the initial draft to the CEO and CFO within a preset schedule.

For example, about a week after the initial meeting with management, IR should have a first draft of the release and script ready to go. 48 hours later, management should agree to give comments back to IR, and the whole process should be repeated as the financials come together and the auditors do their job.

Then, about a week before the call, the conference call invitation should be sent to the wire utilizing the distribution list that was compiled in the earlier stages of delivery. Once the CEO, the CFO, and IR have turned two or three drafts of the script, with each party adding and subtracting ideas, the final draft should be shown to legal and the audit committee for final approval.

Being proactive: IR and management must collectively decide which issues to emphasize during the quarter. IR may encourage a reluctant management team to discuss a tough issue in the script rather than address it in Q&A because it's a proactive way to control the information and mitigate risk. If, for example, the issue is ignored in the script because the CEO deems it too uncomfortable to discuss, she may find herself off balance in Q&A, fumbling for an answer that's scribbled down on a cheat sheet. If scripted from the beginning, however, the CEO can simply refer back to her prepared remarks on the topic and move on to the next question. An example of a tough issue for a CEO might be downward margin trends in the face of rising sales or the loss of a major customer or why the company doesn't give guidance. Allowing sophisticated portfolio managers or analysts to lead a company down a line of questioning that the CEO is already uncomfortable with can only make management look bad, and unfortunately the entire dialogue will be transcribed for the world to see. That's too much risk, and there's no reason to incur it.

Be prepared: Given the opportunity to be extemporaneous and not follow a script, management might get off message and use a phrase, or even a qualifier like "significant," to describe a new initiative. A simple word or nuance can send an unintended signal to analysts and portfolio managers who are trained to quantify everything they hear from management. For example, on a conference call, management might be talking about an initiative for the upcoming year, and although it won't be a contributor to earnings, the CEO who's not scripted might say, "it's going to be a significant part of our business going forward." This might encourage analysts to incorporate the new business line into their models and increase their earnings estimates. If this unwanted analysis skews the average First Call estimate upward, the company has just put itself in position to miss estimates. For these reasons, management must be very careful even with what it believes is mundane language.

Therefore, the point of a script is to stick to it, and management and IR should practice to ensure that the executives can deliver the prepared remarks with familiarity and ease. Additionally, IR should know, from its Street reconnaissance and industry knowledge, the questions that are likely to be asked. These questions can be subtly addressed in the script with some pre-emptive language to nullify the question altogether. At the very least, they should be written and reviewed so that management can prep for the interaction.

In this preparation, IR should highlight specific *talking points*, as well as issues to avoid, so that management can steer back to port if the call gets bumpy. Preparation helps management present well and build credibility, which is the name of the game when it comes to valuation. Ultimately, the CEO and the CFO must come across as confident, answer all questions thoroughly, and articulate a clear vision for the future.

Front and Center: Topics and Their Speakers

The voices on the conference call become the public voices of the company, and the public role of the company executives should reflect their jobs.

Therefore, have two or three speakers at most represent the company.

The first is the CEO. Not too many investors would buy a stock without listening to, if not sitting down in person with, the CEO. The next individual on the call might be the chief operating officer, who handles the day-to-day operations. Finally the CFO should be on the call.

On an obvious level, this introduces the sell- and buy-sides to the executives in charge, putting a voice to the vision, operations, and numbers. On a subliminal level, it shows a cohesive, connected team in which the members understand the business and their roles. By giving each executive specific issues to cover, IR helps senior management put their best face forward to The Street.

For purposes of disclosure and liability the company should be very particular about who is on the call and who will interact with the investment community on a day-to-day basis. One of the oldest analyst techniques is to call different executives in the company—the CEO, the COO, and then the CFO—and ask the same few questions to each, and look for points of discrepancy that reveal incremental information.

To avoid this, a formal policy should be in place. The best analogy to help clients understand the ramifications of no policy is to imagine the conference call as a trial. If IR is the defense attorney, he must decide who will be put on the witness stand. There are pros and cons for each person. For example, it would be great to have the head of marketing explain the new program for the upcoming year or the head of human resources talk about the latest batch of hires. Better yet, the head of technology could talk about the new Web initiative. Of course, if only IR were doing the questioning after prepared remarks, it would be an easy choice to let these people speak, but the line is filled with money managers, hedge funds, and short sellers. Much like a trial, allowing someone to speak during prepared remarks opens them up to questioning on the conference call, phone calls after the conference call, and potentially questions during the quarter via email or phone. The head of marketing would be viewed as another company source from whom to gather information, and analysts and portfolio managers may start calling multiple senior-level workers within the company. Therefore, to control the information that is directed to Wall Street, IROs must limit the number of participants on the call and make sure everyone has a unified message, particularly intra-quarter.

What to Watch For on Conference Calls

Conference calls can succeed or fail for several reasons, and success relies on preparation and management's ability to hone in on content and delivery. For analysts and portfolio managers, some things just don't sit well.

Tell just enough: A company that spends five minutes on prepared remarks and leaves the rest to Q&A gives too much room for analyst interpretation. It can also send a message that the company isn't taking the call seriously or that they'd rather not share their information. On the other side of the spectrum, a company that spends 45 minutes on prepared remarks is simply taking up too much time, and that drain prevents investors and analyst from participating in a Q&A session afterward, which is critical. Forty-five minutes shows that a company doesn't know how to concisely tell its story to the world. When in doubt, companies that want to disclose many variables should put them in a supplemental disclosure section of the press release for all to see.

Stay on point: The script should help management address specific topics and avoid irrelevant or confusing tangents and trouble spots. Executives must spend time on the focus of the call, possibly an earnings miss, in great detail, before moving on to strategy and the company's outlook. Glossing over these points positions the CEO as unrealistic and a potential investment risk. That's why the script, with related investment community feedback built in, is so important.

Don't hype: Executives work hard all year with few moments to stand up and garner recognition for the company's operating results. The call may seem like the perfect time for this, although in actuality, it's not the right forum. Management must allow the analysts and portfolio managers to characterize the performance. Management should keep it somewhat matter of fact and stay even-keel, whether times are good or bad. The Street wants to hear the explanation behind recent performance and the essence of what will happen for the remainder of the year.

Don't hide: Regardless if the management team decides to be proactive or not in the script, problems can't be glossed over. Executives who talk about positive issues when a big negative is looming are making a big mistake and jeopardizing their own credibility. Management should state the facts, the reasons behind them, and the actions being taken to fix the problem. Management shouldn't take the siutation personally because quarterly misses happen every day on Wall Street. Management should be up-front and overly available. How a management team handles the bad times on their conference calls can define their public company careers and be a major determinant of valuation.

Watch words: As stated earlier, it's not just what is said, it's how it's said. In conference calls, the littlest things might matter the most. The Street always pays close attention to nuance, innuendo, and tone. Their job is to quantify everything that management says, and determine what that means to EPS.

Believe it or not, a certain word or a shift in tone or inflection can affect the interpretation of information and shift the investor's mindset up or down. The difference between "very good" and "good" has meaning to the analyst and portfolio manager. If these words are not quantified, the meanings can be widely interpreted.

Analysts and portfolio managers cringe when they hear certain words or phrases. Phrases such as "explosive earnings" or "our guidance might prove to be very conservative" can ruin IR's plan. The phrases are factored into the share price immediately and many times set an unintended bar by which management will be judged.

Dealing with shorts on the call: Short sellers are not necessarily the enemy, although they certainly don't brighten management's day. They are usually short-term players who have made a bet against the company because the stock has increased in value, and in their minds the earnings don't justify the multiple. There's risk involved in shorting stocks, however, so if they borrow and sell short, they've probably done some solid research to arrive at their bearish opinion.

If IR knows that the short interest in the stock is high, they need to prepare the script with proactive explanations that address each point of the bear story. Because the company does not want to enter a public debate on a conference call, short sellers should not be confronted. Management should simply put forth its counterarguments and then, if necessary, agree to disagree.

Although someone betting against management can lead to an emotional situation, executives need to be matter-of-fact on the call and understand that it's not personal. The shorts may think the company is great, just too expensive. Or they may be making a short-term bet. At the end of the day, however, management shouldn't waste time confronting short sellers on the call. Delivering solid EPS growth over time is the only way to send these players on their way.

Other Interested Parties

The earnings announcement and conference call typically get beyond the sell-side and the buy-side. In fact, there are several constituencies to consider, and management should have a systematic procedure in place to disseminate and explain the quarterly information.

Stakeholders: Employees, vendors, and customers should be notified first and foremost on any important company news. The employees are the heart and soul of any organization, and one way to keep them motivated is to keep them involved and educated. Any procedure for communication should include an internal process that precedes, within Regulation FD constraints, the external one. The CEO, not the local media or the Internet, should be the first source of information for employees on company news.

If it's feasible, and if it would underscore goodwill in a relationship, strategic partners such as vendors and customers should also have an announcement tailored toward them. An announcement after the market closes and moments before the call to The Street keeps the team in sync. This is especially important if it's a cost-cutting measure or a merger that will result in the closing of certain operations or layoffs. No one wants to hear about their plant closing on the radio in the carpool.

Other agencies: Sometimes additional phone calls are required following the announcement. A company with a pending lawsuit was about to announce the judgment. IR called NASDAQ and told them to halt trading; then the company made the announcement. The judgment was going to be considered material to shareholders, and trading volume would definitely be affected. To encourage an orderly market and decrease volatility, IR wanted to make sure the news was evenly disseminated.

IR's responsibility is to know who has to be called and when on any announcement that may have a consequence for that agency, even if the market is closed.

It's All in the Timing

Just as important as the content and structure of the release and conference call is the timing. Many companies may not give the issue much thought, but it's an important part of reducing risk in the overall communications process.

Analysts see companies release their earnings throughout the day. Some would be the first ones out at 7:00 a.m., others at 11:00 a.m., a few at 3:00 p.m., and many at 4:00 p.m. or later. The subsequent conference calls might also be scattered throughout the day. This shotgun approach just isn't smart, and IR should take control of the process and educate management on timing.

The first series of checks IR should make are to competitors' schedules. Look on any of the information services and determine when the competition is reporting. Most companies make that information public well in advance. If they don't, IR might look at prior-year releases to get a feel for timing. Once a reporting grid is composed, IR should evaluate timing with management and pick a release date that's relatively vacant from peer reporting. There's no need to rush. It's more important to be ready, on a date when none of management's competitors will be releasing results.

Rushing to get auditors in and out so that earnings can be reported quickly just doesn't seem to make sense, particularly in the new age of information. In fact, there are no negative ramifications of reporting four weeks after the quarter closes rather than three. The better route is to take the time to ensure that results are accurate, sign off on them feeling confident, script the call, practice Q&A, and listen to other industry calls. To that last point, reporting later rather than sooner gives IR and management time to gather competitive information by listening to other industry conference calls. IR can read each competitor's release and conference call transcript and get a feel for industry results as well as perceptions and tones on Wall Street. As a result, management is more prepared, and the risk of surprise is materially reduced. Therefore, being one of the last companies in an industry to report can be a good thing. If there is a risk in waiting, however, it would manifest itself during a quarter where peers are reporting bad news. Under this circumstance, the company's stock would likely trade down with the group before it has a chance to put out its earnings and control the information. Pre-announcements can take care of this problem, a topic that is addressed later in the chapter.

So how about time of day?

Many companies report earnings in the morning before the market opens at 9:30 a.m., then conduct their conference call at 11 a.m. Better yet, some companies release earnings at 11 a.m. and conduct the call at 1 p.m. In theory, management probably thinks that it would lose the audience if it reported either before the market opened or after it closed. That theory, however, is just a guess on management's part, and IR should do some educating based on its capital markets perspective.

When the earnings release hits the tape during market hours—let's say, 11 a.m.—traders, institutional salespeople, and investors immediately call the analyst to decipher the information. Since the analyst hasn't talked to management yet, and legally cannot until the conference call because of disclosure issues, they really can't give an informed opinion to the world.

"[XYZ Company] is planning to report its 16 week Q1:04 EPS before the market open on May 13, with its conference call after the close. The gap between the EPS press release and the conference call could create material volatility during the day of May 13 if there are ambiguities in the press release."

—From an analyst's email, April 28, 2004.

Therefore, the trading desk will make a snap judgment on its stock position without company comment and without analyst comment. With that judgment can come volatility in the stock. This process becomes even more complex when the earnings release is complicated. If Reuters or Bloomberg picks up the wrong headline or misinterprets the release, for example, the market may move unnecessarily, which can have a serious effect on the stock price, and whipsaw shareholders.

Companies should distribute their releases and conduct their conference calls after the market closes. Specifically, the announcement should hit the tape at 4:01pm and the call should start at 4:30 p.m. or 5:00 p.m. EST.

This method is good for several reasons, including the fact that there's less distraction on the trading floor and less opportunity for an unnecessary reaction, based on a confusing release. For example, a retailer might have inventory levels that appear higher than sales can sustain. Investors who see this on the balance sheet might hit the sell button if the release is distributed during market hours, prior to a conference call. But if the market is closed and the company has a chance to explain that these inventory levels are built into the projections for new store openings, investors may hesitate before selling the stock, or not sell it at all.

The other advantage of distributing the release after the market closes is that the sell-side has time to collect its thoughts, ask management questions, and prepare a written conclusion for their First Call update. During the day, the analyst is barraged with calls, the market is open, and the stock freely moves as the conference call is being conducted. In addition, traders may be out to lunch and institutional salespeople may be focused on other ideas or they may be escorting management teams to buy-side meetings. In other words, the release and the subsequent analyst call are diluted in the commotion of the day. If the market is closed, none of these issues are present and management is maximizing the opportunity to tell its story in a risk-free environment.

Therefore, understanding the atmosphere on the other side of the capital markets, the life of the portfolio manager, and the day of the sell-side analyst helps to clarify why IR should choose this approach. To further maximize the effort, it's extremely beneficial to understand how the day of the sell-side begins.

The Morning Meeting

To truly understand the analysts, their obligations, and their relationships with the sales force, one has to understand the morning meeting at an investment bank.

The morning meeting is the primary means of formal communication between an analyst and the institutional sales force. This is ultimately where investment ideas are introduced, debated, and delivered. For example, the analyst makes his/her argument to buy or sell a stock, and if it's persuasive, the sales force, which can number from 10 to 50 individuals, will pick up their phones and call roughly 10 or more institutional investors each (Fidelity, Putnam, and Capital Research to name a few). This communication channel is very powerful, to say the least, and one that IROs should take advantage of.

Every day, Monday through Friday, from 7 a.m. to 8 a.m. or thereabouts, investment banks and brokerage firms conduct the morning meeting. Picture a large trading floor, fluorescent lights, rows of desks, stacks of computer screens, and the buzz of suits and skirts adjusting their headsets, folding their newspapers, finishing off their coffee, getting ready for the day. At the front of the room is a podium with a microphone that will connect the speaker's voice to the vast network of salespeople who listen to the investment bank's ideas on any given morning.

Controlling the proceedings is a facilitator, the morning meeting gatekeeper. He runs the show on a daily basis, and along with the director of research preselects a handful of analysts to present their ideas each day. Competition to present one of those ideas is fierce, and analysts must lobby for a spot on the schedule. This selection is important to analysts for a couple of reasons. First, getting on the morning meeting and having their investment ideas supported by the sales force makes a name for the analyst among institutions, and these institutions vote for analysts and determine a portion of their compensation. Second, being on the morning meeting means that the analyst in question is most likely upping or lowering their rating on a stock, and those actions facilitate commission business on the trading desk. Again, this is a determinant of analyst compensation. Therefore, the analyst is always looking for undervalued or overvalued ideas and to bring those ideas to the morning meeting.

So the key for IR is to understand the analyst's mentality and find a way to be one of those few Buy ideas on the morning meeting. That's how to fully maximize an earnings release and conference call and how to maximize the relationship with any investment bank.

The first lesson on how to make the cut for the morning meeting is to be an undervalued, interesting company with trusted management. Hold-rated stocks aren't presented in the morning meeting. Why? Because, a Hold rating doesn't generate a nickel of commission business. Therefore, it's imperative to be a Buy.

Getting to the Buy Rating

Positioning a stock as a Buy rating is the reason that IR must go to such lengths in the definition stage to craft a message and package it in the way analysts and investors can relate. The objective is to have it play out something like this:

IR joins a quirky consumer company, refines its comp group, and determines that it should be valued on EBITDA versus earnings. It's a more accurate valuation method for this capital-intensive company and casts it as undervalued in the new peer group. Then, IR garners feedback from management, the buy-side, and industry sources, drafts the earnings release and conference call script, and prepares thoroughly for Q&A. IR, along with management, also sets conservative guidance and conducts the conference call at 5 p.m. EST, thereby controlling the dissemination information.

After the call, the analyst likes management and their approach and views the numbers as conservative relative to the peer group. With time to collect his or her thoughts, a well-thought-out research report is written, incorporating management's conservative guidance. Given the fact that estimates are low, a great argument can be made that the stock is a Buy. The analyst lobbies the gatekeeper to get his or her idea on the morning meeting, and because management and IR have packaged the product conservatively in both the release and the call, the green light is given and the analyst is awarded the lead-off spot for the morning meeting.

The result: IR, along with management, has almost made the stock a Buy through a strategic approach that fully understands how an investment bank operates. If these practices are followed every quarter, particularly conservative guidance, the institutional profile of the company will no doubt be raised, volume will likely increase, and a higher valuation will ensue.

On the other hand, a promotional management team with aggressive guidance doesn't stand a chance of getting on the morning meeting because of the increased risk to earnings estimates. The institutional sales force and the buy-side will rarely support the stock when management has established a pattern that is not conservative. There's just too high a risk of losing money. Whereas in the case above, management has essentially made the analyst look good to the sales force because earnings are positioned to exceed guidance. This in turn generates a buying opportunity and commissions for the analyst's firm. For the company, the multiple increased and the cost of capital declined.

Had the company stretched with its guidance and released earnings during the day, the stock would have immediately moved to a level commensurate with the perceived risk to earnings, and by the next morning there would have been no investment call to make.

Putting It Together

Here are a couple of examples of how the entire process works.

Zippa!, the popular apparel brand mentioned earlier, discovered after the IR audit that not only wasn't it being clear in its definition, specifically with regard to its product diversification, but that it hadn't clearly communicated this reality to The Street. Once the company had packaged this "new product" for the investment community and established earnings guidance, IR scripted a call that would clarify their old-to-them, but new-to-The-Street, position.

After delivering the new message, backed up by numbers, in an after-market-hours conference call, analysts walked away with a new understanding of Zippa!. The company was clearer about its business and conservative in its guidance. New analysts picked up coverage and delivered the new thesis, old analysts changed their views, and despite the fact that Zippa! missed its sales estimate, the stock increased nearly 20 percent the day after the call. The PR group was thus positioned for positive stories in the media, articles that could speak to the financial strengths and diversity of the business.

This approach took much of the risk perception out of the stock. None of this was new, nothing had changed with regard to the way the company did business. It was just delivering the critical information to Wall Street in a way it could understand. Erasing the disconnect between perception and reality.

After the call, several analysts called to thank the IR team, saying it was one of the best messages they'd ever heard. Analysts and investors had unknowingly foundered when it came to Zippa!, although the fault was really in the company's historic communications practices. IR made the analysts' job much easier because issues were formally addressed in an open forum with plenty of time for questions and answers. With access to new information that before wasn't readily available, the investment community recognized a new positioning for Zippa!, right up there with a more mature, global businesses. The conference call improved The Street's perception of the company, took risk out of the stock, and positioned it for a higher multiple, creating tens of millions of dollars in value for shareholders.

Soft Sofas, a company in the home furnishings sector, had slow sales one quarter and achieved Wall Street's expectations only through a one-time gain because of an asset sale. This result was technically a miss and would be viewed negatively by analysts. They began their conference call talking about new initiatives and glossing over the financials. Big mistake.

The analysts and portfolio managers on the call, professionals at dissecting financials, took notice. Management obviously missed estimates and was trying to take attention away from that fact. Nothing could penalize management more, and the odds that Soft Sofa would get on any morning meeting schedule at any investment bank for the foreseeable future were seriously jeopardized (other than as a Sell recommendation).

Soft Sofas should have started the conference call by announcing that sales were down and then talk about the problems that contributed to this slump and what factors were offsetting hoped-for growth. If management had acknowledged the problem, identified its source, and given new guidance, Wall Street would have handicapped the company's ability to fix the problem, lowered estimates, and if the stock dropped materially, had the analyst on the morning meeting schedule to talk about the equity as undervalued. By communicating this understanding, along with a strategy for change, management could have built the kind of credibility that can never be attained by trying to avoid issues with hype.

PRE-ANNOUNCEMENTS

The last agenda item on delivery is the pre-announcement. Management competency is measured by more than the strategic vision to build a business; it also includes the ability to understand the audience and communicate the business. As far as Wall Street is concerned, earnings guidance is a great indicator of management capacity because it tests the budgeting and forecasting process and shows that management isn't afraid to set the bar for performance.

Granted, Wall Street also understands that factors beyond management's control cause earnings to drop. When the problem is the economy, the weather, competition, or a national security incident, an earnings miss is usually explainable. What is not easy to explain, however, are hiccups in the core business where management should have had control. Managing the unexpected is part of the job, and management that has been conservative in setting the bar, even if it means a lower short-term stock price, has given its estimates breathing room to deal with the unexpected.

The reason the market rewards upward earnings revisions is the perception, right or wrong, that the executives are operationally sound and that systems are in place to measure and predict financial performance. Wall Street 101: the market likes predictability and certainty, not risk and volatility.

Take, for example, this quote from a March 18, 2004, analyst's report on a restaurant conglomerate. "We have low confidence in our EPS estimate of $1.46 and $1.56 for FY04 and FY05 respectively, due in part to management's frequent guidance revisions, none provided in press release, and also to the ongoing and much discussed traffic volatility at (one of the company's restaurants)." The analyst maintained his Hold rating.

Missing estimates also puts the analyst in a precarious position. In addition to his own research, the analyst counts on management for reliable guidance, and if credible, the sales force and investors also buy into those numbers. If a company misses estimates during a quarter and the earnings are trending lower, the analyst is going to lose credibility when the quarter sinks beneath them. Though a number that materially beats estimates is positive for investors in the short term, any experienced analyst will wonder how well management is able to forecast.

Missing the Number, but Mitigating the Penalty

> "The tech stock rally deflated yesterday due to weaker than expected earnings from [a Web commerce company] that torpedoed the sector on fears that similar companies were overvalued."
> —*The New York Times*, October 2001.

"Weaker than expected earnings" was the key phrase. A trader was quoted in the article, saying: "Frankly, expectations were too high. Companies haven't released many pre-earnings announcements and analysts were backing out numbers, and no one was telling them otherwise."

If, during the quarter, management can see that the company is going to materially miss or exceed earnings estimates, the best thing to do is to pre-announce a new guidance range as soon as possible. Getting information out early, in good times and bad, keeps Wall Street in the loop while minimizing surprises. And yet, while we recognize management's obligation to get news out as soon as they know about changes, releasing news too early can be costly. For example, if business is trending down during the quarter and halfway through the three-month period management revises guidance, that's fine—unless the company misses revised guidance, which is totally unacceptable. Therefore, management should wait until three-quarters of the quarter has passed, when a tangible range is known. That way, management is not adjusting guidance without feeling 99 percent confident in the new range.

The second part of any pre-announcement strategy is announcing the date and time of the earnings call, probably three or four weeks later, and making sure that it's clear that annual guidance will be addressed again at that time. Why is this important? If, for example, management brings down second quarter guidance on May 30th, a month before the end of the quarter, with no corresponding conference call, analysts may be left wondering what to do with their annual estimates. By announcing that annual guidance will be addressed on the upcoming call, management has just bought time with the analysts and will likely be given the grace period before the analysts move numbers.

Less so these days, but certainly in the late 1990s, most stocks had a *whisper number* circulating. This number is exactly what it sounds like: the estimate that the market believes as information buzzes around Wall Street. It's always higher or lower than First Call published consensus, but for discussion purposes, let's say it's higher.

Pre-announcements help mitigate the whisper number by defining expectations into a range. This is particularly critical with a growth stock that's performing well, because in the absence of an earnings pre-announcement Wall Street is free to manufacture information leading up to the conference call. This is the ultimate in losing control of the communications process and allowing rumors to define expected financial performance. It not only creates volatility but most likely puts management in position to fall short of expectations. By pre-announcing a range, the whisper number is eliminated.

Another reason to pre-announce earnings is if an upcoming shortfall is caused by industry-related problems. If that's the case, getting the news out as soon as possible is even more important, but again, not before management is comfortable with the revised range. On such industry-related news, companies in the same industry will tend to move up and down together. Because a company's peers are likely also feeling the same effect, it's best, if possible, to be the first in a peer group to adjust expectations. That way, management is on the offensive rather than reacting to a competitor miss and any Reg FD issue is eliminated. To that point, if management is the first to pre-announce the industry issue and new earnings estimates, they are free to discuss it, within reason, with the buy- and sell-side. The industry peers who don't pre-announce will likely get a large volume of calls that they won't be able to field because commenting would risk a Reg FD violation.

Ultimately, pre-announcing every quarter, even when there isn't a material variance from expectations, is a good policy because it doubles the amount of communications with Wall Street from four (earnings releases) to eight (earnings releases and pre-announcements). By increasing the communication, consistency and transparency are increased, and management's credibility can follow. The eight communication points also free management of potential Reg FD violations, as referring back or forward to the latest communication is very easy. In other words, the more communication, the fewer windows to talk about material, nonpublic information.

Exceeding the Number, and Increasing the Reward

Many CEOs have realized the hard way that being better than expected does not always turn out to be better than expected. In most cases, when a company materially beats earnings estimates and waits to announce it until the release date—for example, the First Call consensus is $0.10, and the company reports $0.20 on earnings day—they will see their stock increase that day.

However, Wall Street veterans look at that behavior and wonder if the same policy goes when management misses numbers. The smart portfolio managers ask themselves if the company can also surprise on the downside by that much, and come to the conclusion that the company cannot forecast its business. This can be disconcerting to the analyst or portfolio manager relying on management for consistency and guidance. The pattern, more than the content in this case, becomes discounted into valuation.

When an analyst recommends a stock, he or she wants to address their sales force as many times as possible, particularly when the stock is behaving in line with the rating. The morning meeting section taught that conservative guidance, and meeting or exceeding guidance, can start a powerful cycle of addressing the sales force and penetrating institutional accounts.

Octagon Inc. was in the last third of its quarter. The First Call consensus estimate was $0.20, and the company's own forecast, as disseminated on the last conference call, was $0.17 to $0.20. If management believed there was absolutely no way that earnings would be lower than $0.22 and they'd probably be $0.25, an appropriate move would be to pre-announce earnings and increase the range to $0.20 to $0.22.

That way, when reporting the actual quarter three to four weeks later, management would have already known that it would report $0.22 at minimum and most likely $0.25. If $0.25 it would be an upside surprise, and if management reported $0.22, it would still be within the increased range.

Therefore, if IR and management are conservative, and use pre-announcements to raise guidance and update the market each quarter, the analyst has that many more times to address the sales force and reiterate conviction about the stock. Each case becomes an opportunity to generate commissions, create a payday for the firm and analyst, build credibility for management, bolster valuation, and reduce the company's cost of capital.

Pre-announcing elevated to an art form can be about breaking one piece of good news into two: giving the analyst two good data points to talk to clients about and two pluses for addressing the sales force.

Without conservative guidance, however, management doesn't have the leverage to do this. Rather, they only introduce risk into the stock and increase the company's chance of missing estimates. Pre-announcing regularly, particularly when times are good, reinforces the company's upward trend, labels management as conservative, and builds credibility.

Safety First—The Pre-Announce for Prevention

Sarbanes-Oxley and Reg FD reduce volatility in our view, because all analysts and investors receive the information simultaneously. Unlike the Wild West atmosphere of the 1990s, when analysts regularly extracted material information in closed-door meetings with management teams, strict enforcement limits incremental information.

Therefore, why wouldn't companies pre-announce every quarter, if for nothing else to reduce the chances of a material slip up in a one-on-one call? With four set pre-announcements, the public information is always fresh and management can breathe easy in casual conversations.

Another safeguard is Stock Watch, an organization that keeps an eye on trading. If there is heavy trading volume, Stock Watch is going to call the company and ask if they have any news. If the company says no, then they better not come out with new information in the near future. And if the company has a practice of pre-announcing whenever it thinks it's going to miss or exceed the estimate, or just in the normal course of business, then The Street believes management and stays with guidance.

Road shows, which are discussed in the next section of the book, should always be scheduled after the earnings calls so that the information is disseminated before management begins the process. But in cases when that's not feasible, companies may want to consider pre-announcing quarterly results or material news before the scheduled events so that management can speak freely. If a pre-announcement is not feasible before presenting publicly, management should be counseled to refer back to material in the last public conference call. Legally, the company can't break any new ground.

How to Pre-Announce

For all pre-announcements where there is a material miss—that is, actual earnings are off by more than 20 to 30 percent—a conference call is in order to quickly explain the problems and potential solutions. Although the last thing management wants to do is talk about it, that's exactly what it must do.

The conference call gives analysts and investors a chance to ask questions and, for the misses, vent their frustration. The conference call also benefits the analysts who have the luxury of hearing the details in an open forum with the buy-side. Less pressure is then on the analyst because everyone has heard the information in this forum. The analyst need not figure it out from a short press release and a 10-minute follow-up.

When a company supports a pre-announcement with a conference call, the odds are that the stock will decline less than it otherwise would have. The signal also goes out that management is visible in bad times as well as good, which is critical.

A Feel for When

Because of The Street's estimate hypersensitivity, pre-announcements can be a tricky business.

In the middle of its second quarter, a company in the apparel industry was on target to hit its estimates, but felt that it would miss the third quarter and had uncertainty about the full year. Management was reluctant to change anything. IR urged them to bring down the fourth quarter, even though they weren't sure. Management took our advice and the stock dropped that day.

However, it gave management a slight cushion to focus on the business and not the stock price, because the new full-year guidance was conservative. If the company had maintained the original fourth quarter estimate they would have been in a nail-biting situation for six months, wondering if estimates were too high. They would also have been in a Reg FD pickle when asked about their comfort level with annual estimates.

Getting It Right

The approach to pre-announcing must be consistent because the behavior of management oftentimes, more so than the actual event, will be factored into long-term valuation.

If a company only pre-announces when there is a material variance from the consensus estimate, then Wall Street knows that if there's no pre-release during any particular quarter, then the company is tracking toward the number. On the other hand, if there's never a pre-release and the company falls into a potential "make a quarter, miss a quarter" pattern, Wall Street will be tentative to get involved and the multiple might suffer. Therefore, to mitigate volatility and the guessing games on Wall Street, and prevent management from violating disclosure laws, a consistent pattern of pre-announcing and refining conservative guidance is recommended. Management can also use other, non-earnings-oriented releases—for example, an announcement of a new marketing initiative—to update the market on numbers.

Putting It All Together

The following case study of a real company with a fictional name engaging in the delivery stage of IR illustrates how consistent and conservative earnings guidance, combined with pre-announcements and the right message, completely engaged Wall Street via research and the morning meeting, created commission business, made management look great, and drove the multiple to premium status.

Rebuilding Credibility

Orange Foods was a large restaurant chain that had a history of inconsistent performance relative to earnings expectations. They'd hit their number and then lowered guidance regularly. Analysts were generally negative on the company because of this inconsistency, and management was universally perceived as not managing The Street properly.

Orange Foods began working with our IR team on October 1, 2001. The assessment of the problem was that the CEO was very wrapped up in communicating a growth story on par with the best of the industry, rather than acknowledging the limitations of his own concept. In reality, this company just wasn't capable of hyper-growth despite its underlying quality, reputations, and brand.

This unrealistic communication led IR to plot a more conservative strategy. On October 24, management took the advice and formally brought earnings guidance down again. Only this time, it was not a small adjustment. IR suggested lowering guidance by at least 20 percent.

The IR advisors told management that the stock would likely drop materially and, in fact, that happened. It sparked the following comments from four analysts:

(continued)

Analyst A: "Orange Foods reported Q3 earnings that were $0.01 below our estimate and more importantly revised Q4'01 and FY 2002 downward. Orange Foods cited choppy sales and margin pressure. We are revising our estimates downward although our 2002 estimate is at the top of the company's revised range. We reiterate Buy rating."

Analyst B: "We are lowering estimates and our rating to Market Perform from Buy. Orange Foods trades at 24.9x our 2002 EPS estimate and a discount to the group multiple of 30.7x"

Analyst C: "Despite drastic and likely conservative stance by management, we are maintaining our BUY rating (although lowering estimates) given that the new guidance will likely become immediately embedded in the stock—moving it to relatively attractive valuation levels."

And then there was this:

Analyst D: "We are reducing our rating from Strong Buy to Buy. Although the guidance reduction is more aggressive than we believe is necessary, we prefer to have a base to work with and be in position to only make positive changes to our EPS estimates as our analysis dictates."

Analyst D offered IR's desired result. Despite an initial 15 percent dip in the stock price, management was now viewed by the sell-side as conservative rather than aggressive, and all of the analysts revised their estimates to the exact range set by management.

Though two of the analysts lowered their rating, there seemed to be an awareness that the estimates were conservative. The helpful observation, especially to institutional investors, was that Orange Foods was trading at a discount to its peers.

Most rewarding, between the lines of what they wrote, both analysts C and D were telling investors to take a second look at the stock despite the ratings downgrade in Analyst D's case. These situations make a company interesting to Wall Street.

A month later, in November 2001, several analysts wanted management out on the road to visit investors. Why? Because the stock's risk profile had been greatly reduced, thanks to conservative guidance. The sell-side knew it and felt comfortable that management was positioned to meet or exceed estimates for the next few quarters. Because analysts' credibility is linked to the companies they bring to investors on non-deal road shows, they always look for companies with conservative estimates—that is, stocks that are Buys.

This stock was now a Buy largely because of management's own actions. The new conservative guidance was responsible for the analysts having a higher level of conviction in their writing and when talking to their sales force or to investors.

Analyst C, who took management to buyers in early November, said, "We hosted Orange Foods management in San Francisco and Denver earlier this week. Despite recently lowered FY 2002 outlook and some near-term loss of top-line momentum, we still believe that the underlying business model is robust, providing ample, high return growth for several more years. Our $0.80 FY 2002 EPS estimate is predicated on 1% comps and should prove conservative."

Conservative guidance also brought new analysts to the table because they knew their chances of being wrong on their recommendation were very low. Accordingly, another analyst, Analyst E, launched coverage in November and said, "We are enthusiastic about the longer-term prospects for the stock, but believe an increase in consensus EPS estimates will be necessary to move the stock out of its current period of malaise." We knew this was more likely than not given the guidance, meaning management and the analyst would look great as the year wore on.

In the meantime, IR felt that management was clearly delivering on expectations. All of the research reports were extremely positive in their outlook, despite the ratings, and that was what mattered most.

The buy-side worries less about the actual rating then the text. After all, what's the difference between Strong Buy, Buy, Accumulate, or Outperform? These are, as mentioned earlier, investment banking ratings designed not to offend management teams so that investment bankers can pitch their wares. The buy-side knows this, and for that reason they look more at the text and the estimates than the rating. *The moral of the story for the CEO is not to worry about any rating short-term; worry about what's written.*

To that point, on December 11, 2001, Analyst D reiterated her Buy Rating after taking the company out on the road. The analyst wrote: "Company has news to talk about. We are raising our target price to $25 and reiterating our BUY Rating." The analyst also said, "We believe that our current EPS forecasts for both Q4'01 and FY 2002 are likely to prove conservative. We are therefore raising our target P/E multiple to 30x to reflect the company's return to 30% EPS growth."

(continued)

This was the first time an analyst had increased the target multiple for the stock to 30x. Before this, Orange Foods had, despite higher earnings estimates, been trading at a discount to the group. Here the analyst argued for 5 extra multiple points on the stock, and with the 20 million shares outstanding, this was an argument that the company was worth an incremental $100 million.

On January 10, 2002, Analyst D reiterated her Buy Rating again when Orange Foods announced preliminary Q4 results, confirmed comfort with the current Q4 EPS estimate range, and established a range for Q1. In the release IR stated that: ". . . based on these preliminary results, management is comfortable with fourth quarter 2001 earnings per share guidance at the high end of the previously announced $0.14 to $0.16 range." IR also announced that Orange Foods had "established guidance for the first quarter ended March 31, 2002. Based on current visibility, management expects a first quarter 2002 earnings range of approximately $0.17 to $0.19 per share based on . . ." Also, ". . . its comfort with previously announced 2002 EPS guidance of $0.80 to $0.84 per share."

This announcement allowed IR to share another positive data point with The Street: that management was comfortable with the previously announced range. The management sell-side relationship was blossoming. Analysts who took the company on the road and recommended a Buy looked great, and investors were happy with management's certainty.

Things were even better in reality. Management had set themselves up to release several positive data points down the road. For one, they were fairly confident that they would at least hit the very high end of the fourth quarter range, although it looked as though they might beat it by a penny. Two, the earnings guidance range set for Q1'02 was very conservative with virtually no risk. Three, 2002 estimates were conservative and beatable, if business stayed the same.

Even though the First Call estimates were going up, they were going up in line with management's guidance and comfort level. Management was in full control in this case, never having to worry about the estimate, meaning fewer phone calls from concerned analysts and buysiders and more time to run the business, which was invaluable.

"Conservative" in this case meant realistically looking at the business and factors in management's control and taking a discount to that estimate for factors outside of management's control—factors that inevitably have an effect every year. These consensus estimates gave Orange Foods a safety net to deal with unforeseen circumstances.

On January 29, 2002, the company announced Q4'01 EPS a penny better than the range with which they were comfortable on January 10. They reiterated conservative guidance for the March quarter, all of fiscal 2002, and fiscal 2003 despite pressure from the sell-side to raise guidance.

Analyst E maintained the market perform but on valuation only, cited 30.2x the 2002 estimate, and wrote, "Because Orange Foods is accelerating its unit growth, margins may be under pressure, creating slightly above average risk regarding negative EPS surprises."

Analyst C maintained the Buy. "Estimates for 2002 look conservative. We believe our '02 estimate of $0.82 is conservative by at least 5%. Therefore, we continue to believe that EPS estimates will continue to be upwardly revised." But he did not raise his estimate, which was key. He followed management's guidance, so he and his firm were positioned to look good. He had a Buy, and he would look great if the company increased earnings.

Analyst A maintained the Buy Rating, arguing for 30x 2003 $1.01 estimate.

And then another nation was heard from. From a research firm with no investment banking that, in an effort to gain credibility, only carried Buy or Sell recommendations, Analyst F recommended a Sell. He wrote, and this is a Sell recommendation mind you, "We believe there is minimal earnings risk to the story but the valuation is high. Shares have rocketed back to 30x consensus. We continue to be a believer in the long term prospects of the company but would wait for a more attractive entry point." Victory for IR and management.

For the first time in awhile, Orange Foods felt it had nothing to worry about with The Street. They'd kept expectations low, left behind their traditional "make a quarter, miss a quarter" pattern, and kept several "arrows in the quiver," meaning there was a good chance guidance would increase in the future. Instead of blindly communicating aggressive guidance at the beginning of the year, management would start off lower, and as the year went on and results came in, only then would they raise guidance, and only when they were sure.

This approach would reduce risk materially and attract investor

(continued)

interest. *The company might arrive at the same actual earnings at the end of the year, but the way they got there built credibility and valuation.*

Analyst E wasn't buying it, however, and felt the chances were slightly higher than normal for an earnings miss. Behind the scenes, IR knew this analyst was at risk as Orange Foods would continue to revise upward throughout the year. Additionally, Analyst F had written what we read to be a very positive Sell report. The analyst downgraded based only on valuation and argued to buy on the dips. On the other end of the spectrum, Analysts A and C had written about how conservative management was and how consensus would go up over time. This was very powerful and a direct result of the strategy.

The next month, February 4, a recommendation from Analyst G caught IR's eye. This analyst had been following the industry for a long time and would not recommend a stock if he thought management credibility or earnings were shaky. Management's constant reiteration of conservative quarterly and yearly guidance was the difference. He raised the stock to a Buy, saying, "We have seen steady improvement in stores and believe that the company is setting itself up to steadily out-perform on an earnings basis. . . . The bar has been lowered sufficiently to provide an easy platform for management to exceed."

In March, another analyst came on board, initiated coverage and recommended a Buy. Analyst H said, "The balance sheet is sound and financing is in place, allowing management the ability to execute their growth plan without raising additional equity."

This phrase came verbatim from the conference call script. *By providing the analysts with specific, reliable, and quotable information, IR made it easier for the analysts to write what the company wanted them to write, and management took control of its Wall Street destiny.*

Another analyst covering the stock, Analyst I, wrote a 30-page re-port on the company with an Outperform Rating. "Orange Foods is currently trading at 24.1x our 2002 estimates (stock traded down 20% recently), a premium valuation, yet one that reflects investor confi-dence. . . ." This quote was great and showed a 360-degree turn on Wall Street. Whereas prior to our engagement with the company, ana-lysts argued that Orange Foods should trade at a discount to the group, they were now arguing for a premium valuation to the group. This stance implied a lower cost of capital, which was key.

Obviously, at this point, the strategy was really taking hold. All of the analysts were speaking very highly of the company regardless of their ratings. *They knew management's conservative stance on guidance would ultimately make them look good.* Additionally, the quote from Analyst I showed IR that *management was being rewarded with a higher multiple because they understood how to manage The Street.*

In early April, Orange Foods announced that it was comfortable with the high end of the previously announced range of $0.17 to $0.19 per share for the first quarter ended March 31, 2002. On April 23, 2002, Orange Foods beat that range and announced $0.20 as the quarterly result. Management knew in early April that $0.20 per share was very likely, but not guaranteed, and reiterated comfort with the $0.17 to $0.19 per share range to maximize the announcement and generate two positive data points versus one. One of those announcements, possibly generating the $0.20 per share, would be perceived as an upside surprise relative to expectations, although if they earned $0.19 it would have been viewed positively as well. If $0.20 was the result, analysts would have a boost and Orange would have created two opportunities for analysts to share good news with their sales force.

In fact, $0.20 was the ultimate result after the auditors had closed the books. Analysts raised numbers by $0.01 (the "overage") and estimates were revised upward. But management kept a tight leash and conveyed specific guidance for the upcoming quarter, the full year 2002, and 2003. At this point, the stock hit $26, up from $17 in October, just six months before.

IR also found that the company now had more buy-and-hold investors than traders who fed off volatility. The new investor base loved the slow and steady philosophy. Moreover, the First Call numbers were still at the range set by management, keeping the stock interesting to everyone on Wall Street.

In May, two new sell-side firms came in with coverage. Both rated Orange Foods a Long-Term Buy. More analysts were attracted to Orange Foods because they knew management was being conservative. If these analysts thought First Call was too high, they would have thought twice about risking their reputations and publishing on the stock. If they did, it would likely have been a lower rating, and the conviction level most likely would have been suspect. In June another firm initiated coverage with a Buy recommendation.

(continued)

On July 2, Orange Foods raised its guidance for the second quarter from $0.19 to $0.21 to $0.21 to $0.23 per share versus First Call, which was $0.21. The company also increased full-year 2002 guidance to $0.85 to $0.88 per share and 2003 guidance to $1.01 to $1.05 per share. On July 3, Bloomberg's Starmine service published a report targeting Orange Foods as one of several companies with the propensity to surprise on the upside. On July 19, another analyst rated Orange Foods a new Buy.

On July 23, 2002, Orange Foods posted earnings of $0.23 per share, achieving the high end of the range. Again they reiterated conservative 2002 and 2003 guidance and encouraged analysts not to move numbers. Analysts followed suit.

By the end of the year, of the 10 analysts who published Orange Foods research, 70 percent maintained some form of Buy rating versus 30 percent prior to this strategic IR initiative. All continued to be within the desired First Call range, and the analysts benefited greatly as Orange Foods rounded out the year beating numbers for three consecutive quarters.

Commissions were generated for the sell-side, returns were generated for the buy-side, and credibility (and plenty of it) was generated for the CEO & CFO. Based on this performance, these executives would be candidates to eventually move on to bigger public companies and really build their careers and personal wealth.

After initiating strategic IR efforts, Orange Foods' management team took control of Wall Street and repositioned its stock conservatively relative to expectations. As the stocks outperformed, the analysts looked smart, the buy-side was happy, and management was perceived by investors as savvy, thereby raising its credibility. The company stayed the course and consistently matched or overdelivered on what they promised. Finally, this had vast, positive effects on media coverage and employee morale.

DEFINITION AND DELIVERY

There are many nuances to strategic IR that come together in the delivery stage. The content, method, and timing of disclosures is a culmination of uncovering value, building or redefining the investment thesis, and targeting the landscape in a conservative manner. IR starts with honing in on the definition and moves on to polish a delivery that is effective, as well as time- and cost-efficient for management.

CHAPTER 21

From Delivery to Dialogue

Each of the three parts of IR—Definition, Delivery, and Dialogue—overlaps in a cycle that supports management's objective of continuously defining and effectively communicating its value to The Street. A lot of intelligent planning and effort are needed for a company to build bridges with the institutional community, and once these bridges are established, the company should do everything it can to maintain them. A misguided estimate, a misspoken word, or a mishandled situation can break a company's valuation in one shot.

Dialogue continues the conversations that were positioned in the definition stage and planted in the delivery stage and helps companies react to events on a day-to-day basis. The dialogue stage calls on IR to be flexible and adapt quickly to the ebbs and flows of the capital markets.

The following chapters cover dialogue and include ways in which IR should help management:

■ *Maintain and build relationships with the sell- and buy-sides.* Maintaining relationships can only come once management understands the delicate interaction on The Street between companies, the sell-side, and the buy-side. Once established, however, effective ties to The Street should position management to build long-term credibility. New relationships are also a part of this section as IR reactively manages inquiries from investors and analysts who have shown an interest in the business.

■ *Meet The Street.* The second part of Dialogue includes non-deal road shows (one-on-ones), company visits, teach-ins, and conferences.

■ *Conduct effective event management,* which discusses information flow and how the proper information is critical to plotting short- or long-term strategy or reacting to positive or negative events. In this case, the issues are not only third-party information systems but also investor perception and feedback.

■ *Adopt the banker mentality.* This thinking, which focuses on building shareholder value, aligns IR's thought processes with the CEO's and can proactively assess value creation strategies, like share repurchases and dividends, not to mention the implications of a strategic acquisition. In this case, IR isn't necessarily impeding on the finance function; it is actually educating the CEO and CFO how best to position an initiative like this and how to communicate it over time. Part of that job is searching for precedent in market reaction to any of these events so when the decision is made, shareholder reaction is likely known in advance.

KEEPING THE COURSE

Having the right relationships can ease a company's dialogue with the investment community. Management and IR can continually garner feedback, choose a strategy, and address difficult situations in a manner that Wall Street is accustomed to. Accordingly, because best practices ensure that management's communication pattern is in tune with what Wall Street is expecting, benefit of the doubt is earned. That stored-up value can come in handy in difficult times when, for example, a complicated earnings miss might need to be communicated. Analysts and portfolio managers can be far more forgiving if management had a preexisting pattern of communicating effectively and transparently.

Regardless of specific situations, though, if IR knows its objectives and has relationships that help support those objectives, then the long-term journey should run a bit smoother. To keep the course, IR needs a prize on which to keep its eye, and it starts with a question:

"Regardless of the event or issue, how can it be handled so that long-term equity value is enhanced or preserved?"

If this is the over-riding goal, rather than what will happen to the stock price, the right decision will almost always be made.

BUMPY ROAD AHEAD

The dialogue stage can be the most turbulent, as management and IR deal with everything that comes their way. On any given day, stocks can rise and fall with no real explanation, so all companies must be in a position to react. Anchoring that process is IR, and that person must have enough capital markets knowledge to discern an emergency from a simple day-to-day fluctuation when there are more sellers than buyers.

The dialogue stage is continuous, but different for each company. For example, a company that is growing at 20 percent with a 10 P/E, with limited sell-side coverage and institutional ownership, can be very conservative with regard to setting financial expectations, because Wall Street is basically disengaged and the stock is interesting (based on its valuation) without promising too much. But a company with a 50 P/E, in hyper-growth mode, with a lot of analyst coverage must be very particular in the dialogue stage, maintaining a constant flow of communication that allows analysts and portfolio managers to make their investment decisions. Conservative financial guidance is certainly a part of that, but for the company is that highly valued, accelerating earnings are already discounted into the stock in all likelihood, and other information about future strategy might be needed. For the investment community, this would go a long way in mathematically supporting the current stock price.

A CONTINUOUS PROCESS

IR in the dialogue stage is a continuous redefining and repositioning of the company and its performance. IR needs to manage this process and make it as simple and time effective as possible, including providing management with knowledge, experience, and options when engaging the investment community.

CHAPTER 22

Maintaining and Building Relationships

The capital markets, like any business, are driven by relationships, and there is no better way to maximize the process for everyone involved than a long-term commitment to transparency and consistency. Investors depend on analysts, analysts rely on management, and management teams rely on investors.

Successful long-term interactions between companies and the capital markets are not one-sided and depend greatly on building mutual trust. This mating dance between company and analyst or company and portfolio manager is at the core of building that trust. Over time, if each party understands and respects one another's job, shareholders are positioned to come out on top.

MUTUAL RESPECT AND TRUST

To build long-term relationships, strategic IR must respect the interaction and trust that the analyst maintains with both investors and management teams. If senior management is unaware of the importance of this relationship, IR should lay out concrete examples of how a lack of understanding in this area can cost the CEO and shareholders millions.

One way IR can protect the relationship is to continually educate analysts, through honest and frequent communication. In that spirit, IR might suggest to senior management that a schedule of earnings pre-announcements would heighten and improve the ongoing dialogue. It would ensure that the market is updated eight rather than four times per year, and more frequent information means less risk for an analyst. That's protection brought on by IR policy.

197

Management may find that the analyst is equally motivated to return that protection. This subtle protection can be as basic as the analyst being upfront with management about her rating system and how it works, price targets, estimate changes, and under what circumstances she might downgrade the stock. This in turn helps the CEO and CFO to better understand the analyst and her job and makes it less likely that management will take the analyst's action personally, which always plays poorly in public forums.

To that point, IR professionals see many management teams that are overly focused on their day-to-day stock prices when they should actually be focused on their businesses. What these management teams need to realize is that stocks go up and down based on many factors, from a shift in an investor's position to a strategist's call on the economy. But because analysts hold such sway with the investment community, their negative opinions can grate loudest on a CEO's nerves. In our experience, management teams that take analyst downgrades personally are only setting themselves up to look bad.

Ultimately, analysts have a job to do, to give unbiased opinions, right or wrong. A CEO who doesn't understand that fact, or understand that analysts' opinions are part of the double-edged sword of being public, should probably be working for a private company. IR must educate management personnel to check their emotions and make them understand that the only way to counter analyst's negative opinions is to consistently produce solid earnings relative to expectations.

Below is an example where the CEO's lack of understanding positioned the company in a very negative light.

Building bridges from IR and management to Wall Street can prevent this type of unnecessary and unproductive antagonism. It's harmful to everyone, hurts shareholders, and would have been a non-event had the CEO been better educated when it came to the analyst's job and the way perceptions are created on Wall Street. Management should have ignored the downgrade and focused on running the business. If management was right, the analyst would have been proven wrong eventually anyway.

MAINTAINING AND BUILDING RELATIONSHIPS— THE SELL-SIDE

IR should have a plan to improve its relationships with key sell-side analysts while cultivating relationships with new ones. The first step in this process is to establish policies that position the company as more forthcoming and transparent, which in turn reduces risk for analysts. The key to actually im-

A June 19, 2003, article in *The Wall Street Journal* portrayed the consequences of not establishing a trusting relationship between management and The Street and shows a lack of understanding when it comes to the IR Dialogue stage. It cited the case of Fresh Del Monte Produce Inc. when an analyst at BB&T downgraded the company's stock, citing risks from litigation and her perception of threats to the core business. On the day of her downgrade, the stock fell more than 10 percent.

As the *Journal* tells it: "In a February 2003 conference call with the company, the analyst asked a question about pricing and the company's chief executive said: 'Let me tell you one thing, please. You are covering us without our will and we would not like you to ask questions on this conference call.' When the analyst asked why, the CEO said: 'We don't want you to ask questions. You can make your own conclusion. You can cover us the way you want, but you have not been covering us in any objective way and we thank you for being on this call, but we don't like to answer your question.'"

The article stated that the analyst was surprised by this and even more surprised when "Fresh Del Monte named her in a lawsuit a month later. A part of a complicated dispute with the company's former owners, Del Monte Fresh filed a suit in State Supreme Court in New York in March, charging that certain business people were part of a 'conspiracy' that caused the company's stock to drop precipitously."

plementing these policies, however, is management's understanding of why they are so important. In other words, if analysts understand that they will get honest information on a systematic basis, their career risk and their firm's risk is materially reduced.

Policies that help maintain a solid relationship include conducting conference calls after the market closes when material positive or negative events occur. This allows the analyst to understand the events and ask questions while the market is closed and formulate an educated opinion. The policies can also include regularly scheduled pre-announcements, which ensure timely information at the end of each quarter but before the earnings release. Finally, extra tables in a company's press release that describe historical drivers of the business would be helpful.

Ultimately, IR and management must work together to understand analyst concerns—what information they need and when they need it—and out of that process better communication will likely result. Better communication can often buy management an edge in getting its point of view across to Wall Street.

IR should seek out new analysts as well, and the timeliness of this outreach may depend on the company's relative valuation. For example, if the price of a company's stock has been forced down because of a temporary setback, each multiple compression and each dollar drop may represent an opportunity for analysts looking for ideas. For that reason, IR must make it a point to constantly educate all the analysts in advance rather than wait for a problem to reach out. If that course is taken, the likelihood increases that an analyst will move quickly with a recommendation. Without that groundwork, the analyst would likely take many weeks, if not more, to learn about the company, visit management, and talk to vendors and consumers before gaining the comfort level to publish. Therefore, as part of the relationship process, IR must be aware of analyst movement around The Street, investment banks that are starting an industry practice, or analysts who are free to publish on multiple groups of stocks.

Additionally, an investment bank occasionally drops research coverage altogether. This move can be the result of many factors, including a company that doesn't seem to fit into a particular coverage universe or a company that doesn't fit with the philosophy of the investment bank's organization (another company might be a better fit with research/trading/and investment banking). Finally, stocks that languish are also candidates for the revolving door.

IR must be aware of why analysts drop stocks and attempt to prevent it. Because most analysts are looking for something that will lead them to believe the stock will move either up or down, it's simply a matter of engaging the analyst and conservatively communicating the story. But if there's no news to tell, IR has to be clever. By feeding analysts industry information like new products or promising consumer trends, IR gives the analyst incremental intelligence, which can be a huge help. Why would an analyst want to stop that flow of information by dropping coverage, even if the company isn't the most exciting?

The next chapter covers in-person meetings, but just in terms of information sharing, analyst tracking, and policies, IR has many ways in which it can add value to the process.

MAINTAINING AND BUILDING RELATIONSHIPS— BUY-SIDE

The buy-side approach to relationships is essentially the same as the sell-side approach, but involves a bit more guesswork and a dramatically longer list.

IR can never know on a daily basis who actually owns stock in his or her company. That exact information is only issued four times per year, about six weeks after the close of each quarter.

IR should take this information, identify the contact information for the appropriate portfolio manager, and create a master distribution list that will be adjusted and updated each quarter. Regardless of what accounts on the buy-side own the company's stock at any given time, however, they should all be on the distribution in an effort to educate them on an ongoing basis. IR's job is to fight for shelf space with the buy-side, and regardless of ownership, portfolio managers should always have a flow of information.

Unlike the sell-side list, which may only involve 10 to 20 names at any given time, institutional buyers can be segmented into multiple categories. They can be growth or value buyers or some variation on those themes. In addition, they can be mutual funds or hedge funds with long- or short-term orientation. IR's job is to constantly create relationships with these buyers and make sure that they receive a steady stream of company information.

Again, as stocks move up and down, any one of these groups can gain in importance. In other words, while the stock is increasing, IR shouldn't overlook educating value investors whom the company may need if unforeseen events sharply decrease valuation. Such knowledge comes too late if IR waits for the negative event to happen before understanding who the value players are and educating them on the company story.

HANDLING AND PRIORITIZING NEW INQUIRIES

Although not highly strategic, handling and processing inquiries is extremely important. First, this activity brings structure to the process so management isn't just reacting to requests. Second, dealing with new inquiries efficiently saves money and time. For example, having the tools to identify callers prevents management teams from spending time with the wrong investors or with potential investors who misrepresent themselves. Bob James might call one afternoon and request an hour with management. Mr. James seems to have all the right credentials as he manages over $1 billion for a reputable mutual fund. The only problem, as it turns out, is that Mr. James is the largest shareholder of the company's competitor. Not that the meeting is a waste, because Bob James could be converted into a shareholder. Our point is that it's important to know who management is talking to and prioritizing those conversations because Bob James might be meeting only to protect his investment in the competitor. It comes down to access to software that can quickly and easily identify the financial caller, his fund, the amount of money he manages, and his recent behavior in the sector. Before any calls are returned or any meetings are taken, the company should know the answers to those questions.

SHORT SELLERS

Unfortunately, IR relationships should extend to those groups that don't necessarily have the company's best interests at heart. At the top of that list are short sellers, who bet against the company's outlook and hope that the share price will go down. Although normally short-term in nature, these bets are nonetheless infuriating to most management teams as emotions get the best of senior executives. Therefore, it's important to identify short sellers whenever possible and counsel management on the best course of action for dealing with them.

An SEC rule is that short sellers must report their holdings and through various databases. The Short Interest Ratio (SIR) records the short interest outstanding over the average daily volume of shares traded. If that number is 2, for example, that means it would take two full days of average trading for short sellers to cover—that is, buy back the shares they borrowed and sold. If this number goes up, a company can look at it as a group betting against them, although many look at a high SIR as bullish because of the built-in buying if fundamentals take a turn for the positive.

If short sellers are active in a company's stock, IR first and foremost should counsel management as to what the approach should be. A cool and detached mind-set is preferable. Waging a public battle trying to prove them wrong is almost always a losing game.

In fact, according to a January 26, 2003, article in *The New York Times*, Professor Owen A. Lamont, associate professor of finance at the University of Chicago's graduate school of business, analyzed the returns of 270 companies that waged public battles with short sellers. He found that their stocks lagged the market by 2.34 percent in each of the 12 months after the battles began. The study, which covers 25 years, not only found that the companies involved were generally overpriced, but also found that the short sellers were consistently right. Professor Lamont went on to divide the tactics used against short sellers into three types:

1. Belligerent statements which include claims of a conspiracy
2. Taking legal action against the short sellers
3. Undertaking technical maneuvers to prevent short selling (like urging shareholders to register shares in their own name to prevent borrowing)

The study included companies like Conseco, Samsonite, and Micro-Strategy, and more recently Allied Capital, MBIA, Farmer Mac, and Pre-Paid Legal Services. What seems to be the common thread is that when stocks begin to fall, "companies, investors, and even regulators often attack short sellers."

"But short sellers are not the enemy of investors. The fact is, short sellers actually reduce volatility in the market. Their selling helps keep stocks from flying too high, and when they close out their trades, the buying often gives beleaguered stocks support."

Therefore, with historical proof that companies locking horns with short sellers is the wrong move, IR might question pursuing the relationship at all.

- Staying close to shorts and finding out their arguments allows management to confront issues head-on in conference calls and earnings releases.
- Short interest can be bullish and useful, because short sellers invariably cover (buy the stock back), and when they do, the stock will likely be "squeezed" upward.
- Shorts can often force irrational management teams to be realistic about guidance. However, some management teams have actually promised a higher earnings growth rate in an attempt to scare the shorts away. This tactic only adds risk to the stock and is totally the wrong way to go.

Big Muscles, a company in the fitness sector, had a significant short interest position. Through some reconnaissance IR was able to discover that the shorts were betting against Big Muscle for four specific reasons: the core product was 95 percent of revenues, the market was approaching full penetration, their financing of customers was a perceived risk, and the cost of their primary source of promotion—TV advertising—was rising.

The shorts' presence also signaled a lack of faith in management and fueled the CEO, along with IR, to discern what might have been broken in the business and fix it. Big Muscles ultimately lowered its financial guidance to The Street, admitted some mistakes, and articulated the plan to get back on track. Over time the shorts covered, and the company's valuation improved.

IR is the ideal group to craft a short seller strategy. As a third party outside of the executive suite, IR will likely be less emotional about hearing the short story and know best how to use those points. Though bringing down overly optimistic guidance can often solve the short seller problem, IR's job is to dig deeper, discover the underlying short argument, and make sure each point has a counterpoint in every communication to The Street.

Ultimately, maintaining relationships with the capital markets is about sharing information and laying the groundwork for introductions when out-of-the-ordinary events occur. That might include meeting growth versus value investors once operations pick up. Similarly, it could mean targeting value investors as the stock decreases and short positions grow. These value investors will be looking for a turn in the business, knowing that when it does, built-in buying pressure will exist as short sellers cover their open positions.

CHAPTER 23

Meeting The Street

Whereas the Delivery stage of IR dealt with basic disclosures like earnings releases and conference calls, the Dialogue stage includes in-person events geared toward interaction with the sell-side and the buy-side. Through these events, most savvy management teams are able to maintain a sound relationship with The Street and offer systematic information that benefits existing analysts and portfolio managers as well as those who are new to the story.

THE NON-DEAL ROAD SHOW

At the top of the list of these events is the non-deal road show. This is a series of one-on-one meetings with the buy-side over a one-day period or over multiple days in several cities. As the "non-deal" aspect of the name implies, management is not raising money at the time (unlike an IPO or secondary offering). It's simply a forum to update money managers on the company's progress.

The non-deal road show is the most effective forum to develop interest in a stock because the portfolio manager can ask questions, look management in the eye, and share concerns in a private setting. This is very different from a well-attended conference call where a portfolio manager might not even be able to ask a question, let alone five or six like she wants. The one-on-one meeting usually lasts 45 minutes to an hour, and there can be anywhere from five to eight meetings in a given day.

Management and its IR department should plan the year in advance and specify which dates work best for the non-deal road show. Four times per year, directly after each quarterly conference call, is a good start, although management may want to layer in one or two other opportunities. The reason post–conference call road shows are best is basically for Reg FD purposes. Because all new company information and financials will have been released and discussed on the call, management will be free to talk about the latest developments and do so without disclosure risk.

However, circumstances may cause management to hit the road intra-quarter. A small acquisition may have to be explained or the stock may have fallen without any change to the underlying financials. Under either of these scenarios, management can elect to meet with the buy-side. However, if any chance exists that a material initiative will be discussed, a press release announcing that initiative should be distributed prior to the meetings.

With dates in hand and topics fresh, IR must then decide which buy-side accounts to target. This task can be daunting for IR, but a capital markets perspective makes it easy.

Analysts increase their compensation levels in a variety of ways. They can be good stock pickers, publish volumes of research, or call 300 portfolio managers every month with their latest idea. One of the biggest determinants of compensation, however, is the non-deal road show: delivering management teams to the buy-side on a regular basis. This helps the buy-side cost-effectively meet management teams and of course helps the company tell its story. It also helps the sell-side, because after the meeting, if the portfolio manager likes the company and management, and buys the stock, he or she will usually buy it through the sponsoring investment bank.

This outcome is much more likely for smaller, over-the-counter stocks, where only a handful of sell-side investment banks make a market. In that scenario, if Fidelity were to buy the stock they'd have to go through one of the handful of firms anyway. However, with NYSE-listed companies, the buy-side will find a way to pay back the sponsoring firm in all likelihood. For example, if Fidelity ends up buying stock in a company that Wachovia Securities brought through town on the non-deal roadshow, but didn't execute the trade with Wachovia for whatever reason, odds are that another large trade will come Wachovia's way. More than ever, with investment banking fees eliminated from analyst compensation, these commissions are invaluable.

Therefore, in the case of a non-deal road show, a company should never target the buy-side directly (unless there is no current analyst coverage) and certainly never use a third-party, outside IR agency looking to take ownership of the process. Unfortunately, this scenario happens all the time, and results from a lack of capital markets expertise on management's part and a total lack of expertise on the part of the outside IR agency. Whenever possible the company should enlist the sell-side to shepherd the process and create an economic event. That economic event, in this case, is commissions that will invariably be steered to the sponsoring bank. Multiplied by 300 non-deal road shows annually, the economics become fairly powerful.

Once the company has determined which analyst or analysts will put the one-on-ones together, IR must ensure that the meeting schedule is optimized, which means double-checking the quality of the appointments that the sell-side has made and adding any others that may seem appropriate. Because of the lack of a relationship, the sell-side can sometimes leave critical meetings off the agenda. Through its own search, IR must have the appropriate investors in each city at hand, and insert one or two as the schedule permits. Once those meetings are set, however, IR should make sure that the sponsoring bank gets credit because it will likely lead to a solid relationship and commission business down the road.

IR that has this perspective, always looking to create paydays for the sell-side, is much more inclined to garner coverage and have a better, more interactive relationship with the analyst. This latter point can mean the difference in an upgrade or a downgrade or simply receiving the benefit of the doubt in a situation where an analyst might otherwise reduce the rating.

If the road show is in multiple cities, IR must quarterback the process. We would suggest giving the larger investment banks New York and Boston (one city for each analyst), and if the company intends to visit Philadelphia, Baltimore, Chicago, Denver, or the West Coast, split those dates with the remaining sell-siders. This approach allows the company to keep an auction atmosphere with multiple sell-side firms vying for time. It also serves to create an economic event for every analyst involved. If, for example, management visited every city with its two largest investment banks, the smaller analysts wouldn't have much incentive to recommend the stock and might become disengaged. Make no mistake that investment banks exist to make money, and for many smaller firms with no notable investment banking business, the non-deal road show is a primary source of their top-lines. Therefore, when orchestrating the road show process, IR should maximize the event, which tends to maximize value over the long run.

One more point on choosing investment banks for road shows. Through a summary of the trading reports of the investment banks, IR departments can see on a week-to-week basis which investment banks are trading the highest volumes in their stock. Year-to-date results might show SG Cowen to have traded the most and Piper Jaffray close behind. However, Lehman Brothers also covers the stock, is constantly tenth or below in trading volume, yet is always asking to escort the company to premier cities like New York or Boston. Our view is that an investment bank must earn that right, and trading volume can be a great indicator of the investment bank's willingness to support a stock. In this hypothetical example, IR could split New York and Boston with Cowen and Piper, and give Lehman Brothers a secondary city until it shows improving numbers.

TEACH-INS

Another important event that all companies should adopt is the teach-in. Before explaining the actual teach-in, however, a review of how analysts launch coverage on stocks would be helpful.

After discussing the investment idea with the director of research and after writing his or her report, a time is usually scheduled with the institutional sales force to present the idea, almost always after market hours. The analyst steps to the podium and makes his or her argument on why the company and the stock are interesting, and a question-and-answer session ensues.

As stated in earlier chapters, a lot rides on each stock pick. Certainly the analyst's reputation with the buy-side and the analyst's reputation with his or her own sales force is at stake. Also, those stakes move up a notch if the analyst's last pick went awry, with investors losing money and the sales force losing points with buy-side accounts.

For that reason, management should actually be part of the teach-in when a new analyst launches coverage. This is not only a show of support for the analyst by management (impressing his or her bosses), but it can temper any existing ill will with the sales force, particularly if the analyst's last pick was a poor one.

In this scenario, the analyst would conduct the teach-in like any other stock pick, but management could conduct its own brief presentation after the fact, or simply be available for the question-and-answer session.

This IR technique can markedly help the analyst in terms of credibility and compensation and invigorate the sales force to call accounts and recommend the stock. It gives the sales force increased motivation if they are able to make a call and say "we met with management today," which is not very common.

A teach-in takes the risk out of a launch and maximizes the event for everyone involved. In addition, because management will be in town after the teach-in anyway, IR should schedule, along with the launching analyst, a series of one-on-one meetings in that city to further maximize the time and money spent traveling.

CONFERENCES

Throughout the year, numerous investment banks hold large investor conferences. Often centered around industry themes, they attract many important buy-side players. Management teams should, selectively, make themselves available for these sell-side gatherings to present or even fill slots in an industry panel or topical discussion.

This effort creates awareness and helps investors better understand the company. Management's presence also supports the analyst and the investment bank by indirectly generating a payday. After all, analysts are paid on commissions, and a great conference line-up leads to high buy-side attendance and increased commissions.

Therefore, IR should track which conferences are well attended and by whom and which are not. To that point, if there are six people in the room, it may not be worth the CEO's time, unless those six people are from Fidelity, Capital Research, T. Rowe Price, Dreyfus, Trust Company of The West, and State Street Asset Management. Similarly, there could be 50 "investors" in the room, but they are individual brokers offered a free lunch to fill the seats. IR's responsibility is to screen and prioritize management's time, and conference planning must be highly selective.

One last point: to maximize management's time at the event, IR can use the sponsoring investment bank to set up one-on-ones, and then utilize another investment bank to set up the following day should management elect to stay. This could be in-filled with media opportunities so that the time and money spent to attend the conference are maximized with events that the CEO would have to travel again to do.

INVESTOR DAYS

Investor days that feature tours of the company's operating facilities and a schedule of meetings with senior management members can be highly successful methods of building bonds with the investment community. Not only do these days get the investor or analyst into the business environment, but they allow management to describe the business with visual references.

For example, a CEO can take a group of analysts and portfolio managers through his headquarters to explain a new initiative. Upon seeing the plan and the workers executing the plan, they are much more likely to have a better recollection of the concept, versus seeing it explained on a presentation slide. After the tour, the head of design might speak about plans, trends, and the competitive market. Then, off to marketing and distribution, where the products are physically packed and stored.

These visits also provide the investment community with the opportunity to meet company personnel beyond the CEO and CFO, which is especially helpful for a company that may not have the most dynamic executive at the helm, but has an exciting and enthusiastic team of professionals and employees and a depth of management that puts the company in a positive light.

All of these images are highly valuable for the sell- and buy-sides and tend to stay in their minds. For this reason alone, companies should plan one or two investor days per year and open the day to new and existing investors. Finally, the event should be Web cast to ensure that material information isn't being selectively disclosed.

TRADE SHOWS

Trade shows are a good arena for management to meet various stakeholders and capital markets players and usually offer a more relaxed environment than an industry conference. To make the most of the event and all the attendees, IR should engineer a cocktail hour or dinner, sponsored by one of the sell-side analysts in attendance to foster better relationships. The company gets the visibility, the buy-side attends another meeting where he or she can access management, the analyst gets credit for the event and positions his or her firm for a commission payday, and IR slips away, knowing the job was well done.

CANCELING AN APPEARANCE

Management should never cancel a scheduled appearance. Management teams sometimes become aware, just before a road show or panel, of a problem that will hit their earnings. The instinct is to not attend, thinking no news was better news. But if a company cancels a scheduled appearance, The Street assumes something is wrong. As a result, even if in actuality everything is fine, the stock is likely to take a hit.

This scenario happened with a company in the branded consumer products sector prior to its scheduled appearance at a conference. IR strongly advised them to pre-announce the earnings miss on the morning of the conference and still show up for their presentation, which they did. Their stock took a small hit, but after they stood up and faced a room full of analysts and portfolio managers to discuss the issues, the dust quickly settled. Management also earned significant credibility points.

THE PRESENTATION

IR must always have up-to-date presentation slides with which to attend these types of meetings. Unfortunately, after numerous uses and revisions, these presentations can often evolve into something that's long and unmanageable, ending the interaction process with Wall Street before it begins. For this reason, IR needs to keep the presentation fresh and current and practice delivering it in no more than 25 minutes. This time limit holds for one-on-ones, but these days, some sell-side conferences allow only 15 minutes and in some cases, 10. It goes without saying then that the Wall Street time crunch is behind this compression, and most analysts and portfolio managers believe that if management can't present its business in 15 minutes, then there is a communications problem.

Contrary to this thinking, management teams sometimes show up with a 55-page slide presentation that lists each company's product, backed up by pages of the technology and management bios. This sure sign of an inexperienced management team will more likely than not result in the analyst or portfolio manager tuning out, politely showing management the door, and not buying the stock. Unfortunately, snap judgments are made every day on Wall Street, and IR's job is to know in advance how the sell- and the buy-sides are used to seeing management presentations. In other words, IR must package the product for Wall Street, or the result will often be reflected in valuation.

In addition, presentation skills are important because The Street naturally judges one management team relative to the next. Management should be enthusiastic and dynamic, yet avoid being promotional. In addition, companies should always refrain from addressing valuation. In other words, hearing management make an argument that its stock is undervalued is a turnoff. This is the domain of the professionals in the audience, and conclusions on valuation should be left to them. Management's job is to generate financial performance and deliver results in the most consistent and transparent manner possible.

Below is a suggested outline for the presentation slides and is by no means the only way to construct them. However, it might be a successful guide in tailoring a presentation for a specific company. A solid presentation should include:

Market data: stock symbol, exchange, current price, and shares outstanding, which leads the viewer to market capitalization.

Company overview: the description of the business, management and experience, market position or niche, and historic EPS growth.

Strategic initiatives: the plan for earnings growth.

Company financials: a snapshot of the numbers with quarterly, year-to-date, and historical (last three years) information. It also includes gross margins and operating margins (sometimes by segment), and current status of the balance sheet. For companies that use significant debt to expand their business, this might be interest coverage, while debt-free businesses, like retailers, might profile the current ratio (current assets divided by current liabilities).

Key investment highlights: The five or six points on why the company is a good investment.

MEETING MANAGEMENT IN BAD TIMES TOO

No matter the forum, nothing builds management credibility more than showing up and facing the music when things are bad. When an event occurs that pushes the stock down, management should consider going on the road with an analyst to visit institutions or attending a conference.

This might seem counterintuitive, but the action itself can add to long-term valuation. A portfolio manager who knows that management will be available during bad times knows he'll be able to have access and get the information needed to make a decision. Management teams that hide when times are bad may never get a second chance with an experienced investor. Also, in many of these meetings, the audience will be welcoming, because they'll likely see the drop in the stock as an opportunity and potentially soak up some of the share supply as its being dumped on the market. Therefore, as unpleasant as it may seem, organizing a road show when the company may be at its worst can make management look its best.

THE STREET AND THE COMPANY

Meeting The Street is about building and maintaining the dialogue, in good times and bad. A solid relationship between management and the investment community can only help a company when the inevitable, unpredictable event occurs.

CHAPTER 24

Event Management

As part of the Dialogue stage, IR must react appropriately to positive and negative events, in order to enhance or preserve valuation at any given time. To best anticipate and negotiate the inevitable, IR must (a) always have the proper information available in the form of market data and market feedback, (b) have a relationship with the CEO based on respect so that management can absorb and take direction from IR depending on the circumstances, and (c) help management plan its short- and long-term strategies with an understanding of the potential effects on the market.

INFORMATION FLOW

In order to make an informed decision based on unexpected events, IR must have the proper information available at all times. For internal IR at a larger company, this means subscribing directly to third-party information vendors. A smaller company can depend on agencies for these services. In addition to the important real-time data, IR must also gather investor perception and feedback, and combining the two should make any tough decision that much easier.

Third-Party Information Systems

In order to monitor the markets and the unexpected events that invariably occur, IR must have access to the following:

- *Stock quotes:* Not only the company's day-to-day stock price movements, but its peer group's. This is the first line of defense in keeping an eye on market perception of an individual company or group.

- *First Call*: A company can gauge the effectiveness of its message and guidance by checking analyst research and recommendations and, of course, the First Call earnings estimates. IR should also gather research reports on competitors and the sector, and process any new information that surfaces.
- *Trading*: The Autex Rankings gather trading volume in stocks by investment bank and shows which banks are active in any particular stock at any given time. These figures can be an indicator of company or sector expertise, or the banks' willingness to commit capital on the trading desk.
- *Ownership*: IR needs to extract, from shareholder databases, a list of the new owners, existing owners who have added to their positions, and those who have sold their stock. This is mandatory when performing a cross-ownership analysis for targeting, particularly when a stock is dropping.
- *Conference call transcripts*: Transcripts are the best way to track material events in the industry.

IR should package this information for management, so they can glimpse a quarterly scorecard of sorts and form an idea of how the company is being perceived against its peers.

Garnering Feedback

Part of that packaged information should also include old-fashioned buy- and sell-side feedback. This information, in the form of informal conversations, estimate revisions or recommendation changes, or the actual buying or selling of stock, is the purest form of judgment. But feedback sometimes can be tough to find.

Analysts

In terms of the sell-side, even a 15-minute conversation during earnings season can be asking a lot, so IR must come across as an informed peer who can talk credibly about valuation and industry events. Also, if IR can be a gate-keeper to a deeper relationship with management, that will also earn respect. Ultimately, IR must use whatever leverage it has to engage the analyst and extract the market's current perception. An inexperienced subordinate, with a checklist list of questions will almost always be ineffective.

Investors

Investors purchase stocks because they believe the financial outlook is positive relative to the current price, and they sell stocks when they believe the opposite is true.

Investors with large stakes in companies have a particular interest that the company do well financially, and this objective gives IR an opportunity to reach into the thought processes of the buy-side and garner any perception that's relevant, such as the investment highlights as the PM sees them.

Information from an institution that has not purchased stock in the company, but is buying the competition, is equally valuable to IR. Obtaining this investor's insights can lead to uniquely helpful and constructive criticism. These are tough-to-access, unique opinions because the investor is obviously interested and bullish on the sector, but has some reservations about the company in question. Perhaps the investor is harboring reservations about the success of the business or even skepticism about management.

Short Sellers

Similarly, IR should always be aware of short interest and why certain investors are betting that the company won't live up to expectations. Although short sellers are tough investors for IR to pin down directly, even the second-hand story can give management the ammunition to prepare a counter argument.

Wall Street's Hot Buttons

In any given sector at any given time, companies are doing business and generating news. Because the stock market moves on how that news might affect financial performance, it's safe to say that there is always something to react to in the IR department. Examples are foreign exchange rates, a pending port strike, back to school's shaping of inventory levels, a shift in demographics, a thrust in teen spending, or the overcrowding of a market that stalls expansion and suppresses growth. IR should always be prepared to tailor dialogue based on the issues affecting the company's sector.

This awareness is especially important when drafting the conference call script and deciding which issues require emphasis or even inclusion.

Another method of handling unforeseen events is to launch a *pre-emptive strike* and take control of the information. Tread Lightly, a footwear

Swell Sweaters Inc. and Sophisticated Shirts Corp., two companies in the clothing industry, were trading at similar multiples. Then Swell Sweaters started doing very well based on an emerging sports trend while Sophisticated Shirts was pulled down by a portfolio that, by contrast, seemed outdated.

Timeless Tops also competed in this sector. They had the preppy image as well, but their value and quality stayed popular with teens. Yet, Timeless Tops' stock was trading at a discount, and IR's information (stock performance, First Call, shareholder analysis) pointed to the fact that the preppy image was probably the reason.

IR wasn't sure, though, and reached out to The Street for reconnaissance. After talks with several portfolio managers, IR found, instead, that the concern was low inventory and faltering sales. This news was delivered back to Timeless Tops and a strategy emerged.

Their next communication to The Street immediately addressed these issues and articulated current initiatives as part of the company's strategy. The misperception was corrected, but without the proper information, handling this event would have been impossible.

manufacturer, had a large amount of its business flowing through one retailer. Thanks to Regulation FD, companies can't disclose anything to The Street that IR professionals can't also access.

The IR community discovered that the retailer was receiving certain exclusive agreements from a competitor, Putya Foot Down. We knew that the retailer was not receiving any such agreements from Tread Lightly, and that these agreements would give the retailer incentive to feature Putya Foot Down products to shoppers with price reductions and special displays. This would, of course, hurt Tread Lightly's volume and presumably its stock price.

Given that the retailer was Tread Lightly's biggest customer, investors and analysts would estimate a drop in sales. Tread Lightly's IR advisors had the company consider this possibility before The Street did so that they could reconcile it with their strategy, make adjustments, and address the issue with the investment community.

Another reason to stay on top of industry events is to *draft off of others' momentum*. A company had recently licensed a hot brand for one of its product lines. IR heard from The Street that a huge retailer was touting this particular brand, cheering its recent volume in its stores. The opportunity arose for the company to capitalize on the buzz and start communicating its success with the brand but in a context that included conservative guidance. This easy, quick maneuver gained significant IR and PR attention, positioning the company to exceed estimates and create long-term value.

Analysts and investors see many companies fail to stay in touch with trends that affect valuation within their own sector. IR needs to remain diligent for management, collect the information, interpret it, and determine what course is best to maximize valuation.

If IR doesn't already know the sector's overarching messages each quarter, it's bound to discover them too late. Anticipating these hot buttons keeps the company ahead of the audience.

THE IR/CEO RELATIONSHIP

The most crucial element for productive dialogue with The Street is the management/IR relationship. IR must be an effective and reliable liaison between The Street and the company, and the CEO must believe that IR lends him or her a new perspective. Too many yes-men around the CEO can be awful for shareholders, but sometimes a domineering CEO has no interest in hearing critical feedback. The role of the IRO or the outside IR counsel is to bridge the gap between the company and the capital markets, stand up to the CEO when no one else will, and bring Wall Street's perspective to the discussion.

The Emperor Has No Clothes

For IR to be effective, management and the board of directors must trust the function and give IR full immunity to create a secure conduit to and from The Street. Given the fact that access is king on Wall Street, and criticizing a CEO jeopardizes that access, some management teams become insulated from reality, particularly when the CEO's ego is an issue. This situation demands a strong, objective hand to come in for a reality check.

In 2002, a fairly new, but very successful technology company saw its products gathering momentum. As a result of its success, the company publicly set high financial goals, which seemed set to garner a high short-term valuation. Subsequently, executives felt pressure to meet those goals and were trapped in a make-the-number pattern that crushed so many companies at that time.

Management, as well as IR, failed this company in several respects. There was no managing of expectations, guidance was aggressive, short-term goals were overemphasized, and no one stood up to the CEO and educated him on how these tactics would damage his credibility and his career. An objective third-party view was necessary, and neither IR, the sell-side, or the buy-side would jeopardize their access to the CEO by raining on his parade.

Draw an Analogy

How, then, does IR delicately deliver critical feedback to a CEO with a strong personality? One way is to draw the analogy that the CEO's company is essentially a product to Wall Street. Therefore, why not treat Wall Street like a buyer of the product, no different than any other customer? Ask CEOs, "If you walked into one of your retail stores and the counters were dirty, tags were on the floor, and the neon sign outside was on the fritz, what would you do?" Most executives know the answer. They'd immediately move heaven and earth to fix up the store so that the customer experience would improve.

Although, if IR said to the same CEO that analysts think the CEO's presentation was weak or the last conference call wasn't thorough enough, he might dismiss the analyst as clueless. Amazingly this happens all the time. If CEOs were as open to Wall Street feedback as they are to their own customers' feedback, valuations across the board would likely improve. With that analogy in mind, the CEO can be more open to IR's opinions on dealing effectively with day-to-day events.

A Case of Credibility

The following is the story of a real company, with a fictional name, that realized the importance of management in preserving value.

Paperclip Partners, a small B2B in the office supply industry, was experiencing a sudden fall-off in revenues that partially resulted from cyclicality in its sector. But management had not articulated this possibility in its most recent earnings guidance to Wall Street because the company thought one of its new divisions would have higher-than-average gross margins, thus countering that cyclicality.

Unfortunately, the company couldn't reconcile the subsequent cash shortfalls with its debt obligations, and it had broken some of its bank covenants. Additionally, The Street had already recognized that management had not been forthright throughout the process. Downward pressure hit the stock price.

Bankers came to management with a few solutions. One suggested that Paperclip consider an acquisition to build the business. Another thought that management should refinance the bank debt with an issue of high-yield bonds. Yet another suggested selling the company.

An IR audit included a discussion with the buy- and sell-sides. Both analysts and investors felt that management had an antagonistic attitude toward the capital markets and was unwilling to listen to feedback, often fighting back when analysts shared criticism or shutting off investors who had complaints. The Street also felt that quarter after quarter, the company would hold back bad news, even when they knew they were going to hit unexpected, one-time charges that would cause the earnings to fall short.

This management team was fighting the entire credibility checklist. Within the company there was no accountability, the numbers were not transparent, the managers didn't anticipate problems, and they were hardly visible to The Street. The Street didn't care what the value proposition was, because management had no standing with the investment community.

IR brought the information back to management. The good news was that The Street felt Paperclip's stock could be very attractive if management pulled its act together. The bad news was that management's lack of credibility had sunk the valuation to such depths that each of the capitalization maneuvers they were considering offered only symptomatic relief; none, even selling the company, would bring the shareholders the value that the board felt was appropriate.

Paperclip needed to reposition its story and regain Wall Street's trust. IR suggested making the following changes and communicating them on the next conference call:

- Change the tone of all communications from defensive and arrogant to conciliatory.
- Streamline the profile to reflect a simple, organized business model.
- Organize an internal audit to create department-by-department accountability.
- Direct valuations to focus on EBITDA, not earnings.
- Begin cost-cutting initiatives.

(continued)

Each of these moves sent a signal to The Street that Paperclip's management team was accountable, transparent, credible, and candid. The bankers stepped back and investors stayed with the stock or became newly involved.

This company had a good business, a good story, and a good plan. IR helped them adapt short-term goals that would stay true to the long-term strategy and keep the company honest with The Street. The dissemination of this story to The Street gained the company increased coverage and new sell-side distribution and buy-side volume.

Other credibility cases don't turn out as well. Inevitably, despite the best strategies, negative opinions surface. Because a lot of money is on the line when analysts make a positive or a negative recommendation, they are very careful in their assessment of management and in their valuation argument.

One thing that some management teams fail to recognize, however, is that nothing personal is involved in the process. It's simply an opinion based on assumption. Companies that fail to understand this and publicly antagonize analysts simply end up looking foolish, demonstrating a lack of capital markets savvy and, ultimately, hurting shareholders.

Executives must find a way to absorb negative opinions and not get into a defensive volley with analysts, although it happens frequently. Several instances of management-analyst antagonism have occurred in the past few years. According to a June 19, 2003, article in *The Wall Street Journal*, after two Morgan Stanley analysts questioned Qwest Communications' accounting, Qwest denied analyst access to Morgan Stanley and wouldn't consider the firm for banking business. The *Journal* also stated that a former chief executive "publicly derided the analysts and questioned the integrity of their work." Morgan Stanley continued to downgrade the stock to a Sell rating.

The *Journal* article also reported on a telecommunications analyst at J.P. Morgan Chase who questioned whether Nextel Communications was lowballing its bad debt estimates. Within hours, the *Journal* said, Nextel's CFO was on the phone to the analyst's boss, "accusing the analyst of faulty work."

In these situations, the companies looked foolish, management lost credibility, and the shareholders suffered because the stocks dropped. IR with an understanding of the research process could have headed off this antagonism and subsequent damage to valuation.

Ultimately, if a company wants to be public and benefit from raising capital and selling shares, CEOs and CFOs have to understand Wall Street and also accept the negatives.

> "One of the most important things a CFO must do is articulately com-
> municate what is going on in the company to outside constituents and
> do it with credibility. That's always been important, but it's even more
> so today.
>
>   —David Viniar, CFO, Goldman Sachs
>
> "You get no pretense with David. He's the opposite of slick. In evalu-
> ating a complex company that takes on a lot of risk, like Goldman,
> that makes me comfortable,"
>
>   —anonymous investor on David Viniar.
> *Source*: February 2004 *Institutional Investor*

Being Upfront with Information

Human nature is to want to position any event in the best light possible, but
analysts are skeptical about promotion. Using superlatives that generate
high expectations puts more risk in the public domain than most analysts or
investors are willing to tolerate; more often than not, analysts and the buy-
side steer clear of a heavily promoted stock. For that reason, any company
that tries to spin an obviously negative event into something positive will be
found out in due time. Management credibility and company valuation will
be erased.

HANDLING BAD EVENTS (AND LOWERING GUIDANCE)

Three basics apply to IR's handling of bad events: don't delay, don't divide,
and don't diminish.

1. *Don't delay*: Management should weigh the benefits against the risk of
   being one of the last companies in an industry to report. If a material
   event occurs and there are risks of rumors in the marketplace, management wants investors to hear the news from them first. It's far better to
   take control of the situation and define the problem rather than sitting
   on bad news and allowing rumors to define the company's reality. Management should get a handle on what the news means to the bottom line
   and deliver it.
2. *Don't divide*: Telling the whole story to all constituents at once helps

take the risk out of the news, even if it's bad. Ideally, management should never allow another shoe to drop. If bad news does dribble out, the analyst has no choice but to negatively comment on every announcement. This painful, drawn-out process will affect future earnings and the stock's multiple will likely compress.

A slow roll-out of bad news has a ripple effect as the media latches on to the problems, and as employees and vendors lose confidence in management. These factors can fundamentally weaken the business, leading to a low valuation and a high cost of capital.

Companies need to get all bad news out at once if possible. Explain it, quantify it, boil it down to conservative earnings guidance, and rebuild the share base through effective targeting.

3. *Don't diminish*: Management must be transparent and accountable because analysts ultimately listen to management teams that own up to mistakes. They don't want to hear excuses that downplay the news.

We knew a company that treated earnings releases as an opportunity to promote the business. They glossed over financial results in favor of promotional language that always cast the business in the best light. The fact was, management was viewed poorly by The Street despite their chronically rosy outlook that attempted to perpetually mask poor earnings. That game can be played only so many times without investors running for the exits. In fact, they did.

Another often-used excuse is blaming poor earnings on events outside of management's control, such as the economy, weather, or our recent favorite, "geopolitical issues." This type of deflection, although sometimes very true, can often be a management crutch. One company had for several quarters had been blaming sub-par performance on the economy. At the same time industry peers were announcing positive results in those same markets due to a rebounding economy. IR's job is to monitor competitor results because, as in this case, it can avoid embarrassment. Had management blamed the economy again when others were doing well, credibility would have been further damaged. This is just another example of a proactive IR effort managing an unexpected event.

THE OPTIMAL TIME TO LOWER GUIDANCE

One of the most important events that a management team faces is lowering guidance. In determining the best time to do so, IR should take into account stock price and valuation. That check can be the difference between the stock getting trounced and the stock increasing on high volume.

If the stock price is at a 52-week low, the valuation is at a big discount to its peer group, and the analyst community is relatively disengaged—that is, no one has a Strong Buy rating—management has greater leeway to reduce guidance without hurting the analyst, the investor, or its own credibility. In all likelihood The Street is expecting very little from management performance-wise given this scenario, and the market might just be waiting for management to reassess its expected earnings guidance. Bringing guidance down under these circumstances would result in lower risk, more attention, and probably an increased stock price.

However, if the valuation is high—say, because the CEO wanted to use 25 percent EPS guidance rather than 15 percent as the IRO suggested—management must take its medicine and lower expectations. To minimize the risk, the company should do this after the market closes in a press release with a simultaneous conference call to explain the factors. This is the best way to lessen the risk of a situation that management and IR both know will result in a falling stock price.

When readjusting guidance, management cannot be married to a best-case number. In fact, given the choice of lowering a $1.10 estimate by $0.05 or $0.10, management should always take the latter, particularly if the stock is drifting downward. The reason is that another $0.05 reduction isn't going to matter as much to The Street as if the company positions itself to miss revised guidance. Additionally, when setting guidance, management must do so with an eye to the future. Most events are usually not a one-quarter phenomenon, and The Street will suspect that subsequent quarters may come in low. When the company sets guidance, it needs to establish a conservative cushion for the rest of the year, without, of course, setting itself up to materially exceed the number either. To set the company up for success, guidance must be both realistic and achievable.

HANDLING GOOD EVENTS

One quarter after another of terrific results is every company's dream, but this is where IR hits the double diamond trails of keeping a check on management ego and managing The Street's expectations. In order to stay on course and not be dissuaded by the stock price, IR must script a bit of conservatism or push back in every quarter when there is great success. Management must always be in control of its numbers via guidance, and an analyst or two over-hyping the company is an analyst or two too many.

Another by-product of positive news is the invariable analyst downgrade. As mentioned throughout this book, analysts are in the business of generating commissions; therefore, a large part of their job is to upgrade and downgrade stocks. In theory, this activity guides the decisions of the buy-side and in the process drives trading volumes for the investment bank.

The analyst downgrade should never be taken personally, and CEOs should understand that when his or her stock price reaches the analyst target, action will be taken. Either the analyst will up the price target and reiterate her Buy rating or downgrade the stock, saying it's fully valued.

IR's task, through conservative guidance primarily, is to manage expectations to the point where the company has built significant credibility. At that point, an analyst typically downgrades based on valuation only. In other words, the analyst isn't lowering his rating because the business model is flawed or because management has lost credibility. He is lowering is because the stock hit the target price.

This downgrade is the best that a company can hope for, and it might read something like this:

> *Analyst Paul Hewson from American Securities writes, "Based solely on valuation, we are lowering our rating to Underperform from Market-perform. We continue to view this as a good company that has met or exceeded our expectations. However, with the sharp run-up in share price, we believe the stock is considerably ahead of current expectations. Victory's stock has appreciated by more than 40% in the last couple of months, from the mid-teens to more than $20 per share. Our 12 month price target remains unchanged."*

Again, managing the analyst community relative to good news is just as important as doing so when the news is bad. Because the buy-side pays more attention to the content of any report versus the rating, a downgrade such as the one above is a big victory for the company and IR.

How does a company control investor expectations when the business is on fire? An article in *The Wall Street Journal*, March 25, 2004, was titled "Investors Cut Starbucks Some Rare Slack." With the subhead, "Coffee Chain's Decade of Frothy Performance Overshadows Chairman's Growth Warning."

The article states: "When a top executive warns investors that his company won't be able to sustain its rate of growth, the result is usually a stock sell off. But that didn't happen on Feb. 25th when Howard Shultz, chairman of Starbucks Corp., announced that the world's largest chain of coffee shops couldn't keep getting larger at rates as fast as 32%. Sure the stock slipped, but only 3.4%, and then it bounced back a day or two, perhaps because the company nevertheless stood by double-digit sales-growth expectations. As for analysts, their recommendations remained neutral or positive, with most of them predicting that Starbucks would outperform the market. This faith in Starbucks certainly doesn't arise from any sense that the stock is under-valued. In recent days, the price-to-earnings ratio of Starbucks stock has flirted with 50, making it one of the most expensive stocks on Wall Street." . . . "Rather, the market reaction—or lack of reaction—suggests that a rare type of credibility gap is developing between Starbucks and the Street. It is the opposite of the gap that forms between hype-prone executives and share-holders. This type of gap reflects no suspicion, no sense among investors that the executive is trying to fool them or gin up a quick bump in the stock; in-stead, there's a sense that this executive is hard on himself and his company, and therefore his self-effacement isn't entirely credible." The article com-pares this credibility gap with that developed around Warren Buffett and the late Sam Walton.

This approach to restraining, or at least trying to restrain, The Street al-lows management to focus on the business and The Street to worry about valuation.

MANAGEMENT AND LANGUAGE

One of the most important parts of a company's ongoing dialogue with The Street is the actual language that's used on a day-to-day basis. To that end, management and IR shouldn't underestimate the impact of the words they use. For example, if a CEO is asked how he feels about his company's most recent guidance and starts his answer with the phrase, "Several things have to happen for us to deliver . . . ," investors might sell a share or two.

In order to script and oversee a conservative communication's plan, IR has to make sure that all language is tempered and delivered in terms that The Street is used to hearing. A company should never say emphatically that "we will," but rather "we believe," "we should," or "we expect."

Nor can the language be nebulous. A company which states that they are going to "make a significant investment in cap ex" or "generate sub-stantial earnings potential" without quantifying such terms is giving open-ended guidance, which is dangerous. Analysts and investors must translate words to numbers or any number of variations could come out of those phrases. For example, "substantial earnings potential" from a new initiative might mean 5 cents in one analyst's model and 15 cents in another analyst's model. The result would be a wide-ranging, higher than intended, First Call consensus estimate that management, deep down, knows is unattainable. Words, whether referring to guidance or when issuing new news, should always be quantified, with an earnings per share range and a time frame that foots with that financial guidance.

Words are just the beginning. As we mentioned earlier, in the late summer of 2003, the SEC cited a Reg FD violation based on "tone, emphasis and demeanor" to Schering-Plough. The IRO was present at the time of the infraction, which illuminates the fact that even some of biggest IR executives can't be expert enough on the ever-changing regulations on financial disclosure. Staying within the limits of the right words and phrases, not to mention the appropriate body language is not easy. That's what makes systematic, scripted disclosure, with clear and quantifiable guidance, essential.

Finally, it's also helpful in the Dialogue stage if everyone is speaking the same language.

Big Hand Accessories, a consumer products company, kept telling The Street that their business wasn't seasonal, and that, in fact, the reason the company was so profitable was because it was not seasonal, which was confusing to IR consultants who worked with them. Their accessories clearly sold better in summer than winter.

When we asked the CEO about this, he explained that when they were not selling in North America, they were selling in Australia at a different time of year. He was quite surprised when we told him that by using the word "seasonal," not only was he not clearly explaining the situation, but he was creating the impression that he didn't understand it either.

Curious that this didn't come up in calls, the IR team asked some of the analysts and investors why they had never questioned the CEO on his use of this word. They said that they thought that they were missing something obvious and they were waiting to figure it out before asking.

IR decided to clear this up and scripted the next call to do just that. In the call, the CEO explained that the business adapts to the market with less SKUs by creating products that avoid obsolescence because they transfer easily.

That solved that problem.

THE MARKET EFFECTS OF SHORT- AND LONG-TERM STRATEGIES

On a quarter-to-quarter basis, P&L and balance sheet items change with financial performance, and each change is another event that must be properly explained to Wall Street. Although this book certainly couldn't address every possible variation, in most situations strategic IR is able to clarify the issues and communicate them properly.

State of Affairs and Their Effects

LIFO, FIFO: Inventory levels send strong signals to The Street and may be misinterpreted if they're not backed by a logical story. For example, slower inventory turns can sometimes foretell an earnings slowdown, or a retailer may experience inventory levels that appear higher than sales can sustain.

In many industries, inventory levels and turns are cyclical, but sometimes they indicate a particular shift in the marketplace. This situation can be specific to a particular company, because of something that's happened to its product or service or those of its competitors. Or the situation can be specific to the industry, like a shift in demographics or the economy that affects buying tendencies or consumer tastes.

Investors that smell an inventory problem on the balance sheet may be prompted to sell shares. But if the company has the chance to explain that these inventory levels are built into the projections for, let's say, new stores coming on line, a shifting marketplace, or a proven strategy, the investors will see a viable asset, one that will be monetized and benefit the bottom line.

A/R and COGS: There are times when expenses, specifically cost of goods sold (COGS), are contested. This can happen when companies do not believe that they owe their suppliers or vendors certain expenses or that they were overcharged for expenses that are directly related to the cost of making the products they sell.

Some companies, when they contest this number, may assume they are either not going to have to pay the contested amount or that they are going to get a refund on payments already made. Then they don't even recognize this expense as a cost at all, deleting it altogether from COGS. Those who expect a refund may go so far as to book it as a receivable. This type of expense refuting or refund claim inflates earnings. If Wall Street sees this tactic in the footnotes of the financials, or hears that it is surfacing as a practice of a management team, The Street will very quickly penalize the stock and subtract credibility points from the CEO.

Such talk arose among several portfolio managers who owned big chunks of real estate in the form of REITs. They thought this accounting issue was occurring among tenants and landlords of certain commercial properties and might become a material revelation. Concerned their stocks would fall if news of the problem were true, they sent a ripple of warning out to the companies. The companies now knew that The Street strongly disagreed with the practice and that there was a chance that valuations would be adversely affected if the issue came to light.

Obviously, both sides of the business-to-business relationship were vulnerable. If the landlords in this case had overcharged, then they had over-reported revenue for that period. If the tenants were underreporting the COGS expense, then they were possibly hiding millions of dollars of gross margin expense. Both sides were potentially enhancing earnings.

The fact is that in these scenarios, where a business or a division is playing an accounting game to shore up numbers, the CEO and CFO will be exposed every time. Wall Street is always checking the notes and assumption behind COGS and other line items, and management must always acknowledge it. Though an income statement can be somewhat manipulated, the discrepancies will always come out in the cash flow statement. To that end, earnings quality should always be identified by IR and expressed accordingly.

NOLs: Net operating loss (NOL) carry forwards are one of the subjects that create confusion among management teams with regard to communication. Many companies intentionally report and highlight the untaxed number because of the net operating loss, but fail to mention the NOL outright because the reported number might not be viewed as very high after all.

This approach works in management's favor, until they've run out of the net income sheltering NOLs (when earnings will again be fully taxed). This fully taxed year will not compare favorably to the untaxed year, and the company's year-over-year comparisons will look as if the underlying business experienced serious erosion when, in reality, pretax net income increased. Unfortunately, this company put itself in an awkward situation for a perceived short-term gain, and it all could have been avoided if the company had presented earnings as pro forma fully taxed despite the untaxed GAAP number. A simple GAAP-to-pro forma reconciliation would have kept the communications sound and within the current rules.

Any decent analyst will see the NOLs as temporary anyway, and value them on a present value basis (because it's real future cash that the company can invest over time).

Cash

Cash on the balance sheet can be viewed as positive or negative. A lot of cash can peg a management team as too conservative, unwilling to undertake prudent risk. It can also signal a business that legitimately has few reinvestment opportunities. Therefore, analysts should know that the company has plans for its cash, whether it be for share repurchasing, dividends, research and development, or capital spending. After all, the stock market is about return on investment over and above the bond market, and over and above the 1 percent or 2 percent that can be generated in savings.

By investing in a new project, a company and investors expect a return in the form of free cash flow. This, in turn, fuels a perpetual investment cycle of cash generated from operations being invested in yet higher return projects. That's why investment pros look for management teams who can consistently and over time drive return on equity and return on assets.

If a company is going to redeploy cash to increase shareholder value it has to consider how each decision affects each type of investor and how the cumulative action will affect value. The hope is that management is assessing which alternatives can generate the greatest return on invested capital for shareholders, and IR's job is to position the outcome to buy- and sell-side analysts.

Light Bulb Ideas, a consumer electronics company, had just come out of a cyclical downturn in its core business with a solid balance sheet, lots of free cash flow, and numerous potential investment opportunities, including acquisitions. The company recently initiated a dividend in light of favorable dividend tax legislation.

Light Bulb Ideas had three large institutional shareholders. One was a growth fund that was urging management to reinvest in the business aggressively via capital expenditures and acquisition opportunities. A second fund was a value fund that wanted management to utilize its growing free cash flow and cash on hand to buy back stock to enhance returns. A third fund was an income-oriented institution that wanted management to increase the dividend.

Management posed the question, "What should we do when three large shareholders are asking for three different things?" After some

(continued)

careful analysis and in-depth discussions with senior management, an IR team suggested they do what they have been doing best: run the business. But they also needed to communicate better to shareholders just how they were running that business.

To knowledgeable observers, the company seemed overfocused on what shareholders had to say and factored these cluttered messages into their decisions. What they should have been sharing with investors, however, was the rigorous hurdle process they had for committing investor capital, regardless of growth, value, or income orientation. Their practice, before any of the company's capital was ever put at risk, was to complete a detailed rate of return analysis; managers were held to performance standards based on that analysis. Before capital was reinvested in the business or used for an acquisition, those returns were compared to the benefits to shareholders of a stock buyback or an incremental dividend.

Not only was this information very important to shareholders, but it needed to be communicated to them. That information would serve as the foundation to keep all three shareholder constituencies—growth, value, and income—satisfied, because they would know that they had a management team that was already looking out for their best interests by taking shareholder input into consideration regarding capital allocation decisions.

Similarly, if a company in mid-strategy changes tactics for its cash, it needs to communicate the story behind that decision. For example, if a company pulls back a dividend to use the cash for an acquisition, or invests in a new product development instead of pursuing acquisitions, the effects of each of these, to each type of investor, must be calculated and quantified. Management should articulate its strategy and decision making with all shareholders' interests in mind.

Debt

Debt requires a continuous search for the lowest cost of capital to support the optimal return on equity. Although good earnings or excess cash can be used to pay off debt, companies are often wiser to maintain certain levels of debt, as debt can be the cheapest money around (particularly in the past few years).

However, The Street's perception of different debt levels can have a significant effect on valuation. If debt is too low, investors may believe management is playing it too safe with no pressure to be efficient. If debt is too high, investors may feel interest payments are too burdensome to bring much to the bottom line. What Wall Street likes is an optimal capital structure that includes debt and equity, because the returns for shareholders can be that much more magnified.

Dollar Sense, a company with a top-notch product offering and business model in the finance sector, was trading at a heavy discount to its peers. It was obvious that the company carried a lot of cash on their balance sheet and had very little inventory, but it also had significant high-yield debt. The Street saw this as a threat to profitability.

Some IR professionals, on the other hand, saw this as a terrific opportunity. What we knew was that Dollar Sense had been forced to take this high-yield debt after two banks consolidated and lumped Dollar Sense's debt into a sub-credit group, and Dollar Sense just assumed this was par for the course. They could recapitalize their debt at a better rate, which seemed like a terrific communications gem and a catalyst for improved earnings.

The first step was to clear the high cost of capital cloud hanging over Dollar Sense and tell the story so that The Street would not think that the interest-coverage threat was as real as the debt levels would suggest.

Once articulated, via a conference call, investors and analysts clearly realized that the high cost of debt was not a liability to equity holders. Rather, the debt was a catalyst for improved earnings because once the capital markets realized that the company was now going to actively refinance this debt, the cost of capital would eventually go down and there would be a financial bump to earnings. In addition, the refinancing opportunity also was a "public broadcast" that the company would recognize prepayment penalties, so no investor would be surprised when it actually occurred.

By reconciling the balance sheet to the overall growth story we shifted a perceived weakness into a strength. A strong company was signaling that it was going to recapitalize, the bankers smelled opportunity to garner a client, and the sell-side became further engaged. IR from a capital markets perspective knew how to make the most of this information, attract bankers, and position the company for enhanced visibility.

HORIZON THINKING

Ultimately, the stock market may overreact, either positively or negatively, to any of the events or conditions we've mentioned in this chapter. But if the company believes that the underlying financial outlook hasn't changed, then the short-term consequences of these overreactions shouldn't be an urgent matter. Stock prices don't stay up or down forever, so if the company is confident in the future, it should simply reposition relative to its peers, understand that one investor's weakness is another's buying opportunity, and rely on IR strategy to re-engage the market, albeit at a lower valuation. With the proper guidance, the price will recover, assuming the financial results match expectations.

CHAPTER 25

The Banker Mentality

The final part of Dialogue is the *banker mentality*. This name applies because IR must ultimately be nimble enough and educated enough on the capital markets to have parallel conversations with both analysts and investment bankers. These conversations can still lead to analyst coverage or at least a closer relationship with an investment bank. They can also lead to suggestions and tactics that will increase shareholder value over time.

Investment bankers are in the business of helping companies raise capital to achieve their goals. They also are transaction facilitators that show CEOs potential acquisition or merger candidates. Across the board, however, whether raising capital or suggesting M&A opportunities, the transactions must be beneficial to shareholders over the long run.

Therefore, IR must have the ability to think like an investment banker, aligning IR's goals with those of the CEO and the board of directors. Every tactic or strategy should relate back to building shareholder value over the long run. Whether it's an acquisition, a capital raise, implementing a dividend, or repurchasing shares, IR must be able to stand shoulder-to-shoulder with the banker and the CEO and know how to position the event.

INVESTMENT BANKERS

A good connection with the right investment bankers, for both public and private companies, can generate an extremely symbiotic relationship over time, one that involves transactions for the bankers and value-added, accretive deals for management and shareholders.

In order for companies to find the best investment banks, however, companies need to focus on those firms that have a long track record of dealing with companies of similar size. If a company carries a $200 million market cap, there's no need to pursue an investment bank that facilitates transactions for $5 billion–plus market cap companies. IR professionals, along with management, must do their homework in this regard and know all the parties that navigate in their space.

THE CHINESE WALL

The reforms of the last few years have cut ties between banking and research. There is virtually no communication between these two groups, with the exception of analysts being "taken over" the Chinese Wall—that is, the barrier that separates research from investment banking. This would occur when a transaction is pending and the investment banking department must communicate it to the analyst before it is announced.

However, despite these strict rules on communication, all investment banks are allowed to have a strategy where research, sales and trading, and investment banking are aligned. For example, having analysts publishing on mega-cap stocks while banking is focused on small caps makes no sense. It would create a schizophrenic organization where the lack of focus would most likely doom the effort. Therefore, most investment banks blanket companies of similar size, and research and banking both are active in pursuing relationships.

With all that said, there's a myth that the sell-side will only publish on a company if there is a pending corporate finance transaction. Although more true than not in bigger firms during the late 1990s, this myth does not necessarily hold true today. In fact, analysts are actually looking for good stock picks. However, companies that happens to be capital intensive, or active in the equity or debt markets historically, might be more attractive to the entire organization. Analysts and investment bankers understand this fact and no communication is needed.

Therefore, we believe that IR should make an effort to track and establish ties with all logical investment bankers in the sector. This may lead to interesting corporate finance ideas for management, but for IR's purposes, it may be the back door into research coverage, as the company starts to develop a relationship with the investment bank. This is very useful when direct conversations with the analyst are not proving fruitful.

The second reason to track bankers is to be ready in the event that management quickly decides to raise capital or sees a strategic acquisition that can't wait. IR should present management with an evaluation of all the players and discuss the strengths of each organization. Although certainly not a function of traditional IR, it's a critical part of a successful IR approach.

Cast a wide net and evaluate bankers based on the answers to the following questions:

Quality of Distribution and Trading Support

- Which firms have traded the most shares over the last 3, 6, and 12 months? Most active traders tend to have the best order flow; strong order flow usually means good execution; good execution gets the company the best value for its money.
- Can the firm get the stock out there to the buy-side and continuously support the desired liquidity of the stock through volume and trading activity?
- Finally, what are the characteristics of the sales force? Are they professional and experienced, or is it a force simply out for the commission?

Value Creation
- Which firms have done the most to create shareholder value?
- Do the investment bankers call with good ideas, and are they considered trusted advisors?
- Do they have an analyst covering the sector, and, more important, is it a good analyst with whom the management team will get along and who is respected by his or her own brokers as well as the rest of The Street?
- Which firms have the analysts who have written the most comprehensive reports, understand the companies' investment theses, and have followed through on their research by generating investor interest in the companies?

These points fall around the main point: companies want to cultivate relationships with banks that they believe will be in for the long haul, especially considering the size and relative infrequency of investment banking fees.

Management, however, does not have to engage just one investment bank. While needing larger investment banks as the "lead horse" in selling equity or debt, a company also can benefit from smaller, regional banks that may bring analyst coverage and aftermarket support.

Some companies have chosen a lead banker and then think they're done with the job. They're not. There is usually an opportunity for companies to be economic to a few more banks and include them in the process, and create more opportunities to preserve or enhance valuation. To that point, aftermarket support is a major criteria. Does the investment bank fade away after the transaction or are they aggressive with capital on their trading desk and with research coverage?

PICKING THE BANKS

Once IR is clear on the company's objectives, and all internal parties have narrowed down the investment banking choices to a small few, IR should continue its due diligence to make sure the bank fits the company's needs.

To assess a team:

Call their references and make sure they do what they promised on previous deals. The best bankers usually have impeccable references over a long period of time. It's always great to find companies that have not done one deal with a banker, but three or five, like the IPO, secondary, and a merger or acquisition. Repeat business usually means good customer service.

Watch the bank's most recent performance. Many investment bankers thrive off momentum. If the buy-side has made money off the last three deals the investment banker has brought to market, chances are that institutions would be receptive the next time around. When does someone not take a call or meeting from somebody who has a track record of making them money?

Make sure the banking team, or those that expect to service the company, are the individuals who will execute the transaction. It's not unusual for small to mid-cap companies to experience a bait and switch. The bankers that pitch the business, whom management is so enamored with, don't execute the deal. The B Team does, made up of the folks carrying all the pitch books to the presentation who never say a word. After the deal is done, the A Team may want nothing to do with the company . . . until the next deal is available.

While most investment banks are very competent and professional, this problem typically arises when a company's economic value (its fee potential) is not so relevant to an investment banker compared to other opportunities. This situation most frequently occurs among bulge-bracket investment banks chasing deals among small and mid-cap companies.

Does the rest of the firm generally support their deals? Has the *trading desk* remained an active market maker after previous deals? While *research* is now greatly regulated, ask if the firm has a policy in place regarding covering—that is, providing research to—investment banking clients. Make sure the analyst is a credible one, with sector or industry experience. A retail company does not want a former technology analyst covering it. Ask to speak to several of the firm's *institutional salespeople* regarding reference

The Bankers' Scorecard

Score 1–10	Bank 1	Bank 2	Bank 3	Bank 4
Track Record on Previous Deals				
Company Knowledge				
Sector Knowledge				
Aftermarket Trading Activity				
Quality of Research Team				
Quality of Investment Banking Team				

points to previous deals. These people are the ones who have to get orders from the institutions.

Companies should use these transactions to either reward the investment bank with whom they already have a good relationship or to gain the attention of firms where a relationship could be built.

On smaller transactions, IR should huddle with management and evaluate the possibility of using a small, regional investment bank, where an otherwise smaller payday will be substantial. This may lead to analyst sponsorship down the road. With sell-side tracking, IR should be in a pretty good position to enlighten a CEO on the ramifications of choosing one small underwriter over another.

Ultimately, IR has the responsibility of helping companies leverage their capitalization decisions into fruitful, long-term relationships with the investment banks. Unfortunately, most companies do not put enough thought into getting the best execution for shareholders. Traditionally, management allocates transactions to investment banks based on little-to-no analysis and more on gut instinct, which is a missed opportunity to maximize the value of the transaction for shareholders. Smaller companies sometimes think they should be linked with a prestigious big name bank to gain validation, only to get lost in the aftermarket shuffle, and other companies engage three bulge-bracket firms when it would have been more effective to team one bulge bracket with regional and boutique firms. IR must be entrenched in this process and, as a confidant and sounding board for top management, help the company weigh all of its options.

VALUE CREATION

The first part of this chapter dealt with the valuation positives that can result from strengthened investment banker contacts. It also dealt with picking underwriters to widen a company's exposure and maximize the impact of a transaction.

The following section deals more with how management teams use their capital internally to create value for shareholders over time. This is also part of the banker mentality, and IR should always be in position to suggest these strategies to management and the ramifications of going forward.

What may be obvious on some of these value creation initiatives, such as stock buyback, is that the move will have a positive impact on earnings per share. But what may not be so obvious is that these transactions have the ability to boost a company's long-term multiple. This is the domain of IR which, armed with capital markets expertise, should communicate the events in their proper context.

ORGANIC GROWTH

Many clients fight the trade-off between increased spending and bringing profit to the bottom line. The former strategy invests in the future, bucks short-term thinking, and sets the table for long-term sustainable growth. In most quality organizations this is, and should always be, the prevailing mind-set. On conference calls and in one-on-one meetings, however, management might feel pressure to think on a more short-term basis—perhaps from shorter-term investors who care little about the company and a lot about the stock price. Less experienced management teams may react by altering their philosophy, spending slightly less, and focusing on shorter-term goals. IR must interject and counsel management on how best to fight this trade-off.

First of all, articulating to Wall Street that management is spending to improve the long-term competitiveness of the company is tough to dispute. Second, if historic returns back up that statement, short-term thinkers won't have much to say. Finally, if IR wraps the "spending" issue into a comprehensive strategy to increase shareholder value over time, management should feel very comfortable delivering that message to The Street.

One last point on spending: if the stock is materially off its recent high and a majority of the analysts are disengaged—that is, they have neutral ratings—management has more leeway to set a comfortable guidance bar. In other words, if management resets conservative guidance to include increased spending, short-term pressure will never be an issue.

ACQUISITIONS

IR must also understand the implications of an acquisition and learn how to communicate the attributes of the combined company.

First, IR should obtain the term sheet from the CEO or CFO and gain a thorough understanding of the deal terms. Is the transaction an all-stock deal or a combination of cash and stock, and will the transaction accelerate the need for the company to access the capital markets? Once the details are understood, IR must understand the qualitative benefits of the acquisition and the underlying performance of each business.

Lastly, IR must understand whether the transaction is additive to earnings and work with senior management to revise guidance to a conservative range. Conservative guidance sets the stage to exceed estimates, generate buy- and sell-side interest, positive media coverage, and boost employee morale.

One company refused to provide updated guidance when an acquisition closed because management would not have sufficient time to get comfortable with the combined/consolidated numbers. IR thought that was fair enough, but reminded management that in their due diligence on the transaction the investment bankers presented a base case pro forma (as if the acquisition was closed on the first of the year) estimate for the year. Even a conservative version of that estimate would suffice for the outside world. The client moved ahead with no guidance, risking that Wall Street might make its own assumptions, raise estimates, and position the acquisition for financial failure (relative to expectations).

Again, any non-organic growth should be framed in long-term shareholder value creation. To take control of the process and soundly advise a CEO, IR must think like a banker and understand why any given deal would or would not resonate with sophisticated investors.

SHARE REPURCHASES

Moving to a category that could be called "adding value below the operating line," management can drive long-term value by sticking to a philosophy of returning cash back to shareholders. One of the ways management and the board can do this is to opportunistically repurchase shares and shrink the company's market cap. The result is a smaller denominator in the P/E calculation and higher earnings per share assuming the same level of net income.

Share repurchase authorizations make sense if a company's share price is low and its ability to generate cash hasn't been hampered materially. In fact, the company can create a floor for the stock price where management can repurchase shares, particularly if shares are still coming on the market after negative news.

IR's job, again, is to frame out the buyback in terms of long-term shareholder value creation rather than a one-time event. In other words, repurchasing $1 million in stock may be accretive in the coming year, but committing to repurchasing shares opportunistically over time can drive a company's multiple.

DEBT REPAYMENT

Another way management can add value below the operating line is to reduce debt, if appropriate. Again, management can drive long-term value by systematically reducing debt as part of its free cash flow uses and, in the process, reduce interest expense and increase earnings per share. IR's role is to frame the reduction as part of the ongoing strategies described above. In fact, it's a powerful tool to feed the analysts the message that shareholders come first and the company will use its cash to engineer a better bottom line as the core business stays the course.

DIVIDEND

Because of recent tax law changes, dividends have become an attractive means by which to reward shareholders with capital. In constructing a dividend policy with management, IR must read The Street carefully to provide accurate feedback on the potential decision.

The first reason a company might issue a dividend is to simply reward shareholders with capital. In other cases, initiating a dividend can completely reposition a company and broaden its shareholder base to include yield buyers.

In almost every case, a dividend should not be communicated as a one-time payout. Rather, it should be positioned as a regular, dependable allocation of free cash flow back to shareholders. Initiation of a dividend, or in-

In 2003 Big Winner Inc., a successful leisure resort operator, faced a valuation crossroads. They generated superior free cash flow, but the nature of the business prevented significant expansion over time, presumably limiting bottom-line growth. Therefore, in addition to organic growth, management had repurchased stock over the years and dramatically reduced debt, two options that by definition increased earnings. Now Big Winner was considering a dividend that would likely change the way the company was valued and increase the share price.

Big Winner issued a $3.00 dividend and suggested they would target future payouts at approximately 40 percent of free cash flow. In this case, the dividend *and* the strategy of management changed investor's perception. The president of the company was relaying confidence in the business as well as a willingness to reward shareholders with excess cash.

creasing a dividend, is good news to shareholders. Done correctly, it is also news that can be leveraged to support management's views regarding creating shareholder value over the long run.

Figure 25.1 shows how a dividend strategy can combine with guidance to create multiple positive events over several years.

Initiating a dividend also indicates that it's the best use of cash, implying slowed growth prospects or signaling the completion of an event, such as de-

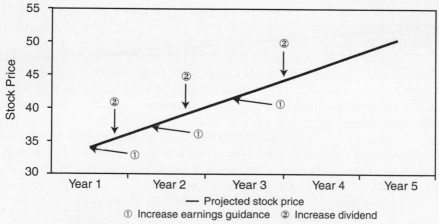

FIGURE 25.1 Dividend and Earnings Guidance Strategy

leveraging. As a company pays down debt and de-leverages the balance sheet, a dividend would signal financial stability and a reallocation of capital to shareholders.

Calculating an appropriate dividend is no easy task and it's a senior management decision. However, IR should play a part in those discussions because depending on the current share price, a full payout may not be needed.

First and foremost, however, a long-term financial forecast should be developed with projected free cash flow. After management is comfortable with the forecast and the amount of free cash flow the business will generate, an allocation of some portion of that free cash should be directed toward the dividend.

When implementing the dividend, management needs to start conservatively and plan out future dividend payments with an eye toward sustainability and increases. The reduction or elimination of a dividend can have a material negative affect on a company's stock price.

In that spirit, IR must also understand whether a proposed dividend, and thus its yield, will mean anything to existing valuation. In a low-interest-rate environment, equity yields are more attractive to income-related investors. However, if one of the objectives of the dividend is to attract additional investor interest, IR should compare similar yields (dividend/share price). Initiating a dividend that yields 1 percent when the sector is paying 3 percent may not attract much attention.

Finally, the strategy can be more effective at attracting investor interest than the actual dividend. That's due to *yield perception*. If a company's dividend strategy is to pay out 30 percent of free cash flow, and free cash flow has been growing at 20 percent annually, investors may be much more fixated on potential growth of dividends versus the actual dividend today. This increases valuation.

Examine a yield range and gauge the appeal of incremental yield within that range to value, growth, and income investors. Look to see what level of enduring yield is necessary to support investor interest. A technical analysis of the stock price at different yield assumptions is important to develop a range where yield matters (see Figure 25.2).

One company was inclined to institute a very large dividend relative to its peers, about 5 percent. The business had a strong, reliable cash flow, and the company was sure they could support this yield on an ongoing basis. It was an emotional issue for management because their stock had been viewed as risky, they were trading at a discounted multiple to their largest competitor, and they felt the whopping dividend would make a big statement.

We recommended that management not show their hand quite so fast.

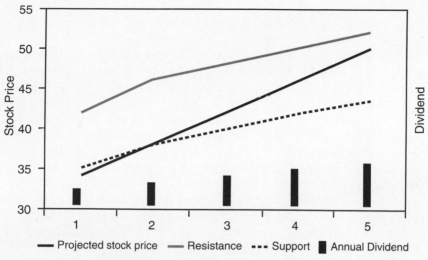

FIGURE 25.2   Yield Perception on Dividend

The company could initiate a conservative dividend and keep the option to increase the payment over a period of time. We suggested a 1 to 2 percent dividend to start, which The Street would recognize positively. The investment community would also understand that it only represented a small portion of free cash flow. Then each quarter, the company would have the luxury of deciding if it wanted to increase the payment or not.

IR pulled together a list of yield investors and added them to the distribution list. The dividend and the philosophy was announced on a conference call after hours, and bottom-line and dividend guidance were established to keep the analysts in check. The upshot of the announcement was to create a floor price for the stock and a "yield perception" that created multiple expansion and strong underlying support. Mission accomplished.

The banker mentality maximizes the company's position in the capital markets at any given time. It maximizes outside transactions, where bankers help management raise capital. It also assesses each dollar spent on the business and frames decisions on free cash flow allocation in a mathematical formula. In other words, if the company is going to spend $1, they need to decide if they spend it on their core business, an acquisition, a share buyback, debt reduction, or a dividend. The exact decision should derive from the CEO and CFO's office or from the company's investment banker, but IR should play a major part in the discussions. IR is in the trenches every day with analysts and portfolio managers, and thus uniquely qualified to gear market reaction. It's a critical part of the Dialogue stage.

Conclusion

A Call for Change

We hope this book has demonstrated that a strong, integrated investor relations program can have considerable impact on how Wall Street perceives and values a business. Information flow between a company and the financial markets needs to be based on a shared perception of the company's business. This is, somewhat surprisingly however, rarely the case. In our minds, solid information flow clearly lowers the risk perception of the investor. By definition, a lower level of perceived risk means that an investor will pay more for the same equity or debt, implying a lower cost of capital.

Maximizing the delta that often exists between a company's current valuation and its potential valuation is a job that falls squarely on the shoulders of the investor relations function. Investor relations, as a practice and as an industry, must undergo some fundamental changes in order to truly fulfill the task with which it's charged.

First and foremost, IR really must be executed by someone who has direct knowledge of the capital markets. Without a real understanding of how the various sales, trading, sales-trading, investment banking, research, and portfolio management functions interrelate and are motivated, many IROs start with a disadvantage.

The traditional agencies continue to approach IR as a largely administrative function and staff their accounts in this manner. Without a capital markets mindset that thinks constantly about the value equation, little value can be added to management's communications, and even further, to its strategic thinking. Rest assured, cost of capital is high on the list of priorities. Of course, the charge of every public company is to operate the business to the benefit of the shareholders.

At our company, Integrated Corporate Relations, we made a strategic decision at the outset that we would turn the industry service model on its head. Instead of following the typical agency model of staffing directors with junior-level account executives, as we grew our business we grew laterally at the top. We hired strong senior managers, who typically have several years of very senior-level capital markets experience. We shared administrative support and demonstrated that it was possible, if you are willing to roll up your sleeves, to provide a whole new level of advisory service on par with the McKinseys and Bains of the world. An IR program is only as good as the person picking up the phone on behalf of the company, day in and day out.

A second imperative for the investor relations industry is that many IROs (if they aren't currently doing so) should change their work processes. They must conduct constant due diligence on a company's financials, strategic initiatives, and competitive posture in exactly the same way as an analyst or portfolio manager—with a skeptical, objective eye and a keen sense of risk. They must move through the looking glass between the company and the markets to ask management the hard questions, evaluate the initial answers, and then advise management on the best positioning for a whole myriad of issues that are of concern to the capital markets. In this way the assassins of value, miscommunication, and misunderstanding can be avoided. Also in this way management's understanding of Wall Street is heightened, which is equally as important.

We often tell a potential client to think about what it would be like to talk to their most trusted analyst about a deal, an earnings report, or an emergency *before they went public with the information*. That is the role we fill; that is what superior investor relations and capital markets advisory is all about. At ICR, we've often brought a whole suite of former analysts or portfolio managers together to puzzle out a complex event or disclosure issue. In our experience, the strategy and solutions that come out of that kind of intellectual capital are of incredible value. Again, that to be forewarned is to be forearmed seems self-evident. Giving management the proper tools is really dependent on the filter through which the investor relations officer views disclosures. Appropriately, that filter is a capital markets viewpoint, facilitated by a process that mimics that of the analyst.

The third way in which the IR industry can change is that it must work much harder to develop relationships with The Street. An investor relations advisor must clearly keep his client as the center of his efforts, but the analysts who follow it, the portfolio managers who own it, and the bankers who can help take it to the next level are incredibly important constituencies. They are also, as a rule, people who are overworked and short of patience for yet another phone call. This is not the case if the investor relations officer appreciates their viewpoint, understands their job, and can speak their language. IR's contacts should not be viewed as a replacement for the relationships that the executive management team must have with The Street, but rather as an enabler. Providing strong color on the views, personalities, and functions of these constituencies to the executive team is critical to maximizing the use of their time and the effectiveness of their contact.

We were fortunate, as former analysts and portfolio managers, to begin with peer-to-peer relationships with The Street. We knew that, as analysts, we often would conduct a call with an outsourced IR representative as a courtesy at best. This was the central reason that we knew there was an opportunity to have an impact on the industry. Traditional investor relations officers at outside agencies call to set up meetings for a company. The new IRO must be able to clearly explain, in under 30 seconds, why it is important for that analyst or banker to take a meeting and to have that message resonate. Even today, when business is incredibly competitive on The Street, we know that many investor relations agencies find ways to actually undercut the potential of an analyst to be compensated and place themselves in a competitive role with one of their primary constituencies. We have good relationships because we know how to help analysts and ensure that they are compensated.

Finally, the industry must change the way in which it integrates its communications efforts. Investor relations, in most cases, must become the tip of the spear for a whole suite of communications functions, including many aspects of public relations, trade relations, business media, corporate communications, government affairs, and even advertising. Traditionally, these functions have been spearheaded by large public relations firms or ad agencies. They have tended to operate from something of an ivory tower and often lack the skill set and unifying vision that makes valuation the ultimate goal. The same analyst on the conference call goes home and reads the paper, watches the news, sees television commercials, and is aware of the regulatory environment of the industry he follows. If the message he is getting direct from management is not properly validated by the other forms of communication that emanate from a company, he will begin to question the credibility of the message. Similarly, the public is aware of the opinion of the market and can sense the disconnection. It's that combination of Wall Street and Main Street perception that drives valuation. Therefore, if the fiduciary responsibility of a CEO is to increase shareholder value, IR should naturally be pushed to the forefront in many communication decisions.

We formed a public relations and corporate communications group at ICR because we witnessed some costly disconnects where value was needlessly destroyed for little benefit. Once again, we looked to hire the best people who had direct experience in the media, in corporate communications, and in government affairs. As a result of careful coordination, we believe

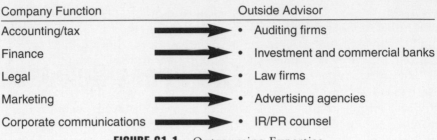

Company Function		Outside Advisor
Accounting/tax	⟶	• Auditing firms
Finance	⟶	• Investment and commercial banks
Legal	⟶	• Law firms
Marketing	⟶	• Advertising agencies
Corporate communications	⟶	• IR/PR counsel

FIGURE C1.1 Outsourcing Expertise

that every communications effort becomes stronger and more credible. This reinforces value and again serves as an enabler for management to control and direct the perception of their business. This approach serves everyone involved—the investor, the analyst, the media, and the public.

Although we cannot claim to be without bias, the ideal investor relations effort is unquestionably a coordinated effort between an outsourced specialty firm and a capable internal investor relations officer. In the absence of the financial resources to support both, the breadth of services and support that an outsourced firm can provide is the first priority. Companies routinely outsource accounting to auditing firms, financial transactions to investment and commercial banks, legal work to law firms, and marketing to advertising agencies. They would do well to look at the highly specialized function of investor relations in the same way. In addition to providing superior personnel and broader understanding of and relationships within the capital market, there is a scalability at play within the agency that provides for access to data and telecommunications services that makes the prospect of outsourcing cost-effective.

Even considering the not-insignificant cost of outsourcing IR, what is a 15, 10 or even 5 percent increase in earnings multiple worth to a company and its shareholders? That answer is often in the tens or even hundreds of millions of dollars. The investor relations professional needs to remain focused on liberating this value. We hope that this book helps to provide a better road map for how to do so and a more appropriate yardstick for us all to measure the performance of the professionals who conduct this essential function.

Two Press Releases

PRESS RELEASE #1

For Immediate Release

Food To Go, Inc. Announces First Quarter Results

Earnings increase 23% to $0.27 per diluted share

Fargo, North Dakota, April 22, 2004 — Food To Go, Inc. (NASDAQ: SYMBOL), today announced financial results for the first quarter ended March 28, 2004. Highlights for the first quarter compared to the same quarter a year ago were as follows:

- Total revenue increased 35.9% to $40.2 million
- Company-owned restaurant sales grew 35.1% to $35.9 million
- System-wide same store sales increased 11.8%
- Earnings per diluted share increased 23% to $0.27

Karen Frey, chief executive officer and president of Food To Go, commented, "We are pleased with our first quarter performance as it demonstrates our ability to drive top-line growth while maintaining a keen focus on operations. In terms of sales at both company-owned and franchised locations, we credit timely and effective promotional activity as well as strong traffic at our restaurants during the Super Bowl and the NCAA tournament. The economy also seemed buoyant during the quarter, and we are no doubt experiencing some of the same positive trends evident across the casual dining and quick casual sectors." Frey continued, "Knowing that potato prices were stubbornly high during the period, we stressed operational excellence throughout the organization. Our team rose to the challenge and the attention to detail and hard work is shown in the year-over-year improvements in almost every key expense category."

Total revenue, which includes company-owned restaurant sales and franchise royalties and fees, increased 35.9% to $40.2 million in the first quarter compared to $29.6 million in the first quarter of 2003. System-wide same store sales increased 11.8% for the quarter. Company-owned restaurant sales for the quarter increased

35.1% to $35.9 million, aided by a company-owned same-store sales increase of 11.1% and 15 more company-owned locations in operation at the end of first quarter 2004 relative to the same period in 2003. Franchise royalties and fees increased 42.5% to $4.3 million versus $3 million in the prior year. This was due to a franchise same-store sales increase of 12.0% and 37 more franchised restaurants at the end of the period versus a year ago.

Average weekly sales for company-owned restaurants were $32,289 for the first quarter of 2004 compared to $28,782 for the same quarter last year, a 12.2% increase. Franchised restaurants averaged $39,678 for the period versus $33,920 in the first quarter a year ago, a 17.0% increase.

For the first quarter, GAAP earnings per diluted share increased 23% to $0.27 versus $0.22 in the first quarter of 2003. On a pro forma basis, the first quarter 2003 earnings per diluted share were also $0.22 per share. This was due to the fact that the Company's mandatorily redeemable Series A Preferred Stock was dilutive in the prior period.

Frey concluded, "Looking to the remainder of 2004, we're on plan with our expansion strategy and excited about our ability to extend the brand. On the development front, we have opened three restaurants in Nashville during the last six months, and we plan to continue this new market growth strategy in Dallas and Los Angeles. In terms of marketing, we're confident that our promotions for the upcoming quarter and full year will drive sales, and we'll continue to innovate our menu. Our efforts remain focused on building a successful national brand and executing this strategy in a manner that grows shareholder value over the long term."

Second Quarter 2004 Outlook

For the second quarter ended June 27, 2004, management expects total revenue to approximate $38 million based on a system-wide same-store sales increase of 5% to 7%. Revenue assumptions are also based on two new company-owned restaurants during the second quarter and six new franchised units. Management also believes that earnings per diluted share for the second quarter will range from $.10 to $.13. This is based on the revenue assumptions mentioned above, average chicken wing prices for the second quarter of $1.58 per pound, and diluted weighted average shares outstanding of 8.6 million.

Information included in this release includes commentary on franchised and system-wide restaurant units, same-store sales, and average weekly sales volumes. Management believes such system-wide sales information is an important measure of our performance and is useful in assessing consumer acceptance of the Food To Go Grill & Bar concept and the health of the concept overall. Franchise information also provides an understanding of the Company's revenues as franchise royalties and fees are based on the opening of franchised units and their sales. However, system-wide same-store sales information does not represent sales in accordance with GAAP, should not be considered in isolation or as a substitute for other measures of performance prepared in accordance with GAAP and may not be comparable to system-wide financial information as defined or used by other companies.

The Company is hosting a conference call today, April 22, 2004, at 5:00 p.m. EDT to discuss these results. There will be a simultaneous webcast conducted at the Company's website. A replay of the call will be available until April 29, 2004. To access this replay please dial (number, password).

About the Company: Food To Go, Inc., founded in 1985 and headquartered in Fargo, North Dakota, is an established and growing owner, operator and franchisor of Food To Go Grill & Bar restaurants featuring a variety of boldly flavored, made-to-order menu items including seasoned and fried potatoes spun in one of the Company's signature sauces. The widespread appeal of the Company's concept establishes its restaurants as an inviting, neighborhood destination with more than 255 restaurants in 30 states.

Forward-looking Statements

Certain statements in this release that are not historical facts, including, without limitation, those relating to our anticipated financial performance and expected store openings for the second quarter of 2004 and the remainder of the year, are forward-looking statements that involve risks and uncertainties. Such statements are based upon the current beliefs and expectations of the management of the Company. Actual results may vary materially from those contained in forward-looking statements based on a number of factors including, without limitation, the actual number of locations opening during the second quarter of 2004 and the remainder of the year, the sales at these and our other company-owned and franchised locations, the cost of wings, our ability to control other restaurant operating costs and other factors disclosed from time to time in the Company's filings with the U.S. Securities and Exchange Commission. Investors should take such risks into account when making investment decisions. Shareholders and other readers are cautioned not to place undue reliance on these forward-looking statements, which speak only as of the date on which they are made. The Company undertakes no obligation to update any forward-looking statements.

* * *

PRESS RELEASE #2

For Immediate Release

BLUE AND GOLD INC. REPORTS 2003 FOURTH QUARTER
AND FULL YEAR 2003 OPERATING RESULTS

— Quarterly Consolidated Revenues Increase 37% —

— Quarterly Earnings Per Share Increase 20% to $0.30 —

— Fiscal Year Revenues Total $975 million —

— FY04 EPS Guidance Increases to New Range of $1.18 to $1.22 —

PEMBROKE, MASSACHUSETTS, DECEMBER 18, 2003 — Blue & Gold, Inc.
(NYSE: SYMBOL), today announced operating results for the fourth quarter and
full year ended October 31, 2003.

Consolidated revenues for the fourth quarter of fiscal 2003 increased 37% to
$269.2 million as compared to fiscal 2002 fourth quarter consolidated revenues of
$196.1 million. Consolidated net income for the fourth quarter of fiscal 2003 in-
creased 43% to $17.4 million as compared to $12.2 million. Fourth quarter fully diluted earnings per share was $0.30 versus $0.25 for the fourth quarter of fiscal 2002.

Consolidated revenues for the full year of fiscal 2003 increased 38% to $975.0
as compared to fiscal 2002 full year consolidated revenues of $705.5. Consolidated
net income for the full year of fiscal 2003 increased 56% to $58.5 million as com-
pared to $37.6 in fiscal 2002, and diluted earnings per share for the full year in-
creased 34% to $1.03 versus $0.77 for the full year of fiscal 2002.

Stephanie Wood, chairman of the board and chief executive officer of Blue &
Gold, commented, "We are pleased to have exceeded our plan for the fourth quarter,
and we finished the year with clean inventories, continued strong sell through rates,
and an excellent strategic position in the marketplace. As we close in on the $1 bil-
lion revenue mark in the upcoming year, we are excited about our prospects both do-
mestically and around the world."

Revenues in the Americas increased 15% during the fourth quarter of fiscal
2003 to $125.6 million as compared to fiscal 2002 fourth quarter revenues of
$109.7 million. As measured in U.S. dollars and reported in the financial statements,
European revenues increased 25% during the fourth quarter of fiscal 2003 to $106.7
million as compared to fiscal 2002 fourth quarter European revenues of $85.3 mil-
lion. As measured in euros, European revenues increased 8% for those same periods.
Revenues in the Asia/Pacific segment, which was added in the first quarter of fiscal
2003, totaled $36.7 million. In constant dollars, overall Spring bookings increased
6% over the previous year.

Revenues in the Americas for the full year of fiscal 2003 increased 18% to
$492.4 as compared to fiscal 2002 revenues of $418.0 million. As measured in U.S.
dollars and reported in the financial statements, European revenues increased 37%
during the full year of fiscal 2003 to $386.2 million as compared to fiscal 2002 re-

sults of $282.7 million. As measured in euros, European revenues increased 15% for the full year. The Asia/Pacific division added $94.2 million to consolidated revenues in fiscal 2003.

Ms. Wood continued, "Over the course of the year, we have been able to properly align our marketing strategies, our product lines, our operations, and our management team to go forward with a singular vision for the future. Clearly, the power of our youth-oriented lifestyle view and the culture of extreme water sports is resonating with consumers everywhere."

Inventories in the Americas increased 25% to 86.4 million at October 31, 2003, from $69.0 million at October 31, 2002, while decreasing $2.1 million from July 31, 2003. European inventories increased 38% in euros and increased 63% in U.S. dollars, totaling $43.8 million at October 31, 2003, compared to $26.9 million at October 31, 2002. Inventories in the newly acquired Asia/Pacific division totaled $16.2 million at October 31, 2003. Consolidated inventories increased 53% to $146.4 million at October 31, 2003, from $95.9 million at October 31, 2002, which is an increase of 45% after adjusting for the effect of the stronger euro in comparison to the prior year.

Consolidated trade accounts receivable increased 33% to $224.4 million at October 31, 2003, from $168.2 million at October 31, 2002. Accounts receivable grew more slowly than sales as average days sales outstanding decreased about three days.

Lily Hamilton, president of Blue & Gold, Inc., commented, "As we move forward into the new year, we are benefiting from a continued position as the leading youth brand in the United States, Europe and Australia, and we have excellent prospects for growth in a variety of markets in Eastern Europe. We are focused on leveraging the strength of our brands and our superior operating platform to take advantage of these opportunities."

Also today, the company increased its guidance to new ranges of $1.06 billion to $1.08 billion for revenues and $1.18 to $1.22 for earnings per share.

Ms. Hamilton concluded, "These results represent our 8th consecutive quarter of exceeding both internal and external expectations, and importantly, we have been able to accomplish all of this in a challenging retail climate. At the same time, we have successfully integrated a number of new businesses that will provide additional growth into the future. The benefits of our strong brands and diversified operating model are clear and compelling, and the combination of innovative product, unique marketing, a cohesive management structure, and world-class execution will allow us to expand our business and drive significant value to our shareholders into the future."

About Blue & Gold: Blue & Gold designs, produces, and distributes clothing, accessories, and related products for young-minded people and develops brands that represent a casual lifestyle-driven from an extreme water sports heritage. Blue & Gold's authenticity is evident in its innovative products, events, and retail environments across the globe.

Blue & Gold's primary focus is apparel for young men and young women under the Blue & Gold label. Blue & Gold also manufactures apparel for boys (Blue &

Gold Boys), girls (Blue & Gold Girls), men (Blue & Gold Men) and women (Blue & Gold swimwear), as well as water sports gear under the Blue & Gold Technologies label. Blue & Gold's products are sold throughout the world, primarily in specialty stores that provide an authentic retail experience for our customers.

Safe Harbor Language
   This Press Release contains forward-looking statements. These forward-looking statements are subject to risks and uncertainties, and actual results may differ materially. Please refer to Blue & Gold's SEC filings for more information on the risk factors that could cause actual results to differ materially from expectations, specifically the section titled "Forward Looking Statements" in Blue & Gold's Annual Report on Form 10-K.

* * *

NOTE: *For further information about Blue & Gold, Inc., you are invited to take a look at our world at (website).*

Also included:

CONSOLIDATED STATEMENTS OF INCOME (Unaudited)

CONSOLIDATED BALANCE SHEETS (Unaudited)

Information related to geographic segments

The Conference Call Script

FINAL - 1

X SPORTS USA INC.

THIRD QUARTER 2003

CONFERENCE CALL SCRIPT

Thank you, Brian.

Good afternoon and thank you for joining us today to review X SPORTS third quarter and nine month 2003 results. This is Taylor Mac, CEO of X Sports and as always, we will open the call to questions after my prepared comments.

Third quarter sales were $221.8 million compared to $261.1 million in the third quarter of 2002. Sales were higher than we expected when we gave guidance on July 24, 2003, mainly due to our aggressive approach to reduce our inventory levels. As we anticipated, this approach to reducing our inventory resulted in lower gross margins and earnings for the third quarter. Our net loss was $5.9 million or $0.15 per share.

In the third quarter, we received positive sell-through data at retail from our larger wholesale customers for the back-to-school season, but we did not experience significant re-order business, and what we did receive was largely close-out merchandise rather than in-line merchandise. We believe the trend toward less reorder business was in part due to retailers having a more conservative approach to inventory planning as well as a recent tendency among some accounts to better plan our brand, as X SPORTS is becoming a more mature and stable business. We believe that our product was, and continues to be, fashion right and in demand by consumers, and that we will continue to be a basic and important part of our accounts' inventory plan. We will continue to focus on our product to ensure that it is on target.

On our second quarter conference call, we stated we were going to be aggressive in our approach to move excess levels of inventory during the back half of the year. We believed, and continue to believe, it was, and still is, prudent to assertively work through our inventory to achieve our year-end goal. We are pleased that we made significant strides in our inventory, reducing it by $66.4 million or almost 31% from second quarter 2003 levels, which resulted in an increase in cash of $39.2 million to

$80.7 million and a decrease in accounts payable of $71 million to $56 million. We believe that we are ahead of our plan of having inventories in-line by year-end 2003 and expect to begin 2004 with inventories that are fresh, current, and on-plan.

For the nine-month period ended September 30, 2003, net sales were $659.7 million compared to net sales of $762.7 million during the first nine months of the prior year. Net income for the nine months ended September 30, 2003, was $476 thousand or one cent per diluted share, compared to net income of $55.6 million or $1.39 per diluted share.

We believe several factors resulted in our reported decline in sales and earnings for the first nine months of 2003 over the same period last year:

- First, the conservative approach to inventory planning by wholesale accounts due to the retail environment. This is not an across-the-board shift as we have seen some key accounts remain strong.
- Second, we have seen more competition at our basic price points and an increase in off-price product purchased vs. in-line merchandise. We believe these will continue to be a factor in the fourth quarter.
- Third, increased marketing expenses associated with the launch of new product lines, and the signing of Anna Amazing as our international spokesperson.
- Fourth, increased expenses associated with opening 28 retail stores in the last 12 months, including 10 stores opened in the third quarter, three of which were international locations.
- And finally, the start-up expenses associated with establishing new international subsidiaries, including the opening of a showroom in Italy and the hiring of sales representatives and marketing teams for Canada, Spain, Portugal, Austria and the Benelux Region, and our European distribution center located in Belgium, which began shipping in December 2002.

We see factors such as the unsteady economy starting to abate somewhat and the cost of our international initiatives starting to balance out as our subsidiaries grow to their planned level. Even so, we believe it is prudent to take steps to better align our expenditures with sales as we become a more mature company. Now that we've made significant strides in reducing our inventory and improving our balance sheet, we have turned our attention to cost-cutting initiatives. Due to the plan still being developed, we are not prepared to give you specifics about the annual savings at this time. However, *I would like to give you some preliminary thoughts on our cost-cutting initiatives going forward*:

- First, by reviewing our advertising and marketing budget. Our goal is to reduce costs without diminishing the impact to consumers. We plan to do this primarily by lowering our production and tradeshow expenditures.
- Second, we are curtailing the expansion of X SPORTS retail stores. We will concentrate our efforts on maximizing our impact and potential within our existing stores. With 124 locations worldwide by the end of 2003, we believe we have al-

ready established X SPORTS retail stores in the prime markets—such as Times Square, Universal CityWalk, Beverly Center, Mall of America, and the upcoming Las Vegas Fashion Show Mall, and Eaton Centre in Toronto, Oxford Street in London, and the Alstadt District of Düsseldorf. We plan to open only three additional locations in 2004.

■ Third, we have no plans to directly expand our international business into new markets. We will continue to support our existing subsidiaries and focus on bringing each subsidiary's expenses in line with its sales.

■ Lastly, we plan on creating a more efficient business in part by looking at our overall expense structure line item by line item.

We believe the majority of our programs will be implemented by year-end 2003. For the most part, the cost saving effects of the plan will have little or negative impact in the fourth quarter, but will better position us for 2004 and beyond. Again, realigning the Company should allow us to continue to design and develop quality footwear and partner with quality licensees; support our existing initiatives in a more efficient manner; grow our recently established ventures to their potential; and remain competitive in the marketplace.

While our focus for the near term is on containing costs and maintaining our position, we do see several opportunities for growth within set initiatives that will require little or no additional capital investment. These include: international, licensing, and recently launched lines.

In regards to our international business:

■ We began directly handling our product in Germany in 2000 when we saw the opportunity to grow our international sales. Shortly thereafter, we established direct operations in the United Kingdom and France, and today, through eight subsidiaries, we handle the marketing, sales and distribution of our footwear in 12 European countries plus Canada. We have made progress in many of these markets, but are most pleased with our position in our first subsidiary, Germany, where we have seen our orders for first quarter 2004 up double digits over last year for the same period. With the introduction of new lines internationally, we have the opportunity to grow our subsidiary business, and are looking to do so in a strategic and controlled fashion. Our recently opened stores in the Alstadt District of Düsseldorf and Kalverstraat Street in Amsterdam, along with existing stores in Toronto, London, Manchester and Paris, will further build the brand in these markets.

■ Furthermore, we believe that our international sales will also be positively impacted by superstar Anna Amazing, our new international spokesperson for our women's lines. The first ads with Miss Amazing in our X SPORTS Star sneakers are appearing in international fashion and lifestyle magazines this month in conjunction with her sold-out European tour.

Moving on to licensing:

■ Since the signing of our first license with Renfro Corporation for X SPORTS-branded socks in Spring 2002, we have signed seven additional licenses. Our arsenal of licensed product now includes: X SPORTS Kids apparel with Kids Headquarters launched in U.S. department stores in August 2003; men's and women's X SPORTS watches with Advance Group Inc., which began shipping in Fall; X SPORTS Collection men's jackets and coats with Garson International scheduled to ship for Holiday; men's and women's apparel in Japan with Mitsui & Co., Ltd., which is scheduled to ship for Spring 04; and most recently This Is It from X SPORTS junior sportswear apparel in the United States and Canada with Great Jeans; This is Good women's apparel with L'Koral Industries, the maker of Good Jeans; and X SPORTS Kids clothing in Canada with Multi-Group—all of which will launch in stores for BTS/Fall 04. We are extremely pleased with the response that X SPORTS Kids apparel received in key department stores; according to licensee Kids Headquarters, our children's apparel is receiving double-digit sell-throughs. We see licensing as an ideal opportunity to extend the brand beyond footwear in key global markets and believe there are additional opportunities for X SPORTS-branded products in the domestic and international markets. As I mentioned on the second quarter call, we expect a minimum of $0.07 to $0.08 per share in pre-tax profit from licensing revenues during 2004.

And finally another area for growth is within our new product lines.

We now have nine product lines branded with the X SPORTS name and four lines that do not include the X SPORTS name. Of those four lines, three are new and one, ABCD, is approximately two years old. For the designer line, we see growth potential occurring with the in-store launch of the ABCD-branded apparel line in Fall 2004 and the recently opened ABCD store on trendy Robertson Boulevard in Los Angeles. For the men's high-fashion line Men ABCD, which just launched in Fall 2003, we are entering a new market for X SPORTS with fashion footwear for men and believe we are making good initial steps with a couple department stores on board as well as boutiques. The additional two lines launching Spring 2004 are footwear licensing agreements with the popular car specialists 123 Go for 123 Go Footwear and Up Unlimited, Inc. for men's, women's and children's Up Footwear, which will coordinate with Up Unlimited and Up apparel. We also believe these will be ideal opportunities to enter targeted markets that X SPORTS presently has little or no distribution in.

Chief Financial Officer:
Now turning to our third quarter/nine month numbers:

For the third quarter of 2003, sales were $221.8 million compared to $261.1 million last year. The decrease was due to lower domestic wholesale sales, which decreased 21.1% to $150.9 million, driven by an 18.6% decrease in average price per pair on 3.1% less volume.

Gross profit declined to $78.6 million versus $108.8 million in the same period a year ago.

Third quarter gross margin was 35.5%, compared to 41.7% in the same period last year. The gross margin decrease was mainly due to our aggressive pricing and a higher level of close outs during the period to bring our inventories more in-line with our plans, and, to a lesser extent, higher freight costs.

Total operating expenses as a percentage of sales increased to 37.9% from 32.5% in the third quarter of fiscal 2002.

Third quarter selling expenses improved to $20.6 million, or 9.3% of sales, as compared to $32.6 million or 12.5% of sales in the prior year period. The reduction in selling expenses is due to lower sales commissions, trade show costs and our planned reductions in advertising and promotional costs.

On a percentage basis, advertising expense was 6.9% of sales in the third quarter of 2003, as compared to 10.5% in last year's third quarter.

General and Administrative expenses were $63.5 million representing 28.6% of sales compared to $52.2 million or 20.0% of sales in last year's third quarter. The increase in general and administrative expenses was attributable to higher salaries, wages and related taxes, rent, insurance, depreciation and legal fees.

Third quarter operating loss was $4.1 million compared to an operating profit of $24.1 million in last year's third quarter.

Net loss was $5.9 million compared to net earnings of $14.1 million in the prior year period. Loss per share was $0.15 on 37,925,000 shares compared to fully diluted earnings per share of $0.35 on 41,926,000 shares in the third quarter of last year. We did not include the dilution effect of the shares that would be issued under our convertible notes for the third quarter of 2003.

For the nine-months ended September 30, 2003, net sales were $659.7 million versus net sales of $762.7 million for the first nine-months of 2002. Gross profit was $258.6 million compared to $317.6 million for the same period of the prior year.

Selling expenses for the first nine months of 2003 were $67.1 million compared to $72.6 million for the first nine months of 2002. G&A expense was $181.7 million compared to $150.7 million in the same period last year.

We provided $4.4 million for income taxes for the nine months ended September 30, 2003, which is an effective tax rate of 90% of earnings before taxes, compared to an effective tax rate of 36.7% last year. The increase in the effective tax rate is due to losses incurred in low tax rate international jurisdictions, offset by higher rate domestic tax provisions.

Net earnings for the first nine months of 2003 were $476 thousand compared to net income of $55.6 million. Diluted earnings per share were one cent on 38,114,000 diluted shares outstanding versus diluted earnings per share of $1.39 on 41,004,000 diluted shares for the same period last year.

Trade accounts receivable at quarter end decreased 16.8% from September 30, 2002. Our DSOs at September 30, 2003, were 41 days versus 44 days in the same period of 2002.

Inventory at quarter end stood at $150.7 million, representing an increase of $21.0 million from $129.7 million at the end of September 2002. Inventory levels continue to be above last year levels but improved substantially from levels at the end of second quarter 2003. We believe that we are ahead of our plan of having inventories in-line by year-end 2003 and expect to begin 2004 with inventories that are fresh, current and on-plan.

At September 30, 2003, cash on the balance sheet totaled $80.7 million compared to $41.5 million at the end of the second quarter 2003. The increase in cash is mainly due to lowering our inventory levels and converting receivables to cash during the third quarter.

Working Capital totaled $284.9 million as of September 30, 2003.

Long-term debt fell to $120.2 million. Of this amount, $90 million is related to our convertible debt offering. The remainder is related to the mortgages that we have on our distribution center, corporate headquarters and capital lease obligations. In addition, there is no outstanding balance on our revolving line of credit.

Cap ex during the first nine months was approximately $18 million primarily stemming from new store openings and leasehold improvements. For 2003, we continue to project total capital expenditures of $25 million with the majority of this amount related to our retail and international expansion.

Now turning to guidance:

We currently expect fourth quarter 2003 sales in the range of $155 million to $165 million compared to $180.8 million in the fourth quarter 2002 and a loss per share of between $0.45 and $0.55. This assumes that fourth quarter margins will be comparable with third quarter actuals.

As we complete 2003 and move into 2004 with a clean inventory, I want to re-iterate our focus: to realign our expense structure with our sales, to maintain our position in the marketplace, and to grow the recently established initiatives, including the licensing arm of our company. We are taking a detailed look at each expense line item and finding ways to lower our cost structure and maximize our operating margins. Once we realign our business and begin generating consistent earnings, we will be looking at ways to enhance shareholder value.

CEO:

In our first 10 years, X SPORTS grew into a global lifestyle brand recognized around the world. Moving into the next decade, we believe X SPORTS is a mature and stable brand that is becoming a head-to-toe lifestyle brand. We believe the steps we are taking now will result in a stronger company and better position us for the long-term.

And now I would like to turn the call over to the operator to begin the question and answer portion of the conference call.

Velocity Inc. 2004 Investor Relations Plan

There are five main objectives of the 2004 investor relations plan:

1. Secure meetings with equity analysts to obtain potential research coverage and sponsorship.
2. Build a full year of investor marketing and conferences and continue to improve the company's visibility.
3. Improve the Velocity Inc.'s investor presentation (ongoing).
4. Develop a Velocity Inc.'s fact sheet and investor package for investors.
5. Improve the Investor Relations web page.

1. RESEARCH COVERAGE AND SPONSORSHIP

Relationships with the sell-side currently exist, and there are two analysts in the process of launching coverage of Velocity. We believe there are several other worthwhile firms and analysts to meet with for an expanded sell-side following. Analysts in the process of launching coverage are shaded light gray, analysts to target for potential coverage are shaded darker gray (see Figure A1.1).

Potential Research Coverage

As analysts roll out coverage, managing expectations will be increasingly important. Obviously, we want analyst estimates to remain within what management feels is achievable. Velocity Inc. will pull interest from analysts in the gaming sector as well as in the payments industry. Because of the cross characterization of the stock, it is important that the sell-side fully understands the business. We suggest conducting sales force teach-ins when new coverage is available so that the an-

TABLE A.1   Potential Research Coverage

Institution Name	First Name	LastName
A.G. Edwards & Sons	Timothy	Willi
Barrington Research Associates, Inc.	Gary	Prestopino
Bear Stearns & Company	James	Kissane
CIBC World Markets	Bill	Schmidt
Citigroup Global Markets Inc.	Walter	Wible
Credit Suisse First Boston	Dris	Upitis
First Analysis	Lawrence	Berlin
Friedman Billings Ramsey Group Inc.	Christopher	Penny
FTN Midwest Research Securities Corp	Kartik	Mehta
Goldman Sachs & Co.	Gregory	Gould
J.P. Morgan Securities (U.S.)	Dirk	Godsey
Jefferies & Company	Craig	Peckham
Legg Mason Wood Walker	Daniel	Perlin
Lehman Brothers (U.S.)	Roger	Freeman
Merrill Lynch Global Securities	Gregory	Smith
Merriman Curhan Ford, & Co.	David	Baine
Morgan Keegan & Company	Robert	Dodd
Morgan Stanley	David	Togut
Oppenheimer & Co.	Michael	Smith
Piper Jaffray & Co.	Peter	Swanson
RobertW. Baird & Company	Carla	Cooper
Roth Capital	Richard	Eckert
Standard & Poor's Equity Group	Scott	Kessler
Sidoti & Company	Michael	Friedman
Sterne, Agee	Danny	Davila
SunTrust Robinson Humphrey Capital Markets	Wayne	Johnson
Thomas Weisel Partners	John	Mihalijevic

alyst and the sales force have a deeper understanding of the business and, ultimately, the valuation.

Sales Force Teach-Ins

We can't stress the importance enough of educating the institutional sales forces of the firms providing research coverage of Velocity Inc. The basic process of getting an institution to buy a stock often begins with research. Unfortunately, a research report and/or meeting isn't always enough to inspire a portfolio manager to buy a stock. That's where the sales force can help. When an institutional sales force gets to meet management and hear the investment story directly, it tends to have a much greater impact on that firm's ability to close orders. (See Figure A1.1.)

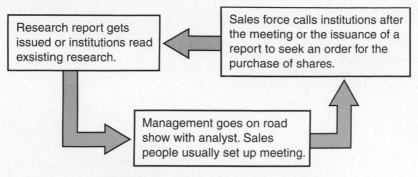

FIGURE A1.1   Sales Meets Management

We believe teach-ins give the institutional salesperson much greater confidence in soliciting meetings and orders from institutions and thus makes the entire marketing process more efficient for management teams.

2. INVESTOR MARKETING AND CONFERENCES

Conferences

We think management should remain as active as possible, without disrupting current management activities. We suggest management consider scheduling road shows around conferences to leverage travel time while maximizing the efficiency of the conference.

There are several conferences we suggest attending, including the Sterne, Agee Gaming Conference (September), the Roth Capital Conferences (September/October—NYC, and February 2005—LA), the ICR XChange (January), and the ABA Small Cap Conference (May 2005—NYC).

Investor Meetings and Improved Targeting

We utilize ownership databases that cross-reference Velocity Inc.'s stock ownership with industry peers. (See Table A1.2.) We believe that effective investor targeting results in improved trading liquidity, as well as a growth in market capitalization.

We will be providing updated analysis of institutional ownership in the gaming industry and payments industry, cross-referenced to Velocity Inc.'s stock ownership. We will do this as ownership statistics are updated (mid-February, mid-May, mid-August, mid-November) or on an as-needed basis.

We believe the comparative analysis in mid-May will indicate a widening potential universe of additional buyers, and we plan on actively working with management, road show sponsors (sell-side firms and their institutional sales forces) and analysts to improve targeting.

TABLE A1.2　Industry Peers

Institution Name	CKN	CSTR	CEY	EQTX	Total
T. Rowe Price Assoicates, Inc.			$280,136,799		$280,136,799
General Electric Asset Management			$203,317,548		$203,317,548
Kayne Anderson Rudnick Investment Management LLC			$161,851,399		$161,851,399
Ariel Capital Management LLC			$157,447,228		$157,457,228
Barclays Global Investors, N.A.		$25,427,841	$58,539,087	$7,543	$83,974,471
AIM Management Group, Inc.		$101,640	$77,115,369		$77,217,009
Denver Investment Advisors LLC			$45,394,845		$45,394,845
Columbia Wanger Asset Management LP		$44,267,850			$44,267,850
Reed, Conner & Birdwell LLC		$19,385,071	$21,528,467		$40,913,538
Vanguard Group		$5,542,538	$35,278,817		$40,821,355
SSGA Funds Management		$6,549,464	$29,007,528		$35,556,992
Trusco Capital Management, Inc.			$31,350,975		$31,350,975
Oak Value Capital Management, Inc.			$29,387,909		$29,387,909
Oppenheimer Capital LP			$26,170,803		$26,170,803
New York State Common Retirement Fund			$22,635,917		$22,635,917
Credit Suisse Asset Management, Inc. (NY)			$20,666,016		$20,666,016
Banc of America Capital Management LLC		$1,808,194	$18,477,086		$20,285,280
California State Teachers Retirement System		$1,146,082	$18,807,954		$19,954,036
Northern Trust Global Investments		$4,263,344	$15,087,627	$261,995	$19,612,966
Timesquare Capital Management, Inc.			$17,538,607		$17,538,607
Teacher Retirement System of Texas		$2,495,625	$14,966,460		$17,462,085
TIAA-CREF Investment Management LLC		$3,394,558	$13,889,080		$17,283,638
Dalton, Greiner, Hartman, Maher & Co.			$17,213,479		$17,213,479
Boston Partners Asset Management LP		$15,761,097			$15,761,097
Fidelity Management & Research Co.		$1,815	$15,099,723		$15,101,538

3. IMPROVE VELOCITY INC.'S INVESTOR PRESENTATION (ONGOING)

We are available to provide updates and changes to investor presentations as needed, or on an ongoing basis.

4. FACT SHEET AND INVESTOR PACKAGE

We will develop a fact sheet after the first quarter of 2004 is reported.

We suggest that Velocity Inc. leverage existing marketing materials (folders and other printed company information) and cross-utilize this for investor relations purposes. This can eliminate unnecessary printing costs. We recommend a basic investor kit that would include the following:

Last 10-K
Last 10-Q
Press releases from the prior six months
Proxy statement
Fact sheet

These materials can usually be mailed in a folder. It is our understanding the Company is currently considering re-doing its marketing materials. We will attempt to make sure some of these materials, like folders, can be cross-utilized.

5. IMPROVE THE IR WEB PAGE

In the past quarter, the Velocity Inc.'s website has become SEC compliant as well as linked to CCBN investor website services. We are continuing to improve the Investor Relations web page, and the next step is to enhance content, such as adding a company fact sheet.

Index